C000146315

The Association of An   ...y Presses

Directory 2004-2005

The Association of American University Presses
71 W. 23rd Street, Suite 901
New York, NY 10010

Phone: (212) 989-1010
Fax: (212) 989-0275; (212) 989-0176
Web site: www.aaupnet.org
E-mail: info@aaupnet.org

Published by the Association of American University Presses
71 W. 23rd St., Suite 901, New York, NY 10010
© 2004 by the Association of American University Presses, Inc.
All rights reserved.
Printed in the United States of America

International Standard Book Number 0-94510-3-18-2
Library of Congress Catalog Number 54-43046

Distributed to the Trade by:
The University of Chicago Press
11030 South Langley Avenue
Chicago, Illinois 60628
USA

Publication of this *Directory* was assisted by a generous grant from Edwards Brothers.

Table of Contents

PREFACE

This *Directory* serves as a guide to the publishing programs and personnel of the 125 distinguished scholarly presses that have met the membership standards of the Association of American University Presses. Updated annually, the *Directory* provides the most comprehensive information on these publishers available from any source. It belongs on the reference shelf of anyone connected to scholarly publishing: scholars preparing materials for publication, booksellers, librarians, scholarly presses interested in joining the AAUP, and, of course, the AAUP's own members.

The *Directory* is organized particularly for the convenience of authors, librarians, and booksellers who require detailed information about AAUP members and their wide-ranging publishing programs. The "Subject Area Grid," for example, provides a quick overview of the many disciplines published by the presses, indicating those most likely to publish a work in a given area. "On Submitting Manuscripts" gives advice to potential authors on preparing and submitting a scholarly manuscript for publication.

For further detail, individual press listings provide information on their editorial programs, journals published, and key staff members. Addresses, ordering information, and information on sales representation for Canada, the UK, and Europe are also included.

The last section of the *Directory* focuses on the association and its purposes, and includes its by-laws, guidelines for admission to membership, and the names of the AAUP's Board of Directors, committees, and staff.

GENERAL INFORMATION FOR AUTHORS

What University Presses Do

University Presses perform services that are of inestimable value to the scholarly establishment, and also to the broader world of readers, and ultimately to society. If you are considering publishing with a university or other non-profit scholarly press, the following list should give you a good understanding of the scholarly publishing community.

• University Presses make available to the broader public the full range and value of research generated by university faculty.

• University Press books and journals present the basic research and analysis that is drawn upon by policymakers, opinion leaders, and authors of works for the general public.

• University Presses contribute to the variety and diversity of cultural expression at a time of global mergers and consolidation in the media industry.

• University Presses make common cause with libraries and other cultural institutions to promote engagement with ideas and sustain a literate culture.

• University Presses help to preserve the distinctiveness of local cultures through publication of works on the states and regions where they are based.

• University Presses give voice to minority cultures and perspectives through pioneering publication programs in ethnic, racial, and sexual studies.

• University Presses bring the work of overseas scholars and writers to English-language audiences by commissioning and publishing works in translation.

• University Presses rediscover and maintain the availability of works important to scholarship and culture through reprint programs.

• University Presses encourage cultural expression by publishing works of fiction, poetry, and creative nonfiction and books on contemporary art and photography.

• University Presses sponsor work in specialized and emerging areas of scholarship that do not have the broad levels of readership needed to attract commercial publishers.

• University Presses, through the peer review process, test the validity and soundness of scholarship and thus maintain high standards for academic publication.

• University Presses add value to scholarly work through rigorous editorial development; professional copyediting and design; and worldwide dissemination.

• University Presses are based at a wide array of educational institutions and thus promote a diversity of scholarly perspectives.

- University Presses encourage and refine the work of younger scholars through publication of the first books that establish credentials and develop authorial experience.

- University Presses make the works of English-language scholars available worldwide by licensing translations to publishers in other languages.

- University Presses commit resources to long-term scholarly editions and multivolume research projects, assuring publication for works with completion dates far in the future.

- University Presses add to the richness of undergraduate and graduate education by publishing most of the non-textbook and supplementary material used by instructors.

- University Presses collaborate with learned societies, scholarly associations, and librarians to explore how new technologies can benefit and advance scholarship.

- University Presses extend the reach and influence of their parent institutions, making evident their commitment to knowledge and ideas.

- University Presses demonstrate their parent institutions' support of research in areas such as the humanities and social sciences that rarely receive substantial Federal or corporate funding.

- University Presses help connect the university to the surrounding community by publishing books of local interest and hosting events for local authors.

- University Presses generate favorable publicity for their parent institutions through news coverage and book reviews, awards won, and exhibits at scholarly conferences.

- University Press staff act as local experts for faculty and administrators, providing guidance on intellectual property, scholarly communication, and the publishing process.

- University Presses provide advice and opportunities for students interested in pursuing careers in publishing.

On Submitting Manuscripts

JOURNAL ARTICLES

University presses have always been associated with publishing books of merit and distinction. This remains as true today as in the past, but less well appreciated is the extent to which university presses are active in publishing scholarly journals.

Journals form a major part of the publishing program of many presses, and more than half of the Association's members produce at least one periodical. (See page 18 for a list of presses publishing journals.) In all, university presses publish over 600 scholarly periodicals, including many of the most distinguished in their respective fields.

Authors submitting papers to a journal should check a current issue for information on where to submit manuscripts and for guidelines on length and format. Editors of journals often have very precise requirements for manuscript preparation and may return articles that do not meet their specifications.

BOOK MANUSCRIPTS

Selecting a Publisher

If you are looking for a publisher for a book-length manuscript, do some research on which press may be best for your book. You should consider the reputation in your field of various presses and their editors, the design and production quality of their books, and the range and strength of their marketing efforts. To take advantage of group promotions and past experience, presses tend to specialize in certain subjects. Occasionally a press may take on a title in an unfamiliar area, but you are more likely to be successful in your submission if you choose one that knows the field. Use the "Subject Area Grid," which begins on page 9, to find out which presses publish titles in your field. You can then find more specific information about their interests under the listings of individual presses or by consulting their catalogs. If your book has a strong regional interest, consider the lists of the university presses active in your state to determine what types of regional books they publish.

You can also learn more about the list of each publisher by studying brochures received in the mail, reading book advertisements in journals, and by visiting press exhibits at academic meetings. At these exhibits you can meet acquisitions editors from the presses most active in the discipline and talk with them about your manuscript. Such talks can be very helpful to you and the editor in deciding if your manuscript would be suitable for a particular press. If you have already decided which press you would prefer for your book, call the appropriate editor before the meeting to make an appointment.

Preparing a Manuscript Prospectus

If you have selected a publisher but do not know an editor, you can use this directory to find the appropriate editor at that press. If you are not sure which editor to approach, write to the director of the press or to its editor-in-chief. Many AAUP member presses describe their submission guidelines on their Web sites. It is best not to send the complete manuscript until you have been invited to do so. Presses vary in the amount of material they want to receive on a first submission, but some or all of the following materials are usually provided:

- a short, informative cover letter including a clear and concise description of your book and its notable features, your opinion of the audience for the book, information on the current status of the manuscript and expected completion date, and some details on the physical characteristics of the manuscript, such as length, number of illustrations, tables, appendices, etc.

- a table of contents

- a preface, introduction, or other brief sample of your manuscript

- a curriculum vitae or biographical notes

If the press is interested, the editor will invite you to submit the complete manuscript or inform you that he or she can proceed to review the materials you sent.

Preparing Your Manuscript for Review

Presses vary in their requirements for manuscript preparation. In general, the manuscript you submit for review should be as accurate and complete as possible. If a manuscript is carelessly prepared, reviewers may take offense at typographical errors or careless citations and spend precious review space discussing these problems instead of attending to the substance of your manuscript. If, for good reasons, your manuscript is incomplete, you should indicate what material is missing and provide your schedule for completion.

Although some presses will accept a single-spaced manuscript for review, it is best to double-space your text. A double-spaced manuscript is easier to read and may be required when your manuscript reaches the copyediting stage. For book publication, every element of the text should be double-spaced (including quotations, notes, bibliographies, appendices, figure legends, and glossaries). Once your manuscript is accepted for publication, your editor will advise you on any special requirements imposed by that press's house style.

The Review Process

Some university presses may give advance (i.e., conditional) contracts to experienced authors on the basis of incomplete or unreviewed manuscripts. Most, however, must obtain one or more reviews of a completed manuscript before presenting a project for the approval of the press's editorial board. As review procedures differ from press to press, check with the editor when you first submit the manuscript to find out what will be involved. He or she should be able to give you a tentative schedule for the review process. It is difficult to predict exactly how long it will take to reach a decision, since often readers' reports encourage authors to make further revisions to the manuscript and the manuscript is usually reviewed again after the author makes the revisions. If your manuscript is also under review at another publisher, be sure to let the editor know. Some editors will not review manuscripts that are under simultaneous consideration elsewhere; others will not object.

Preparing Your Manuscript for Publication

Most publishers will want an electronic version of your manuscript. Your manuscript should be keyboarded as simply as possible. There is no need to change fonts, type styles, and formats to differentiate between sections; in fact, this is counterproductive. The press's copyediting or production department will insert the proper typesetting codes for formatting extracts, different levels of headings, and so on. And keep in mind that your book will be designed by a professional on the press's staff. Many presses will send you their own guidelines for submitting manuscripts.

FURTHER READING

Abel, Richard, Lyman W. Newlin, Katina Strauch, and Bruce Strauch, eds. *Scholarly Publishing, and Libraries in the Twentieth Century.* Indianapolis: Wiley, 2002.

American Psychological Association. *Publication Manual of the American Psychological Association.* 5th ed. Washington, DC: APA Books, 2001.

Appelbaum, Judith. *How to Get Happily Published: A Complete and Candid Guide.* 5th ed. New York: HarperResource, 1998.

Becker, Howard S. *Writing for Social Scientists: How to Start and Finish Your Thesis, Book, or Article.* Chicago: University of Chicago Press, 1986.

Carley, Michael J. "Publish Well and Wisely: A Brief Guide for New Scholars", http://www3.uakron.edu/uapress/pubwell.html, 1999.

Day, Robert A. *How to Write and Publish a Scientific Paper.* 5th ed. Phoenix: Oryx Press, 1998.

Derricourt, Robin. *An Author's Guide to Scholarly Publishing.* Princeton: Princeton University Press, 1996.

Germano, William. *Getting it Published: A Guide for Scholars and Anyone Else Serious About Serious Books.* Chicago: University of Chicago Press, 2001.

Gibaldi, Joseph and Herbert Lindenberger. *MLA Style Manual and Guide to Scholarly Publishing* 2nd ed. New York: Modern Language Association of America, 1998.

Hacker, Diana. *A Writer's Reference: 2003 MLA Update.* 5th ed. Boston: Bedford Books, 2003.

Harman, Eleanor and Ian Montagnes, eds. *The Thesis and the Book.* 2nd ed. Toronto: University of Toronto Press, 2003.

Huff, Anne Sigismund. *Writing for Scholarly Publication.* Thousand Oaks, CA: Sage Publications, 1998.

Katz, Michael J. *Elements of the Scientific Paper: A Step-by-Step Guide for Students and Professionals.* New Haven: Yale University Press, 1986.

Luey, Beth. *Handbook for Academic Authors.* 3rd ed. New York: Cambridge University Press, 1995.

Moxley, Joseph M. and Todd Taylor. *Writing and Publishing for Academic Authors.* 2nd ed. Lanham, MD: Rowman and Littlefield, 1996.

Mulvany, Nancy C. *Indexing Books.* Chicago: University of Chicago Press, 1994.

Parsons, Paul. *Getting Published: The Acquisition Process at University Presses.* Knoxville: University of Tennessee Press, 1989.

Powell, Walter W. *Getting into Print: The Decision-Making Process in Scholarly Publishing.* Chicago: University of Chicago Press, 1988.

Schwartz, Marilyn and the Task Force on Bias-Free Language of the AAUP. *Guidelines for Bias-Free Writing.* Bloomington: Indiana University Press, 1995.

Strong, William S. *The Copyright Book: A Practical Guide.* 5th ed. Cambridge, MA: MIT Press, 1999.

Strunk, William J. and E. B. White. *The Elements of Style.* 3rd ed. New York: Pearson Allyn & Bacon, 2000.

Swain, Dwight V. *Techniques of the Selling Writer.* Norman: University of Oklahoma Press, 1982.

University of Chicago Press. *The Chicago Manual of Style.* 15th ed. Chicago: University of Chicago Press, 2003.

Zerubavel, Eviator. *The Clockwork Muse: A Practical Guide to Writing Theses, Dissertations, and Books.* Cambridge, MA: Harvard University Press, 1999.

For additional citations to materials on scholarly publishing, visit the association's Web site at www.aaupnet.org.

SUBJECT AREA GRID

This eight-page grid indicates the subject areas in which each press has a particularly strong interest.

Some presses are prepared to consider manuscripts of outstanding quality in areas other than those listed. For more detailed descriptions of press editorial programs, consult the individual listings in the "Directory of Members" section and contact the presses that interest you. (See also "On Submitting Manuscripts" in this directory.)

	Akron	Alabama	Alaska	Alberta	A. Psychiatric	Amsterdam	Arizona	Arkansas	Beacon	British Columbia	Brookings	Cairo (American)	Calgary	California	Cambridge	Carnegie Mellon	Catholic	Chicago	Chinese	Colorado	Columbia	Copenhagen	Cork	Cornell	Duke	Duquesne	Edinburgh	Florida	Fordham	Gallaudet	Georgetown	Georgia	Getty
African Studies	•									•				•	•			•						•	•			•			•		
African-American Studies	•	•							•	•				•	•			•		•	•			•				•		•		•	
Agriculture							•	•		•			•	•	•			•		•				•	•							•	
American Indian Studies	•	•	•				•	•	•	•	•			•	•			•		•		•		•	•		•	•	•		•	•	
American Studies	•	•					•	•		•	•			•	•			•		•	•	•	•	•	•			•		•			
Anthropology	•	•	•			•	•		•	•				•	•			•	•	•	•	•	•	•	•			•		•	•		
Cultural	•	•	•				•		•	•				•	•			•	•	•								•					
Physical	•	•								•				•	•			•	•	•								•					
Archaeology	•	•	•				•	•		•			•	•	•	•		•					•	•			•					•	•
Architecture			•				•	•		•			•	•	•	•		•						•	•			•	•		•	•	•
Art & Art History			•				•	•		•			•	•	•	•		•					•	•	•			•			•	•	•
Art Criticism									•					•	•	•		•					•	•	•			•				•	•
Art History							•		•		•			•	•			•					•	•	•			•				•	•
Decorative Arts							•			•				•				•						•								•	•
Design & Graphics													•	•				•						•				•					•
Painting & Sculpture	•						•			•	•	•		•	•	•		•		•	•		•	•	•			•					
Asian Studies	•								•					•	•			•	•	•	•			•	•								
Asian-American Studies							•							•				•	•	•													
Astronomy										•			•	•	•			•		•	•			•	•	•	•		•				
Bibliography & Reference									•				•	•	•			•		•	•			•	•			•	•		•	•	
Biography	•	•	•	•		•	•		•	•	•	•	•	•	•		•	•	•	•	•	•		•			•				•		•
Biological Sciences			•		•		•		•	•			•	•	•			•		•	•			•									•
Botany			•						•	•				•				•						•				•			•		
Genetics				•										•				•						•				•			•		
Marine Biology			•							•				•	•			•						•				•			•		
Microbiology						•								•				•						•									
Physiology														•				•			•			•							•		•
Zoology			•						•	•			•	•	•			•	•	•			•	•				•					
Business			•	•						•			•	•				•						•									
Canadian Studies	•		•	•					•	•			•	•				•						•	•		•						
Caribbean Studies	•	•							•	•				•				•	•					•				•			•		
Child Development			•		•		•		•	•				•				•						•	•		•	•	•				•
Classics						•			•					•	•		•	•						•	•		•	•	•		•		
Communications		•		•			•			•				•				•		•	•	•		•	•	•	•	•			•		
Broadcast Media		•		•						•				•				•				•		•	•	•					•		
Journalism		•						•		•				•				•		•	•	•		•							•		
Computer Sciences																•		•								•						•	
Creative Nonfiction	•	•						•		•				•	•			•			•			•									
Criminal Justice	•								•				•	•	•			•						•					•		•		
Demography								•		•	•			•	•			•						•				•	•		•	•	
Drama							•			•				•	•		•	•	•	•	•			•	•	•		•			•		
Earth Sciences			•						•					•				•						•	•			•					
Geochemistry			•						•					•				•						•				•					
Geology			•											•				•						•				•			•		
Oceanography			•											•	•			•						•				•					
Economics	•		•						•	•		•		•	•			•		•	•			•	•	•		•					
History	•		•							•		•		•	•			•							•	•		•					
Theory											•			•	•			•							•			•			•	•	
Education									•	•	•	•		•				•	•					•	•						•	•	
Counseling									•	•				•						•				•							•	•	
History									•	•				•																	•	•	
Learning Disabilities					•					•		•								•											•	•	
Theory & Method									•	•				•						•				•							•	•	
Engineering													•	•	•	•																	
Environment/Conservation	•	•	•					•	•		•		•	•	•	•		•		•	•			•	•			•			•	•	
ESL															•									•									
Ethnic Studies	•	•	•			•	•	•	•	•			•	•	•			•			•			•	•		•	•	•				
European Studies	•						•			•			•	•	•		•							•	•				•				
Fiction									•			•		•	•	•								•	•	•	•	•		•	•		
Film Studies		•					•		•			•		•	•	•		•		•	•	•		•	•	•		•					•
Gender Studies						•	•	•	•	•		•		•	•			•		•	•	•		•		•		•					
Geography			•				•			•	•		•	•				•		•	•	•		•							•	•	
Gerontology	•	•	•			•	•		•	•			•	•	•	•	•	•		•	•			•	•		•	•	•	•	•		•
History														•	•										•	•							•
African	•													•	•										•								
American	•	•	•				•	•	•					•	•			•		•	•	•		•	•			•	•		•	•	
Asian	•								•					•	•			•		•	•			•	•			•					
British	•								•				•	•			•	•						•	•			•					
Canadian	•		•	•					•					•				•						•	•		•	•					•
Environmental	•	•	•				•	•	•	•				•				•	•		•			•	•	•	•	•					
European	•						•		•					•	•			•		•	•			•				•	•				
Latin American	•	•					•		•					•	•			•		•					•			•	•				
Middle Eastern	•								•	•			•		•	•					•							•	•				

10

	Akron	Alabama	Alaska	Alberta	A. Psychiatric	Amsterdam	Arizona	Arkansas	Beacon	British Columbia	Brookings	Cairo (American)	Calgary	California	Cambridge	Carnegie Mellon	Catholic	Chicago	Chinese	Colorado	Columbia	Copenhagen	Cork	Cornell	Duke	Duquesne	Edinburgh	Florida	Fordham	Gallaudet	Georgetown	Georgia	Getty
History (Cont'd) Ancient														●	●		●	●						●	●								
Classical						●								●	●		●	●						●	●								
Medieval						●									●		●	●				●		●	●								
Modern	●	●	●			●	●	●						●	●	●	●	●	●	●	●			●	●		●	●				●	
History of Science	●	●				●	●								●			●	●	●				●	●			●					
Law	●		●			●				●	●		●	●	●		●	●	●	●				●	●						●	●	●
Language						●	●			●		●		●				●	●									●	●	●	●	●	
Language Arts						●							●		●																●	●	
Linguistics		●				●		●					●		●			●						●				●	●		●	●	
Speech						●							●		●																●		
Latin American Studies	●	●				●		●		●			●	●	●			●		●				●				●					
Library Science						●									●			●															
Literature		●	●			●	●						●	●	●		●	●		●				●	●	●	●	●	●	●	●		●
Literary Criticism														●	●	●	●	●			●		●	●	●	●	●	●	●				●
Literary History		●													●	●	●	●			●		●	●	●	●	●	●		●			●
Literary Theory															●	●	●	●			●			●	●	●	●						
African															●			●															
African American		●						●							●			●			●			●	●			●					●
American		●						●						●	●	●	●	●		●	●			●	●		●	●	●	●			●
Asian															●		●	●			●			●	●	●	●	●	●	●			
British															●		●	●			●			●	●	●	●	●	●				
Canadian				●									●		●									●									
Classical														●	●		●	●						●	●								
Eastern															●			●															
European						●									●		●	●						●	●	●	●	●					
Medieval						●									●		●	●			●			●	●		●	●	●				
Renaissance						●									●		●	●			●			●	●		●	●					
Modern		●													●		●	●	●	●				●	●		●	●					●
Contemporary		●					●								●		●	●	●	●	●			●	●						●		●
Folklore		●				●	●											●					●	●									●
Mythology	●	●				●												●						●									
Translations	●	●						●			●				●		●	●	●	●				●	●			●					
Maritime Studies	●	●				●				●					●			●										●					
Mathematics															●			●															
Medicine		●		●		●								●	●			●	●		●			●									
Ethics				●										●	●						●										●		
General						●								●	●			●	●	●													
History		●	●			●									●									●	●						●		
Medieval Studies	●					●							●		●		●	●			●		●	●	●		●	●			●	●	
Middle East Studies	●					●		●	●		●	●			●			●			●			●	●		●			●			
Military Studies	●	●	●					●		●	●				●									●									
Music		●				●		●	●				●	●	●			●	●					●	●								●
History		●	●			●		●	●				●	●	●			●				●		●	●								●
Theory						●								●	●			●						●									
Near Eastern Studies	●							●		●	●		●	●	●			●						●	●								
Performing Arts						●							●	●	●	●		●						●			●		●	●	●		
Dance						●									●			●						●			●						
Music						●							●	●	●			●						●									
Theatre						●	●					●	●	●		●		●						●				●	●				
Pacific Studies	●		●			●		●	●						●									●	●		●	●			●		
Philosophy						●								●	●		●	●	●		●			●	●	●	●				●		
Ethics						●								●	●		●	●	●		●			●	●	●	●				●		
History of Philosophy						●							●		●		●	●		●				●	●		●						
Logic															●		●	●		●				●									
Metaphysics															●		●	●		●				●			●						
Physical Science		●				●		●						●	●			●			●											●	●
Photography		●													●			●			●										●		●
Poetry	●						●	●				●		●	●			●													●		●
Political Science/Public Affairs	●		●			●	●	●	●	●	●	●	●		●		●	●	●	●	●			●	●		●				●		
Psychiatry					●										●			●	●					●	●						●		
Psychology						●	●			●	●				●			●	●						●	●		●			●		
Public Health						●			●	●				●	●			●						●									
Publishing						●									●			●															
Regional Studies	●	●	●	●		●	●	●	●	●			●	●	●		●	●	●	●	●		●	●	●		●			●		●	●
Religion		●				●	●		●				●	●	●		●	●		●	●	●		●	●	●	●	●	●		●		
Slavic Studies	●		●			●		●		●					●			●						●	●								
Social Work				●	●	●		●	●				●	●				●		●								●			●		
Sociology	●		●			●	●		●	●				●	●			●	●	●				●	●						●		
Urban Studies	●					●		●	●	●	●				●			●						●	●						●		
Veterinary Sciences															●			●				●		●									
Women's Studies		●				●		●	●	●	●		●	●	●			●			●	●		●	●		●				●	●	●

11

	Harvard	Hawaii	Howard	Idaho	Illinois	Indiana	Iowa	Island	Jewish Pub.	Johns Hopkins	Kansas	Kent State	Kentucky	Louisiana	McGill-Queen's	Marquette	Massachusetts	MIT	Mercer	Michigan	Michigan State	Minnesota Hist.	Minnesota	Mississippi	Missouri Hist.	Missouri	MLA	National Acad.	National Gallery	Naval
African Studies	●		●		●																		●					●		
African-American Studies	●		●		●	●	●				●		●	●			●			●	●	●	●	●	●	●	●	●		●
Agriculture				●	●		●																						●	
American Indian Studies	●			●	●							●	●	●			●			●	●	●	●	●		●	●			
American Studies	●		●	●	●	●	●				●	●	●	●	●		●			●	●	●	●	●	●	●				
Anthropology			●	●	●	●	●	●					●				●			●		●	●							
Cultural			●	●	●	●	●	●					●				●			●		●	●							
Physical			●										●				●													
Archaeology			●		●			●		●			●				●			●										
Architecture			●		●					●					●		●	●				●	●	●	●					
Art & Art History	●	●	●	●		●									●		●	●	●		●	●	●	●					●	●
Art Criticism	●	●													●			●	●		●	●							●	
Art History	●	●			●										●		●		●	●		●							●	
Decorative Arts	●																					●							●	
Design & Graphics	●																●			●	●								●	
Painting & Sculpture	●			●													●	●				●							●	
Asian Studies	●	●			●								●														●			
Asian-American Studies	●	●											●				●					●					●			
Astronomy	●								●																			●		
Bibliography & Reference		●			●	●			●	●									●		●							●		●
Biography	●	●	●	●	●		●	●		●			●	●	●		●			●	●	●	●		●	●	●		●	●
Biological Sciences	●	●	●	●	●	●	●	●		●										●								●		
Botany	●	●		●			●	●												●								●		
Genetics	●							●		●									●									●		
Marine Biology	●	●						●																				●		
Microbiology	●							●		●																		●		
Physiology	●							●																				●		
Zoology	●	●		●	●		●	●												●								●		
Business	●	●	●																●		●							●		
Canadian Studies				●											●						●							●		
Caribbean Studies			●										●	●	●		●			●								●		
Child Development	●				●														●									●		
Classics	●			●	●		●	●											●									●		
Communications	●	●	●		●								●		●		●	●					●			●	●			
Broadcast Media		●	●		●								●		●								●							
Journalism	●	●	●										●										●		●					
Computer Sciences																			●									●		
Creative Nonfiction		●					●						●							●		●	●		●					
Criminal Justice				●									●		●	●							●							●
Demography	●																●											●		
Drama	●	●																	●					●		●				
Earth Sciences	●	●		●			●	●												●								●		
Geochemistry								●																				●		
Geology	●	●		●			●	●												●								●		
Oceanography	●	●						●																				●		●
Economics	●	●	●		●			●			●			●			●		●	●	●							●		
History	●	●	●		●						●			●			●		●	●	●									
Theory	●	●	●		●						●			●			●		●	●	●									
Education	●		●		●	●					●			●			●			●	●						●	●		
Counseling																														
History	●		●		●						●			●			●		●	●	●									
Learning Disabilities	●				●																									
Theory & Method														●							●									
Engineering	●		●																									●		●
Environment/Conservation	●	●	●	●	●		●	●			●	●		●	●	●			●	●	●	●	●	●	●	●		●		
ESL																						●								
Ethnic Studies		●	●		●	●	●				●			●		●				●		●	●	●	●		●	●		
European Studies	●				●	●								●		●			●		●			●			●	●		
Fiction		●			●	●		●											●				●	●		●		●		
Film Studies	●	●	●		●	●					●	●		●			●			●	●		●		●	●	●			
Gender Studies	●	●	●	●	●	●	●				●			●	●		●			●			●	●		●	●	●	●	
Geography		●					●	●			●				●	●						●	●	●	●			●		
Gerontology										●																		●		
History	●	●	●	●	●	●	●	●		●	●	●	●	●	●		●			●	●	●	●	●	●	●	●			●
African		●	●		●	●														●	●									
American	●		●	●	●	●	●				●	●	●	●	●		●			●	●	●	●	●	●	●				●
Asian	●	●											●							●										●
British	●			●									●	●							●			●						●
Canadian			●												●					●										
Environmental	●						●	●			●	●	●	●		●	●					●		●						
European	●				●	●			●				●	●						●	●					●				●
Latin American	●		●										●	●	●						●					●			●	●
Middle Eastern	●				●									●																

	Harvard	Hawaii	Howard	Idaho	Illinois	Indiana	Iowa	Island	Jewish Pub.	Johns Hopkins	Kansas	Kent State	Kentucky	Louisiana	McGill-Queen's	Marquette	Massachusetts	MIT	Mercer	Michigan	Michigan State	Minnesota Hist.	Minnesota	Mississippi	Missouri Hist.	Missouri	MLA	National Acad.	National Gallery	Naval
History (Cont'd) Ancient	•	•				•				•							•			•										•
Classical	•					•				•							•			•										•
Medieval	•				•												•			•				•						•
Modern	•	•	•			•				•			•	•			•			•					•		•			•
History of Science	•	•			•		•			•				•				•		•						•		•	•	•
Law	•	•	•		•				•		•		•				•			•						•				•
Language	•	•	•	•	•												•		•	•							•			
Language Arts		•																				•					•			
Linguistics		•		•									•	•			•		•								•			
Speech				•													•										•			
Latin American Studies	•		•											•						•				•			•	•	•	
Library Science				•															•								•			
Literature	•	•	•	•	•	•	•			•		•		•		•	•		•	•	•	•	•	•		•	•			•
Literary Criticism	•	•	•	•	•		•			•		•		•		•	•	•	•	•	•	•	•	•		•	•			•
Literary History	•				•		•			•		•		•	•		•		•	•		•	•	•	•	•	•			
Literary Theory	•	•			•	•				•		•		•	•		•		•	•		•	•		•	•	•			
African			•		•														•			•	•			•	•			
African-American	•		•		•	•							•		•			•	•	•		•	•		•	•	•			
American	•		•	•	•	•				•		•		•	•		•		•	•	•	•	•		•	•	•		•	
Asian	•	•			•														•				•			•				
British	•			•						•			•	•					•				•		•	•	•			•
Canadian															•						•		•			•				
Classical	•				•					•					•				•				•			•				
Eastern															•								•			•				
European	•				•					•					•				•			•			•	•	•			•
Medieval	•			•											•				•			•			•	•				
Renaissance	•														•	•	•		•			•			•	•				
Modern	•	•			•		•						•		•	•			•			•	•		•	•				
Contemporary	•	•			•		•						•		•	•			•			•	•		•	•				
Folklore	•	•		•	•								•		•				•				•		•	•	•			
Mythology		•													•				•				•			•				
Translations		•			•		•								•				•				•		•	•	•			•
Maritime Studies		•													•						•	•						•	•	•
Mathematics	•		•		•	•				•								•									•			
Medicine	•		•		•					•					•					•			•			•				
Ethics	•				•					•					•								•			•				
General	•									•					•								•			•				
History	•	•			•					•					•					•						•				
Medieval Studies	•				•										•				•			•			•					
Middle East Studies	•				•			•			•								•			•			•					
Military Studies	•	•			•	•					•	•	•	•	•			•			•			•		•		•		•
Music	•	•	•		•	•							•	•	•				•	•	•		•	•	•					
History	•					•							•	•	•				•	•			•	•						
Theory		•			•								•						•	•			•	•						
Near Eastern Studies	•				•			•	•										•							•				
Performing Arts		•	•		•	•	•												•			•	•			•				
Dance		•			•	•																•								
Music		•			•	•													•			•	•							
Theatre		•			•	•	•												•			•	•	•		•				
Pacific Studies		•		•										•												•				
Philosophy	•	•	•	•	•	•			•					•	•		•						•			•				
Ethics	•			•	•									•	•		•	•								•				
History of Philosophy	•	•			•									•	•		•			•						•				
Logic					•									•	•		•													
Metaphysics	•				•									•	•		•													
Physical Science	•	•								•							•										•			
Photography		•		•												•		•		•		•	•	•	•					
Poetry						•							•	•		•					•				•	•				
Political Science/Public Affairs	•	•	•		•	•		•		•	•		•	•	•	•	•	•	•	•	•	•	•		•		•			
Psychiatry	•					•																				•				
Psychology	•		•		•					•								•					•	•		•				
Public Health	•		•		•		•							•									•			•				
Publishing					•													•								•				
Regional Studies	•	•	•	•	•	•	•			•	•	•	•	•	•	•		•	•	•	•	•	•		•	•				
Religion	•	•	•		•	•			•	•			•		•	•		•				•	•	•						
Slavic Studies	•				•									•											•					
Social Work			•		•																					•				
Sociology	•	•	•		•					•			•		•								•			•				
Urban Studies	•	•	•		•				•		•		•		•	•	•			•	•					•				
Veterinary Sciences																				•						•				
Women's Studies	•	•	•	•	•	•	•		•	•	•	•	•	•		•			•	•	•	•	•	•	•	•	•		•	

	Nebraska	Nevada	New England	New Mexico	New York	North Carolina	North Texas	Northeastern	Northern Illinois	Northwestern	Notre Dame	Ohio	Ohio State	Oklahoma	Oregon State	Oxford	Pennsylvania	Penn State	Pittsburgh	Princeton	Puerto Rico	Purdue	RAND	Resources	Rockefeller	Russell Sage	Rutgers	Scranton	Smithsonian	Soc. Biblical Lit.	South Carolina
African Studies	●												●																●	●	
African-American Studies	●		●		●	●	●						●		●	●		●	●			●					●	●			●
Agriculture	●					●								●		●						●	●								
American Indian Studies	●	●	●	●		●									●	●	●										●			●	
American Studies	●	●	●	●	●	●	●	●		●			●	●		●	●	●	●	●							●	●		●	●
Anthropology	●	●			●	●	●					●	●		●		●	●									●	●		●	
Cultural	●	●	●		●		●			●		●	●		●		●	●		●		●					●			●	
Physical		●		●		●									●															●	
Archaeology	●	●	●	●		●			●						●		●	●											●	●	
Architecture		●	●	●		●									●		●	●	●												
Art & Art History		●	●	●		●	●						●			●	●	●		●	●						●	●			●
Art Criticism		●	●	●									●			●	●		●	●											
Art History	●		●	●		●							●			●	●	●		●	●							●			●
Decorative Arts	●		●	●		●					●						●			●							●				
Design & Graphics			●														●														
Painting & Sculpture		●	●			●							●	●	●		●	●													
Asian Studies	●												●				●			●		●		●			●				
Asian-American Studies				●									●				●										●	●	●		
Astronomy													●				●	●													
Bibliography & Reference		●	●								●		●	●	●		●	●													
Biography	●	●	●	●	●	●	●	●	●	●	●	●		●	●		●	●	●	●	●		●			●	●		●	●	●
Biological Sciences		●	●										●	●	●		●										●		●		●
Botany	●	●				●							●	●			●										●		●		
Genetics													●				●							●		●					
Marine Biology													●				●												●		●
Microbiology													●													●					
Physiology													●				●							●							
Zoology		●													●		●	●									●		●		
Business		●			●	●			●			●		●			●			●	●	●	●				●		●		●
Canadian Studies	●												●				●														
Caribbean Studies	●			●	●				●				●		●		●														
Child Development													●					●		●		●			●	●					
Classics					●			●		●	●	●				●	●		●	●									●		
Communications		●	●		●	●	●		●				●				●			●						●					
Broadcast Media					●								●													●					
Journalism	●	●			●	●	●		●				●				●		●												
Computer Sciences																															
Creative Nonfiction	●	●	●	●			●			●	●			●		●	●														
Criminal Justice	●			●		●	●		●				●				●		●		●						●	●			
Demography																			●	●		●		●							
Drama					●			●				●	●				●														
Earth Sciences		●	●									●	●	●			●			●		●									
Geochemistry													●				●														
Geology		●										●	●				●														
Oceanography													●				●														
Economics					●		●	●			●		●				●	●	●		●										●
History					●		●	●			●		●				●	●													
Theory													●				●	●													
Education					●								●				●	●				●		●							
Counseling																															
History				●	●																										
Learning Disabilities																	●														
Theory & Method																	●														
Engineering													●						●												
Environment/Conservation	●	●	●	●		●	●					●		●	●	●	●		●	●	●	●	●	●	●			●		●	
ESL													●																		
Ethnic Studies	●	●	●	●	●	●	●	●	●		●			●			●		●		●						●	●	●		
European Studies		●	●			●		●	●		●				●				●			●					●				
Fiction		●	●	●		●		●			●	●	●		●				●												
Film Studies		●	●		●	●			●				●				●										●				
Gender Studies	●	●	●	●	●	●			●	●			●	●		●	●		●								●	●	●	●	
Geography	●	●	●			●						●	●	●	●		●														
Gerontology													●					●	●								●				
History	●	●	●	●	●	●	●	●	●		●	●	●		●	●	●	●	●	●	●	●					●	●	●		●
African													●				●														●
American	●	●	●	●	●	●	●	●	●		●	●	●		●	●	●	●	●	●	●						●	●	●		●
Asian													●				●		●								●				
British			●	●				●		●	●		●			●	●	●													
Canadian	●		●		●								●																		
Environmental	●	●		●		●	●						●	●	●		●	●									●				
European		●	●		●	●			●			●	●			●	●	●	●		●										
Latin American	●			●		●					●			●			●	●	●		●						●				
Middle Eastern		●	●		●	●							●		●					●							●			●	

	Nebraska	Nevada	New England	New Mexico	New York	North Carolina	North Texas	Northeastern	Northern Illinois	Northwestern	Notre Dame	Ohio	Ohio State	Oklahoma	Oregon State	Oxford	Pennsylvania	Penn State	Pittsburgh	Princeton	Puerto Rico	Purdue	RAND	Resources	Rockefeller	Russell Sage	Rutgers	Scranton	Smithsonian	Soc. Biblical Lit.	South Carolina
History (Cont'd) Ancient						●					●		●			●	●			●										●	
Classical						●					●		●			●	●		●	●										●	
Medieval											●					●	●	●		●								●			
Modern			●	●		●	●	●	●	●		●	●	●	●		●		●		●						●	●	●		●
History of Science						●					●						●		●			●					●		●		●
Law		●			●	●	●	●		●		●					●		●	●	●		●			●	●				
Language	●	●		●							●			●			●			●											●
Language Arts																															
Linguistics	●			●							●			●			●			●									●		
Speech																															●
Latin American Studies	●		●	●		●					●	●				●		●	●		●						●	●	●	●	
Library Science																															
Literature	●	●	●	●	●	●			●	●	●	●	●	●	●	●	●		●		●						●	●			●
Literary Criticism	●	●	●	●	●	●			●	●	●	●	●			●	●		●		●						●	●		●	●
Literary History	●	●	●			●			●	●	●	●				●	●		●		●										●
Literary Theory	●				●	●			●	●	●		●			●	●		●		●										●
African												●				●			●												
African-American					●	●						●				●			●								●				●
American	●	●	●	●	●	●	●		●	●	●		●	●	●	●	●		●								●				●
Asian						●										●			●								●				
British									●			●	●	●		●	●		●								●				●
Canadian			●																												
Classical						●				●			●			●	●														●
Eastern																●	●		●												
European			●						●	●						●	●		●												●
Medieval										●						●	●	●													
Renaissance										●						●	●														
Modern			●			●		●	●			●					●										●				●
Contemporary	●	●	●	●		●	●	●	●	●		●		●			●	●									●				●
Folklore		●	●	●		●		●				●	●	●			●									●					
Mythology			●									●	●	●			●														
Translations	●		●	●				●	●			●			●	●	●	●												●	
Maritime Studies			●										●					●													●
Mathematics			●										●				●	●													
Medicine			●	●	●								●											●		●					
Ethics			●	●	●								●													●					
General			●	●									●											●		●					
History			●		●								●											●		●					
Medieval Studies								●		●			●	●	●		●										●				
Middle East Studies				●	●								●		●		●			●			●				●			●	
Military Studies	●			●	●	●				●		●		●		●				●			●					●	●		●
Music	●	●		●		●	●						●					●	●								●				
History	●		●	●		●		●					●					●	●								●				
Theory	●		●										●																		
Near Eastern Studies					●								●	●															●		
Performing Arts			●		●		●	●		●			●				●	●													
Dance	●							●					●																		
Music	●	●		●				●					●					●	●												
Theatre	●		●		●			●				●	●				●	●													
Pacific Studies										●			●																		
Philosophy	●			●		●		●	●		●			●	●		●	●	●	●	●		●	●		●			●		
Ethics			●					●	●	●				●			●	●	●	●		●				●					
History of Philosophy					●			●	●	●				●			●	●	●	●	●					●					
Logic								●	●					●			●	●	●												
Metaphysics								●	●					●			●	●	●	●						●					
Physical Science			●	●										●				●	●	●											
Photography	●	●	●	●	●	●												●													●
Poetry			●				●	●		●	●	●	●					●		●							●				
Political Science/Public Affairs		●	●	●	●	●		●	●		●		●	●		●	●	●	●	●		●	●		●						
Psychiatry																	●														
Psychology	●			●	●	●							●						●							●					
Public Health				●								●				●			●	●	●	●			●	●					
Publishing		●	●							●								●													
Regional Studies	●	●	●	●	●	●	●	●	●	●		●	●	●	●	●	●	●	●		●						●	●	●	●		●
Religion	●		●	●	●	●			●		●			●		●	●	●	●							●	●			●	●
Slavic Studies								●	●				●	●	●																
Social Work			●										●							●				●			●				●
Sociology			●		●		●	●					●				●		●	●		●			●	●					
Urban Studies			●	●		●	●							●			●	●		●	●	●			●	●					
Veterinary Sciences																						●									
Women's Studies	●	●	●	●	●	●	●	●	●			●	●	●		●	●	●	●		●			●			●	●			●

	Southern Illinois	S. Methodist	Stanford	SUNY	Syracuse	Teachers	Temple	Tennessee	Texas	Texas A&M	Texas Christian	Texas Tech	Texas Western	Tokyo	Toronto	United Nations	U.S. Inst. Peace	Upjohn	Utah	Utah State	Vanderbilt	Virginia	Washington	Wash. State	Wayne State	Wesleyan	West Virginia	Wilfrid Laurier	Wisconsin	Woodrow Wilson	Yale
African Studies														●	●	●	●					●	●						●	●	●
African-American Studies			●	●	●	●	●	●			●											●	●	●	●	●			●		●
Agriculture								●							●			●													
American Indian Studies				●		●	●	●					●		●				●	●		●	●	●							●
American Studies	●		●	●		●	●	●	●		●		●	●								●	●	●	●	●	●	●	●	●	●
Anthropology			●	●	●		●	●	●	●				●	●				●			●		●		●			●	●	●
Cultural			●	●			●		●					●	●				●		●			●		●			●	●	●
Physical								●						●	●				●			●									●
Archaeology							●	●	●					●	●				●		●	●	●						●		●
Architecture							●	●	●	●				●	●						●	●								●	●
Art & Art History			●	●			●		●													●	●	●		●			●		●
Art Criticism			●				●															●						●	●		●
Art History				●		●		●						●	●							●	●				●		●		●
Decorative Arts							●															●							●		●
Design & Graphics							●															●									●
Painting & Sculpture							●		●	●	●																		●		●
Asian Studies			●	●		●					●	●		●	●		●	●				●							●	●	●
Asian American Studies			●			●					●											●			●						●
Astronomy																													●		●
Bibliography & Reference														●	●						●		●						●		●
Biography	●		●	●	●		●	●	●					●	●				●		●		●						●	●	●
Biological Sciences	●										●		●	●	●							●							●	●	●
Botany	●			●					●		●		●									●							●		●
Genetics														●																	●
Marine Biology									●					●	●								●								●
Microbiology														●																	●
Physiology								●			●			●															●		●
Zoology								●		●	●			●															●		●
Business			●	●										●			●														●
Canadian Studies														●	●						●		●	●	●			●			
Caribbean Studies					●																	●							●		
Child Development														●										●							●
Classics			●					●						●	●											●	●		●		●
Communications	●		●	●		●	●							●	●														●	●	●
Broadcast Media	●		●	●		●	●				●	●	●	●												●			●	●	●
Journalism			●	●		●	●							●	●														●	●	
Computer Sciences			●																												●
Creative Nonfiction			●	●			●			●																●			●	●	
Criminal Justice	●		●	●		●		●						●								●	●								●
Demography														●	●																
Drama	●	●		●		●								●	●																●
Earth Sciences								●	●			●	●	●		●		●													●
Geochemistry														●																	●
Geology								●	●		●				●			●													●
Oceanography															●																●
Economics			●	●					●					●	●	●		●									●		●	●	●
History			●						●					●				●									●		●		
Theory			●											●				●													
Education			●	●		●	●		●					●	●			●		●	●										●
Counseling					●									●							●										
History				●		●								●							●										
Learning Disabilities						●	●							●							●										
Theory & Method			●			●	●							●	●						●										
Engineering														●																	●
Environment/Conservation			●	●		●	●	●	●				●	●	●		●		●	●		●	●	●				●	●		●
ESL																															●
Ethnic Studies			●	●		●		●	●				●	●	●	●		●		●	●		●	●		●	●	●	●	●	●
European Studies			●	●		●					●			●	●	●													●	●	●
Fiction		●	●	●							●	●															●		●		
Film Studies	●	●	●	●		●	●		●						●										●	●		●	●	●	●
Gender Studies	●		●	●		●	●	●	●					●	●						●				●			●	●		●
Geography				●					●	●	●			●	●	●		●				●							●		●
Gerontology				●										●																	
History	●		●	●		●	●	●	●	●	●			●	●			●	●		●	●	●	●			●		●	●	●
African														●			●					●							●	●	●
American	●		●	●		●	●	●	●	●	●	●		●				●	●		●	●	●	●			●		●		●
Asian			●	●							●			●	●								●						●	●	●
British			●									●		●	●			●							●				●	●	●
Canadian														●	●						●		●	●		●		●	●		●
Environmental			●							●	●		●	●	●								●						●	●	●
European			●		●		●						●	●	●						●		●						●	●	●
Latin American			●					●		●		●	●		●				●										●		●
Middle Eastern			●	●	●				●					●								●			●				●		●

16

	Southern Illinois	S. Methodist	Stanford	SUNY	Syracuse	Teachers	Temple	Tennessee	Texas	Texas A&M	Texas Christian	Texas Tech	Texas Western	Tokyo	Toronto	United Nations	U.S. Inst. Peace	Upjohn	Utah	Utah State	Vanderbilt	Virginia	Washington	Wash. State	Wayne State	Wesleyan	West Virginia	Wilfrid Laurier	Wisconsin	Woodrow Wilson	Yale
History (Cont'd) Ancient								●						●	●																●
Classical								●						●	●														●		●
Medieval				●										●	●														●		●
Modern		●	●	●		●						●		●	●			●									●		●	●	●
History of Science								●						●	●									●					●		●
Law		●				●								●	●														●		●
Language	●		●					●					●	●	●				●						●				●		●
Language Arts	●		●					●							●										●				●		●
Linguistics													●	●	●				●										●		
Speech	●																								●						●
Latin American Studies		●	●			●		●						●	●	●	●				●						●		●	●	●
Library Science														●	●														●		●
Literature	●		●	●	●		●	●	●	●	●	●	●	●	●				●		●	●	●	●	●		●		●	●	●
Literary Criticism		●	●	●			●	●	●		●			●	●						●	●	●		●		●		●		●
Literary History				●			●	●			●	●		●	●						●	●	●		●		●		●	●	●
Literary Theory			●	●				●						●								●	●		●		●		●		●
African																						●									●
African American														●	●							●									●
American	●		●	●	●		●	●	●	●				●	●							●	●		●				●		●
Asian			●											●																	●
British			●									●			●							●	●		●				●		●
Canadian															●												●				●
Classical								●							●																●
Eastern			●																										●		●
European			●	●											●							●	●		●				●		●
Medieval			●	●											●							●				●			●		●
Renaissance															●								●					●	●		●
Modern	●		●	●			●	●		●					●							●	●		●				●		●
Contemporary	●		●	●			●	●							●						●					●			●		●
Folklore			●	●			●	●	●		●				●							●			●				●		●
Mythology								●							●			●	●			●			●		●		●		●
Translations			●	●	●			●						●									●	●	●		●		●		●
Maritime Studies							●							●								●			●		●		●		●
Mathematics														●																	●
Medicine	●	●												●	●												●				●
General		●												●													●				●
History	●													●	●												●				●
Medieval Studies			●	●										●	●								●						●		●
Middle East Studies			●	●	●		●							●										●				●	●		●
Military Studies	●					●		●				●	●	●	●														●	●	●
Music						●	●		●					●							●				●	●			●		●
History						●	●		●					●											●	●			●		●
Theory						●	●							●											●	●					●
Near Eastern Studies			●	●			●							●	●		●												●	●	●
Performing Arts	●	●				●								●											●				●		●
Dance																						●							●		●
Music						●																●							●		●
Theatre	●					●								●								●							●		●
Pacific Studies			●											●		●	●						●	●					●		●
Philosophy		●	●	●	●									●	●												●	●	●		●
Ethics		●	●	●										●	●												●	●	●		●
History of Philosophy			●									●		●	●						●						●	●	●		●
Logic			●											●	●												●				●
Metaphysics			●	●										●	●												●				●
Physical Science														●																	●
Photography						●		●	●	●				●	●																●
Poetry	●													●					●								●	●		●	●
Political Science/Public Affairs		●	●	●		●		●		●			●	●	●		●	●			●	●	●	●					●	●	●
Psychiatry			●											●					●		●										●
Psychology			●											●	●				●		●							●	●	●	●
Public Health			●											●	●			●	●		●									●	●
Publishing														●	●																
Regional Studies	●	●	●	●	●		●	●	●	●	●	●		●	●				●	●	●	●	●	●	●	●	●		●		
Religion		●	●	●	●	●	●	●						●	●			●			●		●		●		●	●	●	●	●
Slavic Studies														●	●							●		●			●		●		●
Social Work														●	●		●	●				●							●		
Sociology		●	●	●		●								●	●		●		●			●				●			●		●
Urban Studies			●			●		●						●	●				●			●					●		●		●
Veterinary Sciences														●																	
Women's Studies	●		●	●		●	●		●	●	●			●	●		●		●			●	●	●	●		●		●	●	●

17

PRESSES PUBLISHING JOURNALS

University presses have always been associated with publishing books of merit and distinction. This remains as true today as in the past, but less well appreciated is the extent to which university presses are active in publishing scholarly journals.

Journals form a major part of the publishing program of many presses, and more than half of the association's members produce at least one periodical. In all, university presses publish more than 600 scholarly periodicals, including many of the most distinguished in their respective fields. The following is a list of those presses that publish journals.

Each individual press listing also gives the number of journals, if any, that a press publishes and usually lists the titles of journals under the press's editorial program. Many journals are available in both print and electronic versions. For information concerning a specific periodical, readers are advised to consult a copy of the publication before communicating with the press concerned.

The following AAUP member presses publish journals.

The University of Alabama Press
American Psychiatric Press, Inc.
American University in Cairo Press
Amsterdam University Press
The University of Arkansas Press
Brookings Institution Press
University of Calgary Press
The University of California Press
Cambridge University Press
Carnegie Mellon University Press
The Catholic University of America Press
The University of Chicago Press
The Chinese University Press
University Press of Colorado
Duke University Press
Edinburgh University Press
Fordham University Press
Georgetown University Press
J. Paul Getty Trust Publications
The University of Hawai'i Press
The University of Illinois Press
Indiana University Press
The Johns Hopkins University Press
The Kent State University Press
The University Press of Kentucky
Marquette University Press
The MIT Press
The Michigan State University Press

Minnesota Historical Society Press
University of Minnesota Press
The Missouri Historical Society Press
Modern Language Association of America
National Gallery of Art
Naval Institute Press
The University of Nebraska Press
The University of North Carolina Press
Northwestern University Press
University of Notre Dame Press
Ohio State University Press
Oxford University Press
The Pennsylvania State University Press
Princeton University Press
The University of Puerto Rico Press
RAND Corporation
The Rockefeller University Press
Society of Biblical Literature
State University of New York Press
University of Texas Press
Texas Tech University Press
University of Toronto Press, Inc.
W.E. Upjohn Institute for Employment Research
Washington State University Press
Wayne State University Press
Wesleyan University Press
West Virginia University Press
Wilfrid Laurier University Press
The University of Wisconsin Press

DIRECTORY OF MEMBERS

This section includes a wealth of information on the AAUP's 125 member presses, including current street and mailing addresses, phone and fax numbers, and Web site and e-mail addresses. Most presses also list their sales representatives/distributors for Canada, the UK, and Europe. (Addresses for these representatives are included at the end of the section.)

Each entry contains important information describing that press's editorial program. This includes a list of disciplines published, special series, joint imprints, copublishing programs, and the names of journals published, if any.

Press staff are listed, wherever possible, by the following departments/order: director and administrative staff, acquisitions editorial, manuscript editorial, marketing, design and production, journals, business, and electronic publishing and information systems. In most cases the first person listed within a department is its head. Readers should note, however, that this method of organization is intended to promote ease of use, and is not always indicative of the lines of authority within an individual press.

Information on each press's membership status follows the staff listing. This includes date of press founding, type of membership (full, affiliate, international, or associate), year admitted to the AAUP, title output for 2002 and 2003, the number of journals published, and the total number of titles currently in print.

The University of Akron Press

374B Bierce Library
Akron, OH 44325-1703

Phone: (330) 972-6896
Fax: (330) 972-8364
E-mail: uapress@uakron.edu
Web site: www.uakron.edu/uapress

Customer Service/Order Fulfillment:
Phone: (330) 972-6953
Toll-free: (877) UAPRESS (827-7377)
Fax: (330) 972-8364

Staff

Director: Michael J. Carley (330/972-6896; e-mail: mjcarley@uakron.edu)
Marketing Representative: Marsha Cole (330/972-2795; e-mail: press@uakron.edu)
Production Coordinator: Amy Freels Petersen (330/972-5342; e-mail: production@uakron.edu)
Distribution Manager: Dustin Meeker (330/972-6953; e-mail: uapress@uakron.edu)

Affiliate Member

Established: 1988
Title output 2002: 10
Titles currently in print: 58

Admitted to AAUP: 1997
Title output 2003: 8

Editorial Program

Scholarly books and poetry, with special interests in environmental studies and regional history.

Special series: Akron Series in Poetry, with Akron Poetry Prize Competition; International, Political, and Economic History; Law, Politics, and Society; Ohio History and Culture; Technology and the Environment.

The Press distributes the publications of Principia Press.

The University of Alabama Press

Street Address:
20 Research Drive
Tuscaloosa, AL 35401

Mailing Address:
Box 870336
Tuscaloosa, AL 35487-0336

Phone: (205) 348-5180
Fax: (205) 348-9201
E-mail: (user I.D.)@uapress.ua.edu
Web site: www.uapress.ua.edu

Order Fulfillment:
The University of Alabama Press
Chicago Distribution Center
11030 South Langley Avenue
Chicago, IL 60628
Phone: (773) 568-1550
Fax: (773) 660-2235

UK/European Distributor:
Eurospan

Canadian Representative:
Scholarly Book Services

Staff

Director: Daniel J.J. Ross (205/348-1560; e-mail: danross)
  Assistant to the Director: Valerie Knott-Hudson (205/348-5180; e-mail: vhudson)
  Rights and Permissions Coordinator: Kathleen Domino (205/348-1561; e-mail: kdomino)
Acquisitions Editorial: Daniel J.J. Ross (history, Judaic studies, trade)
  Acquisitions Editor: Judith Knight (archaeology, anthropology, ethnohistory, Native American studies) (205/348-1568; e-mail: jknight)
  Acquisitions Editor, Humanities: Dan Waterman (205/348-5538; e-mail: waterman)
  Assistant Acquisitions Editor: Kathleen Domino 205/348-1561; e-mail: kdomino)
Manuscript Editorial: Suzette Griffith, Managing Editor (205/348-9708; e-mail: sgriffit)
  Assistant Managing Editor: Joanna Jacobs (205/348-1563; e-mail: jjacobs)
  Project Editor: Jon Berry (205/348-1565; e-mail: jberry)
  Editorial Assistant: Carol Connell (205/348-5183; e-mail: cconnell)
Marketing: Elizabeth Motherwell, Manager (205/348-7108; e-mail: emother)
  Assistant Marketing Manager and Publicity Director: Dennis Lloyd (205/348-9534; e-mail: dlloyd)
  Exhibits and Direct Mail Assistant: Katina Bryant (205/348-1566; e-mail: kbryant)
Design and Production: Rick Cook, Production Manager (205/348-1571; e-mail: rcook)
  Designer: Michele Quinn (205/348-1570; e-mail: mquinn)
  Production Editor and Assistant Production Manager: Sonia Wilson (205/348-9665; e-mail: swilson)
Business: Jill Kramer, Manager (205/348-1567; e-mail: jkramer)
  Accounting Assistant: Allie Harper (205/348-1564; e-mail: aharper)

Full Member

Established: 1945
Title output 2002: 58
Titles currently in print: 785

Admitted to AAUP: 1964
Title output 2003: 69
Journals published: 2

Editorial Program

American history; Southern history and culture; American religious history; Latin American history; American archaeology; southeastern archaeology; historical archaeology; Mesoamerican archaeology; ethnohistory; American literature and criticism; rhetoric and communication; linguistics, esp. dialectology; African-American studies; Native American studies; women's studies; Judaic studies; public administration; theater; natural history and environmental studies; American social and cultural history; sports history; military history; various regional studies of Alabama and the southern United States, including regional trade titles. Submissions are not invited in poetry, fiction, or drama. The Press publishes the journals *Alabama Review* and *Theatre Symposium*.

Special series: Classics of Civil War Fiction; Classics in Southeastern Archaeology; Contemporary American Indian Studies; Deep South Books; Judaic Studies Series; Library Alabama Classics; Modern and Contemporary Poetics; The Modern South; Old French Crusade Cycle; Religion and American Culture; Studies in American Literary Realism and Naturalism; Studies in Rhetoric and Communciation; Theatre Symposium.

Co-Publishers: Edinburgh University Press

University of Alaska Press

104 Eielson Building
Salcha Street
PO Box 756240
Fairbanks, AK 99775-6240

Phone: (888) 252-6657; (907) 474-5831
Fax: (907) 474-5502
E-mail: fypress@uaf.edu
Web site: www.uaf.edu/uapress

Staff

Executive Editor: Jennifer Robin Collier (907/474-6413; e-mail: fnjrc2@uaf.edu)
Manager: Warren Fraser (907/474-6250; e-mail: ffwgf@uaf.edu)
Acquisitions/Marketing: Erica Hill (907/474-5832; e-mail: ffeh@uaf.edu)
Customer Service: Becky Hall (907/474-5831; e-mail: fypress@uaf.edu)

Affiliate Member

Established: 1967	Admitted to AAUP: 1992
Title output 2002: 9	Title output 2003: 11
Titles currently in print: 101	Titles currently distributed: 85

Editorial Program

Nonfiction, all disciplines, relating to Alaska and the circumpolar north.

Special Series: Classic Reprint; LanternLight Library; Oral Biography; Rasmuson Library Historical Translation.

The Press distributes publications for Limestone Press, Spirit Mountain Press, White Mammoth, University of Alaska Museum of the North, the Geophysical Institute, and the University of Alaska Foundation.

The University of Alberta Press

Ring House 2
Edmonton AB T6G 2E1
Canada

Phone: (780) 492-3662
Fax: (780) 492-0719
E-mail: uap@ualberta.ca
Indiv: (user I.D)@ualberta.ca
Web site: www.uap.ualberta.ca

Customer Service/Order Fulfillment:
Phone: (780) 492-3662
Fax: (780) 492-0719

UK and Europe Distributor:
Gazelle Book Services Limited

Canadian Distributor:
GTW Limited
34 Armstrong Avenue
Georgetown ON L7G 4R9
Phone: (905) 873-9781
Fax: (905) 873-6170
E-mail: orders@gtwcanada.com
Web site: www.gtwcanada.com

US Distributor:
Michigan State University Press
1405 South Harrison Road, Suite 25
East Lansing MI 48823-5202
Phone: (517) 355-9543
Fax: (517) 432-2611
Web site: www.msupress.msu.edu

Staff
Director: Linda D. Cameron (780/492-0717; e-mail: linda.cameron)
Editor: Mary Mahoney-Robson (780/492-0718; e-mail: mmahoney@gpu.srv.ualberta.ca)
Acquisitions Editor: Michael Luski (780/492-4945; e-mail: michael.luski)
   Editorial Assistant: Alethea Adair (780/492-7714; e-mail: alethea.adair)
Marketing & Sales Manager: Cathie Crooks (780/492-5820; e-mail: ccrooks)
   Marketing Assistant: Laraine Coates (780/492-7493; e-mail: laraine.coates)
Designer: Alan Brownoff (780/492-8285; e-mail: abrownoff)
Customer Relations: Yoko Sekiya (780/492-3662; e-mail: ysekiya)

Full Member
Established: 1969
Title output 2002: 21
Titles currently in print: 135

Admitted to AAUP: 1983
Title output 2003: 29

Editorial Program
The University of Alberta Press (UAP) publishes in the areas of biography, history, language, literature, natural history, regional interest, travel narratives, and reference books. UAP contributes to the intellectual and cultural life of Alberta and Canada by publishing well-edited, research-based knowledge and creative thought that has undergone rigorous peer-review, is of real value to natural constituencies, adheres to quality publication standards and is supported by appropriate marketing efforts. Please see our Web site (www.uap.ualberta.ca) for details.

   Special series: Alberta Reflections (Alberta 2005 Centennial History series); Bountiful Gardens; cuRRents; The Missionary Oblates of Mary Immaculate in the Canadian North West; Western Canadian Reprint.

American Psychiatric Publishing, Inc.

1000 Wilson Blvd., Suite 1825
Arlington, VA 22209

Phone: (703) 907-7322
Fax: (703) 907-1092
E-mail: appi@psych.org
Indiv: (user I.D.)@psych.org
Web site: www.appi.org or www.psychiatryonline.org

Orders:
Phone: (800) 368-5777; (703) 907-7322
Fax: (703) 907-1091

European Distributor:
Eurospan

Canadian Representative:
Login Brothers Canada

Staff
Chief Executive Officer: Ronald E. McMillen (703/907-7876; e-mail: rmcmillen)
  Executive Assistant: Robin S. Allen (703/907-7892; e-mail: rallen)
Editor-in-Chief: Robert E. Hales, M.D. (703/907-7892)
  Editorial Director, Books: John McDuffie (703/907-7871; e-mail: jmcduffie)
  Book Acquisitions Coordinator: Robin S. Allen (703/907-7892; e-mail: rallen)
Managing Editor, Books: Greg Kung (703/907-7872; e-mail: gkung)
Director of Sales and Marketing: Robert Pursell (703/907-7893; e-mail: bpursell)
  Marketing Manager-Books: Christie Couture (703/907-7877; e-mail: ccouture)
  Assistant Marketing Manager-Journals: Stacie Rodriguez (703/907-7874; e-mail:
  srodriguez)
Editorial Director, Journals: Sandra Patterson (703/907-7894; e-mail: spatterson)
Director of Financial and Business Operations: Kathy Stein (703/907-7875; e-mail: kstein)
  Director of Fulfillment and Circulation: Roger Domras (703/907-8544; e-mail: rdomras)

Associate Member
Established: 1981
Title output 2002: 49
Titles currently in print: 750

Admitted to AAUP: 1993
Title output 2003: 51
Journals published: 8

Editorial Program
Clinical books and monographs in psychiatry and related fields; research monographs;
medical textbooks; study guides; nonfiction trade books in mental health; annual review; and
journals.

Journals: *Academic Psychiatry; American Journal of Geriatric Psychiatry; American Journal
of Psychiatry; FOCUS; Journal of Neuropsychiatry; Psychiatric News; Psychiatric Services;
Psychosomatics.*

Special Series: Concise Guides.

Special imprints: American Psychiatric Association; Group for the Advancement of
Psychiatry; American Psychopathological Association.

Copublishing programs: The World Health Organization.

American University in Cairo Press

113 Sharia Kasr el Aini Street
Cairo, Egypt

Phone: (+20 2) 797 6926
Fax: (+20 2) 794 1440
E-mail: aucpress@aucegypt.edu
Indiv: (user I.D.)@aucegypt.edu
Web site: www.aucpress.com

US Office:
420 Fifth Avenue
New York, NY 10018-2729
Phone: (212) 730-8800 ext. 237
Fax: (212) 730-1600

US and Canadian Distributor:
Books International
PO Box 605
Herndon, VA 20172
Phone: (703) 661-1570

UK & European Distributor:
Eurospan

Staff

Director: Mark Linz (20 2 797-6888; e-mail: linz)
   Administrative Assistant to the Director: Tawhida Sherif (20 2 797-6888; e-mail: tina)
   Associate Director, Administrative & Publishing Operations: Laila Ghaly (20 2 797-6890;
   e-mail: lailag)
   Rights and Permissions Assistant: Hala Ganayni (20 2 797-6889; e-mail: halag)
   Administrative Assistant, Administration and Publishing: Mirette Tobia (20 2 797-6317;
   e-mail: mirette)
Editorial: Neil Hewison, Associate Director for Editorial Programs (20 2 797-6892;
   e-mail: rnh)
   Managing Editor: Nadia Naqib (20 2 797-6887; e-mail: nnaqib)
Marketing: Chris Terry, International Sales and Marketing Manager (20 2 797 6926;
   e-mail: cterry)
   Marketing Manager: Atef el-Hoteiby (20 2 797-6981; e-mail: ahoteiby)
   Sales Manager: Tahany el-Shammaa (20 2 797-6895; e-mail: tahanys)
   Publicity Manager: Nabila Akl (20 2 797-6896; e-mail: akl)
Design and Production Manager: Miriam Fahmy (20 2 797-6937; e-mail: miriam)

International Member

Established: 1960
Title output 2002: 45
Titles currently in print: 500

Admitted to AAUP: 1986
Title output 2003: 50
Journals published: 2

Editorial Program

The Press is recognized as the leading English-language publisher of the region, and publishes a wide range of scholarly monographs, reference works, and general books on ancient and modern Egypt and the Middle East, as well as Arabic literature in English translation, most notably the works of Egypt's Nobel Laureate, Naguib Mahfouz. The Press publishes two journals: *Cairo Papers in Social Science* and *Alif: Journal of Comparative Poetics*.

Special series, joint imprints, and/or copublishing programs: Numerous copublishing programs with US, UK, and European university and trade publishers.

Amsterdam University Press

Prinsengracht 747-751
1017 JX Amsterdam
The Netherlands

Phone: +31-20-4200050
Fax: +31-20-4203214
E-mail: info@aup.nl
Indiv: (user I.D.)@aup.nl
Web site: www.aup.nl

US & Canadian Sales Representative:
University of Chicago Press

UK Representative:
UPM

European Representative:
Andrew Durnell

Staff
Director: Saskia C. J. de Vries (e-mail: saskia.de.vries)
Administration: Frans Havelaar (e-mail: frans.havelaar); Daniela Pinnone (e-mail: daniela.pinnone)
  Office Assistants: Ebisse Wakjira (e-mail: ebisse.wakjira); Floor Onland (e-mail: floor.onland)
Acquisitions Editorial: Senior Editors: Anniek Meinders (humanities, art) (e-mail: anniek.meinders); Vanessa Nijweide (social sciences) (e-mail: vanessa.nijweide)
Manuscript Editorial: Jaap Wagenaar, Editor (social sciences) (e-mail: jaap.wagenaar)
  Assistant Editor: Chantal Nicolaes (e-mail: chantal.nicolaes)
Marketing: Laurens Hartman, Acting Director/Marketing Director (e-mail: laurens.hartman)
Publicity: Marike Schipper, Marketing Manager (e-mail: marike.schipper); Magdalena Hernas (publicity US) (e-mail: magdalena.hernas); Marjan Wynia (publicity NL) (e-mail: marjan.wynia)
Production: Arnout van Omme, Production Manager (e-mail: arnout.van.omme)
Ordering: Jelle Bloem (e-mail: jelle.bloem)
Electronic Publishing: Eelco Ferwerda, Publisher Digital Products (e-mail: eelco.ferwerda)
Computer Systems: Rik Zagers, Chief Technology Officer (e-mail: rik.zagers)

International Member
Established: 1992
Title output 2002: 75
Titles currently in print: 422 (excl. Mercator)

Admitted to AAUP: 2000
Title output 2003: 82
Journals published: 3

Editorial Program
Scholarly work and trade books (English and Dutch language) in anthropology; archaeology; art and art history; Asian studies; classical studies; cultural studies; economics; film and television studies; gender studies; history; Judaica; language and linguistics; law; literature; medieval and Renaissance studies; music; philosophy; political science; social sciences; theater and performing arts; regional titles. Textbooks for universities and higher education.
   Journals: *Academische Boekengids*; *Literatuur*; and *Mens & Maatschappij*.
   Special series (English): Amsterdam Archaeological Studies; Film Culture in Transition; Changing Welfare States; Mare Publications. (Dutch): Alfareeks; Tekst in Context (literary texts for higher education); Licht op Japan (cultural aspects of Japan); Studies in politieke vernieuwing (political science).
   Imprints: Vossiuspers UvA, Salomé, Pallas Publications. Co-publications with Mercatorfonds(Belgium), Princeton University Press, and University of California Press.

The University of Arizona Press

355 S. Euclid Avenue, Suite 103
Tucson, AZ 85719-4140

Phone: (520) 621-1441
Fax: (520) 621-8899
E-mail: uapress@uapress.arizona.edu
Indiv: (user I.D.)@uapress.arizona.edu
Web site: www.uapress.arizona.edu

Orders:
Phone: (520) 626-4218; (800) 426-3797

Warehouse:
330 S. Toole Avenue
Tucson, Arizona 85701-1813

Canadian Representative:
University of British Columbia Press

European Representative:
William Gills

Staff

Director: Christine R. Szuter (520/621-1441; e-mail szuter)
  Assistant to the Director/Permissions: Kristen Hagenbuckle (520/621-3911; e-mail: khagenbuckle)
Senior Acquiring Editor: Patti Hartmann (Chicano/Latino studies and literature, Native American studies and literature, environmental literature) (520/621-7920; e-mail: hartmann)
  Acquiring Editor: Allyson Carter (anthropology, archaeology, environmental sciences, and space sciences) (520/621-3186; e-mail: acarter)
  Editorial Assistant: Kathy Baily (520/621-5919; e-mail: kbaily)
Managing Editor: Harrison Shaffer (520/621-5916; e-mail: hshaffer)
  Assistant Managing Editor: Alan M. Schroder (520/621-5814; e-mail: aschroder)
  Associate Editor: Nancy Arora (520/621-5915; e-mail: narora)
Marketing: Kathryn Conrad, Manager (520/621-9109; e-mail: kconrad)
  Publicity Manager: Jennifer Pinkerton (520/621-3920; e-mail: jpinkerton)
  Advertising and Direct Mail Manager: Wayne Koch (520/621-7918; e-mail: wkoch)
  Exhibits Manager: Keith LaBaw (520/621-8656; e-mail: klabaw)
Design and Production Manager: Anne Keyl (520/621-7917; e-mail: akeyl)
  Assistant Production Manager: Linda Jess (520/621-7916; e-mail: ljess)
Business and Information Systems Manager: Beth Swain (520/621-5815; e-mail: swain)
  Accounting/Contracts: Gilda Guerry-Aguilar (520/621-9865; e-mail: gguerry)
  Customer Service/Credit: Rise Cornelio (520/621-7923; e-mail: rcornelio)
  Accounts Receivable/Payable: Veronica Ramirez (520/626-3041; e-mail: vramirez)
  Order Clerks: Mary Cantrall (520/621-5813; e-mail: mcantrall); Melissa Sotomayor (520/621-5813; e-mail: msotomayor)
  Warehouse Supervisor: Howard Lundholm (520/621-3289; e-mail: hlundholm)
  Materials Handlers: Greg Morton (520/621-3289; e-mail: gmorton); Liz Vargas (520/621-3289; e-mail: lvargas)

Full Member

Established: 1959

Title output 2002: 55

Titles currently in print: 668

Admitted to AAUP: 1962

Title output 2003: 53

Editorial Program

Specialties strongly identified with the universities in the state and other significant nonfiction of regional and national interest. Especially strong fields include the American West; anthropology and archaeology; Chicano/Latino studies and literature; environmental sciences; environmental studies and literature; Latin American studies; Native American studies and literature; space sciences.

Special series: Anthropological Papers of the University of Arizona; Arizona Sonora Desert Museum Series; Camino del Sol; Desert Places; Environmental History of the Borderlands; Mexican-American Experience; The Modern American West; Society, Environment, and Place; Southwest Center Series; Space Science Series; Sun Tracks: An American Indian Literary Series.

The Press also distributes titles from the University of Arizona Mexican American Studies and Research Center; the Crow Canyon Archaeological Center; Ironwood Press; the Southwest Mission Research Center; the Tucson Museum of Art; the Arizona State Museum; Statistical Research, Inc.; SWCA, Inc.; Northern Arizona University Bilby Research Center; Center for Desert Archaeology; University of Arizona Critical Languages Program; and Oregon State University Press.

The University of Arkansas Press

McIlroy House
201 Ozark Avenue
Fayetteville, AR 72701-1201

Canadian Representative:
Scholarly Book Services

Phone: (479) 575-3246
Fax: (479) 575-6044
E-mail: uapress@uark.edu
Indiv: (user I. D.)@uark.edu
Online catalog and Web site: www.uapress.com

Staff
Director and Editor: Lawrence J. Malley (479/575-3096; e-mail: lmalley)
  Receptionist: Meagan Bonnell (479/575-3246; e-mail: mbonnel)
Acquisitions Editorial: Lawrence J. Malley
  Acquisitions/Editorial Assistant: Anna A. Moore (479/575-7242; e-mail: aamoore)
Manuscript Editorial, Design and Production: Brian King, Assistant Director (479/575-6780; e-mail: brking)
  Production Manager: Sarah White (479/575-5767; e-mail: sarahw)
Marketing: Tom Lavoie (479/575-6657; e-mail: tlavoie)
  Marketing and Advertising Designer: Charlie Shields (479/575-7258; e-mail: cmoss)
  Marketing Assistant: Meagan Bonnell (479/575-3246; e-mail: mbonnel)
Business: Mike W. Bieker, Business Manager (479/575-3859; e-mail: mbieker)
  Assistant Business Manager: Carolyn Brt (479/575-3459; e-mail: cbrt)
  Customer Service: Kathleen Z. Willis (479/575-3634; e-mail: kwillis)
  Warehouse Manager: Gail Test (479/575-3858)
  Business Office Fax: (479/575-5538)

Full Member
Established: 1980
Title output 2002: 13
Titles currently in print: 349

Admitted to AAUP: 1984
Title output 2003: 21
Journals published: 1

Editorial Program
African-American history; Civil Rights studies; Civil War studies; cultural studies; history; literary criticism; Middle East studies; music; poetry and poetics; regional studies; Southern history; and women's studies. Submissions are not invited in general fiction, textbooks, or children's books.

Special Series: The Carter Collection; The Civil War in the West; The Histories of Arkansas; Portraits of Conflict; The University of Arkansas Press Poetry; and The William Gilmore Simms Collection.

The Press also publishes the winner of the University of Arkansas Press Award for Arabic Literature in Translation, the winners of the University of Arkansas Press Poetry Series, and the journal *Philosophical Topics*.

Beacon Press

25 Beacon Street
Boston, MA 02108-2892

Phone: (617) 723-2110
Fax: (617) 723-3097
Marketing/Publicity/Subsidiary
Rights Fax: (617) 742-2290
E-mail: (user I.D.)@beacon.org
Web site: www.beacon.org

Canadian Representative:
Fitzhenry & Whiteside

European Representative:
Airlift Book Company

Staff

Director: Helene Atwan (e-mail: hatwan)
  Assistant to the Director & Assistant Editor: Christopher Vyce (e-mail: cvyce)
Editorial: Gayatri Patnaik, Senior Editor (e-mail: gpatnaik)
  Executive Editor: Joanne Wyckoff (e-mail: jwyckoff)
  Senior Editor: Amy Caldwell (e-mail: acaldwell)
Marketing: Tom Hallock, Associate Publisher, Director of Sales, Marketing, and SubRights (e-mail: thallock)
  Publicity Director: Pamela MacColl (e-mail: pmaccoll)
  Publicists: Kathy Daneman (e-mail: kdaneman); Katie O'Neil (e-mail: koneil)
  Sales Manager: Lindsay Goodman (e-mail: lgoodman)
  Permissions Coordinator: Michelle Corcoran (e-mail: mcorcoran)
Production: PJ Tierney, Production Director & Digital Publishing Director (e-mail: ptierney)
  Managing Editor: Lisa Sacks (e-mail: lsacks)
  Creative Director: Sara Eisenman (e-mail: seisenman)
Business: Laura Rutherford, Comptroller (e-mail: lrutherford)
  Business Operation Manager: Greg Kanter (e-mail: gkanter)
  Accounts Payable/Receivable: Charlie Feldman (e-mail: cfeldman)

Associate Member

Established: 1854
Title output 2002: 65
Titles currently in print: 585

Admitted to AAUP: 1988
Title output 2003: 67

Editorial Program

Beacon Press, the non-profit publisher owned by the Unitarian Universalist Association, publishes scholarly works for the general reader, specializing in African-American, Native American, and Asian American studies; anthropology; current affairs; education; environmental studies; gay and lesbian studies; nature writing; personal essays; philosophy; regional books; religion; and women's studies.

  Special series and joint publishing programs: Bluestreak; The Concord Nature Library.

University of British Columbia Press

2029 West Mall
University of British Columbia
Vancouver, BC V6T 1Z2
Canada

Phone: (604) 822-5959
Fax: (604) 822-6083
E-mail: (user I.D.)@ubcpress.ca
Web site: www.ubcpress.ca

<u>US Orders and Returns:</u>
University of Washington Press
PO Box 50096
Seattle, WA 98145-4115
Orders: (800) 441-4115
Fax: (800) 669-7993
E-mail: uwpord@u.washington.edu

<u>Canadian Orders and Returns:</u>
UNIpresses
24 Armstrong Avenue
Georgetown, ON L7G 4R9
Canada

Phone: (905) 873-9781
Fax: (905) 873-6170
Toll-free (in Canada): (877) 864-8477
Toll-free fax (in Canada): (877) 864-4272
E-mail: orders@gtwcanada.com

<u>UK Distributor:</u>
Eurospan

Staff

Director: Peter Milroy (604/822-3807; e-mail: milroy)
   Assistant to the Publisher: Jason Congdon (604/822-4161; e-mail: congdon)
Acquisitions Editorial: Jean Wilson, Associate Director—Editorial (604/822-6376; e-mail: wilson)
   Acquisitions Editors: Emily Andrew (Toronto) (416/535-9670; e-mail: andrew); Randy Schmidt (Kelowna) (250/764-4761; e-mail: schmidt)
Production Editorial: Holly Keller, Assistant Director—Production and Editorial Services (604/822-4545; e-mail: keller)
   Project Editor: Camilla Gurdon (416/762-7361; e-mail: gurdon)
   Editors: Ann Macklem (604/822-0093; e-mail: macklem); Darcy Cullen (604/822-5744; e-mail: cullen)
Marketing: George Maddison, Associate Director Marketing and Operations (604/822-2053; e-mail: maddison)
   Academic Marketing Manager: Elizabeth Whitton (604/822-8226; e-mail: whitton)
   Awards and Exhibits Manager: Kerry Kilmartin (604/822-8244; e-mail: kilmartin)
   Advertising and Publicity Manager: Andrea Kwan (416/538-8043; e-mail: kwan)
   Inventory Manager/Academic Sales: Shari Martin (604/822-1221; e-mail: martin)
   Catalogues and Web Manager: Adrienne Lindsay (604/822-5042; e-mail: lindsay)
   Marketing Assistant: Kate Sheehan Spezowka (604/822-9462; e-mail: sheehan)
Finance/Distribution: Elizabeth Hu, Assistant Director—Finance and Distribution (604/822-8938; e-mail: hu)
   Finance Assistant: Ayda Mehrjou (604/822-5370; e-mail: mehrjou)

Full Member

Established: 1971
Title output 2002: 46
Titles currently in print: 485

Admitted to AAUP: 1972
Title output 2003: 34

Editorial Program
Scholarly books and serious nonfiction, with special interest in archaeology; Asian and Pacific studies; economics; education; environment; fisheries; forestry; geography; history; law; Northwest Coast art; Native studies; Pacific maritime studies; political science; sociology; urban studies; and women's studies.

Special series: Canadian Yearbook of International Law; Contemporary Chinese Studies; First Nations Languages; Nature/History/Society; Pioneers of British Columbia; Sexuality Studies; Sustainability and the Environment; UBC Laboratory of Archaeology Monographs; Urbanization in Asia.

Brookings Institution Press

1775 Massachusetts Avenue, N.W.
Washington, DC 20036-2188

<u>UK Representative:</u>
University Presses Marketing

Phone: (202) 797-6000; (202) 797-6258
Fax: (202) 797-6195
E-mail: bibooks@brookings.edu
Indiv: (firstinitial)(lastname)@brookings.edu
Web site: www.brookings.edu

Staff
Vice President & Director: Robert L. Faherty (202/797-6250)
　Program and Web Administrator: Renuka Deonarain (202/797-6423)
　Web Coordinator: Jessica Howard (202/797-6468)
　Permissions Coordinator/Program Assistant: TBA (202/797-2483)
Acquisitions Editorial: Christopher Kelaher (202/797-6260)
Manuscript Editorial: Janet Walker, Managing Editor (202/797-6253)
　Editors: Eileen Hughes (202/797-6256); Tanjam Jacobson (202/797-6261)
Marketing: John Sherer, Marketing Director (202/797-6254)
　Direct Marketing Coordinator/Copywriter: Tom Parsons (202/797-6265)
　Publicity Manager: Nicole Pagano (202/797-6428)
　Sales, Exhibits, and Advertising Coordinator: Christopher O'Brien (202/797-6107)
Design and Production: Lawrence Converse, Production Manager (202/797-6251)
　Art Coordinator: Susan Woollen (202/797-6101)
Fulfillment Manager: Terrence Melvin (202/797-6429)

Full Member

Established: 1916
Title output 2002: 52
Titles currently in print: 900

Admitted to AAUP: 1958
Title output 2003: 50
Journals published: 6

Editorial Program

Economics, government, and international affairs, with emphasis on the implications for public policy of current and emerging issues confronting American society. The Institution also publishes Brookings Papers on Economic Activity, Brookings Papers on Education Policy, Brookings Trade Forum, Brookings-Wharton Papers on Financial Services, Brookings-Wharton Papers on Urban Affairs, and the *Brookings Review*. The Press publishes books written by the Institution's resident and associated staff members employed or commissioned to carry out projects defined by the directors of Brookings research programs, as well as manuscripts acquired from outside authors.

The Press distributes publications of the Bertelsmann Foundation, the Carnegie Endowment for International Peace, the Centre for Economic Policy Research, the Century Foundation Press, Council on Foreign Relations, Economica, the Hudson Institute, the Institute for Latin American Studies, the International Labor Organization, the Japan Center for International Exchange, the OECD, the Royal Institute for International Affairs, the Trilateral Commission, the United Nations University Press, and the Washington Institute for Near East Policy.

University of Calgary Press

2500 University Drive N.W.
Calgary, AB T2N 1N4
Canada

Phone: (403) 220-7578
Fax: (403) 282-0085
E-mail: ucpress@ucalgary.ca
Indiv: (user I.D.)@ucalgary.ca
Web site: www.uofcpress.com

US Orders:
Michigan State University Press
1405 South Harrison Road, Suite 25
Manly Miles Building
East Lansing, MI 48823-5202
Phone: (517) 355-9543
Fax: (517) 432-2611; (800) 678-2120
E-mail: msupress@msu.edu

Canadian Distribution & Orders
uniPRESSES
c/o Georgetown Terminal
34 Armstrong Avenue
Georgetown, ON L7G 4R9
Canada
Phone (toll-free): (877) 864-8477
Fax (toll-free): (877) 864-4272
E-mail: orders@gtwcanada.com

UK and European Distributor:
Gazelle Book Services, Ltd.

Staff

Director: Walter Hildebrandt (403/220-3511; e-mail: whildebr)
Permissions/Copyright: Wendy Stephens (403/220-3721; e-mail: wstephens)
Editorial Secretary: Karen Buttner (403/220-3979; e-mail: kbuttner)
Staff Editor: Peter Enman (403/220-2606; e-mail: enman)
Marketing Manager: Barb Murray (403/220-4208; e-mail: bmurray)
Promotion Manager: Greg Madsen (403/220-4343; e-mail: gmadsen)
Production Editor: John King (403/220-4208; e-mail: jking)

Designer: Mieka West (403/220-8719; e-mail: amcwest)
Journals Manager: Judy Powell (403/220 3512; e-mail: powell)
Accounts/Subscriptions: (403/220-7736; e-mail: ucpmail)

Full Member

Established 1981

Admitted to AAUP: 2002
(Affiliate member 1992-95)

Title output 2002: 25

Title output 2003: 25

Titles currently in print: 237

Journals published: 7 print, 4 electronic

Editorial Program

University of Calgary Press publishes academic and trade books and journals that engage academic, industry/business, government, and public communities. The Press focuses on works that give voice to the heartland of the continent (the Canadian Northwest, the American West, including the mountain region and the Great Plains). The University of Calgary Press is experimental and offers alternative perspectives on established canons and subjects. The Press strives to bring diverse voices and views to the forefront and endeavors to help new scholars and writers break in to the academic and trade markets.

The Press publishes the following print journals *ARIEL—A Review of International English Literature*; *Canadian Journal of Counselling*; *Canadian Journal of Latin American and Caribbean Studies*; *Canadian Journal of Philosophy*; *Canadian Journal of Program Evaluation*; *Mousieon—Journal of the Classical Association of Canada*; *Torquere—Journal of the Canadian Lesbian and Gay Studies Association*; and publishes 4 online journals *Chieftain: The Journal of Traditional Governance*; *Currents: New Scholarship in the Human Services*; *International Addiction*; *International E-Journal for Leadership in Learning*.

Special Series: African Missing Voices; African Occasional Papers; Art in Profile; Beyond Boundaries (Canadian Defence and Strategic Studies); Canadian Archival Series; Cinemas Off Centre; Industry Canada Research; Latin American and Caribbean Studies; Legacies Shared; Northern Lights; Open Spaces; Parks and Heritage; Supplementary volumes of the Canadian Journal of Philosophy.

Copublishing Programs: The Arctic Institute of North America.

University of California Press

2120 Berkeley Way
Berkeley, CA 94720

Phone: (510) 642-4247
Fax: (510) 643-7127
E-mail: askucp@ucpress.edu
Indiv: (firstname.lastname)@ucpress.edu
Web site: www.ucpress.edu

Journals:
2000 Center Street, Suite 303
Berkeley, CA 94704
Phone: (510) 643-7154
Fax: (510) 642-9917
Journals Web site: www.ucpress.edu/journals

California Warehouse:
1095 Essex Street
Richmond, CA 94801
Phone: (510) 642-4240
Fax: (510) 215-0237

Order Fulfillment:
California Princeton Fulfillment Services
1445 Lower Ferry Road
Ewing, NJ 08618-1424
Orders: (800) 822-6657
Fax: (800) 999-1958
Customer Service: (609) 883-1759, x. 513

UK/European Office:
University Presses of California,
Columbia, and Princeton, Ltd.
1 Oldlands Way, Bognor Regis
West Sussex PO22 9SA
United Kingdom
Phone: +44 1243 842165
Fax: +44 1243 842167

Staff

Director: Lynne Withey (510/642-5393)
  Assistant to the Director: TBA (510/642-0189)
  Assistant Director, Book Division: Sheila Levine (510/642-4246)
  Assistant Director, Journals Division: Rebecca Simon (510/642-5536)
  Chief Financial Officer: Anna Weidman (510/642-4388)
  Director of Development and Public Relations: Deborah Kirshman (510/643-7704)
Acquisitions Editorial: Sheila Levine (food, regional studies) (510/642-4246)
  Executive Editors: Doris Kretschmer (natural history, biology) (510/642-4229); Naomi
  Schneider (sociology, anthropology, gender studies) (510/642-6715); Stanley Holwitz
  (anthropology, public health, Jewish studies) (510/642-4244)
  Sponsoring Editors: Laura Cerruti (poetry, literature) (510/643-9793); Reed Malcolm
  (religion, Asian studies) (510/643-1812); Stephanie Fay (art history) (510/642-6733);
  Deborah Kirshman (art history, museum copublications) (510/643-7704); Niels Hooper
  (history) (510/643-8331); Blake Edgar (biology, archaeology, viticulture) (510/643-4643);
  Mary Francis (music, film) (510/642-4147)
Managing Editor: Marilyn Schwartz (510/642-6548)
  Assistant Managing Editor: Kate Warne (510/643-6858)
  Project Editors: Rachel Berchten (510/642-0133); Suzanne Knott (510/642-8981); Dore
  Brown (510/642-4591); Jacqueline Volin (510/642-0061); Stephanie Fay (510/642-6733);
  Sue Heinemann (510/643-8979); Rose Vekony (510/642-6521); Cindy Fulton (510/642-
  6734); Laura Harger (510/643-9081); Mary Severance (510/643-8555)

Marketing: Julie Christianson, Director of Marketing (510/642-4051)
  Associate Director of Marketing: Laura Driussi (510/643-1036)
  Advertising Manager: Marta Gasoi (510/642-2649)
  Direct Mail Manager: Shira Weisbach (510/642-5054)
  Publicity Manager: Alexandra Dahne (510/643-5036)
  Text Promotion Manager: Erich van Rijn (510/643-8915)
  Subsidiary Rights: Dan Dixon (510/642-4261)
  Permissions: Rose Robinson (510/643-9795)
Sales: Anna Bullard, Director of Sales and New Business Development (510/642-6684)
  Sales Manager: Amy-Lynn Fischer (510/642-9373)
  Special Sales: Don McIlraith (510/643-3467)
Design and Production: Anthony C. Crouch, Director (510/642-5394)
  Production Coordinators: Robin Demers (510/642-9758); Peggy Golden (510/643-6859);
  John Cronin (510/642-4395); Sam Rosenthal (510/642-8102); Janet Villanueva (510/642
  9805); Ann Williamson (510/642-1570)
  Design: Nicole Hayward (510/642-7982); Victoria Kuskowski (510/642-0134); Nola
  Burger (510/643-9167); Jessica Grunwald (510/643-2213); Sandy Drooker
Journals: Rebecca Simon, Director (510/642-5536)
  Journals Marketing Manager: Rebekah Darksmith (510/643-0952)
  Journals Production Manager: Susanna Tadlock (510/642-6221)
  Journals Advertising: Marge Dean (510/642-6188)
Business: Karla Golden, Manager (510/642-7944)
  California Warehouse: Khalil El-Kareh (510/642-8744)
  Human Resources: Doris Floyd (510/642-5338)
Information Systems: Patrick King, Director (510/642-6522)

Full Member

Established: 1893

Admitted to AAUP: 1937

Title output 2002: 180

Title output 2003: 180

Titles currently in print: 3,500

Journals published: 49

Editorial Program

Anthropology, art history, Asian studies, biology, classical studies, film, food, history, music, natural history, poetry, public health, regional studies, religion, sociology, Mark Twain Series.

Journals: *Agricultural History; American Anthropologist; American Ethnologist; Anthropology and Education Quarterly; Anthropology and Humanism; Anthropology of Work Review; Archeological Papers of the AAA; Asian Survey; California Public Employee Relations; City and Society; Classical Antiquity; Contexts: Understanding People in Their Social Worlds; CSAS Bulletin; Cultural Anthropology; East European Politics and Societies; Ethos, Film Quarterly; Federal Sentencing Reporter; Gastronomica: The Journal of Food and Culture; Historical Studies in the Physical and Biological Sciences; Index to Foreign Legal Periodicals; Journal of Latin American Anthropology; Journal of Linguistic Anthropology; The Journal of Musicology; Journal of Palestine Studies; Law and Literature; Medical Anthropology Quarterly; Mexican Studies/Estudios Mexicanos; Museum Anthropology; Music Perception; Music Theory Spectrum; NAPA Bulletin; Nineteenth-Century Music; Nineteenth-Century Literature; Nutritional Anthropology; Oral History Review; Pacific Historical Review; PoLAR, The Public Historian; Religion and American Culture; Representations; Rhetorica; Social Problems; Sociological Perspectives; The Sociological Quarterly; Symbolic Interaction; Transforming Anthropology; Visual Anthropology Review; Voices.*

Submissions are not invited in original poetry or fiction.

Cambridge University Press

North American Branch:
40 West 20th Street
New York, NY 10011-4211

Phone: (212) 924-3900
Fax: (212) 691-3239
E-mail: (firstinitial)(lastname)@cambridge.org
Web site and online catalog: www.cambridge.org

Head (UK) Office:
The Edinburgh Building
Shaftesbury Road
Cambridge CB2 2RU
UK

Distribution Center:
100 Brook Hill Drive
West Nyack, NY 10994-2133
Phone: (845) 353-7500
Fax: (845) 353-4141

Staff

UK Office:
Chief Executive: Stephen Bourne
NY Office: (212) 924-3900
President, Americas & Asia: Richard L. Ziemacki (212/337-5052)
Vice President and Business Development Director, Americas & Asia: Nicholas Reckert
   (212/337-5051)
Editorial: Frank Smith, Director, Academic (212/337-5960)
   Publishing Director, STM: Kirk Jensen (212/337-5992)
   ELT Group Director: Richard Milstein (212/337-5010)
   Publishing Operations Director, ELT: Louisa Hellegers (212/337-5042)
Academic Editors: Lewis Bateman (political science) (212/337-5965); Andrew Beck (linguis-
   tics, religion) (212/337-5941); Lauren Cowles (math, computer science) (212/337-5962);
   Peter Gordon (engineering) (212/337-5944); Philip Laughlin (psychology, cognitive
   science) (212/337-5098); Scott Parris (economics, business) (212/337-5964); Edward
   Parsons (social sciences) (212/337-5961); Beatrice Rehl (classics, philosophy) (212/337-
   5096); John Berger (law) (212/337-5958); Nat Russo (medicine) (212/337-5055); Beth
   Barry (medicine) (212/337-5075)
ELT Editors: Debbie Goldblatt (skills & short courses) (212/337-5003); Lesley Koustaff
   (secondary & primary courses) (212/337-5043); Eleanor Barnes (adult courses) (212/337-
   5005); David Bohlke (adult courses) (212/337-5034); Fiona Kelly (adult ed & Latin)
   (212/337-5044); Paul Heacock (reference, vocabulary, exams) (212/337-5031); Jane Mairs
   (grammar & pronunciation) (212/337-5021); Bernard Seal (EAP); Lise Minovitz (skills)
   (212/337-5015)
Marketing: Liza Murphy, Sales and Marketing Director (212/337-5066)
   Academic Marketing Manager: Catherine Friedl (212/337-5049)
   Promotions Manager: Edward Ryan (212/337-5063)
   Exhibits Manager: James Murphy (212/337-5074)
   Rights and Permissions Manager: Marc Anderson (212/337-5048)
   Publicity Manager: Kira Citron (212/337-5058)

Marketing Manager, ELT: Carine Mitchell (212/337-5006)
Senior Sales and Marketing Manager, ELT: Andy Martin (212/337-5007)
Sales Manager, ELT: James Anderson
Academic Sales Manager: Melissanne Scheld (212/337-5988)
Production: Pauline Ireland, Production Director (212/337-5090)
Journals: Edward Barnas, Journals Manager (212/337-5004)
  Consortia Relations Manager: Andrea Cernichiari (212/337-5022)
  Journals Production Manager: Edward Carey (212/337-5985)
  Journals Marketing Manager: Susan Soule (212/337-5019)
  Journals Editor: Mark Zadrozny (212/337-5012)
  Associate Editor, Journals: Barbara Chin (212/337-5981)
Information Systems: Rob Leas, Information Services Manager (212/337-5060)
Personnel: Carol New, Personnel Director (212/337-5045)

West Nyack: (845) 353-7500
Press Distribution Director: Ian Bradie (ext. 4339)
  Computer Department: Joan Bernstein, Software Development Manager (ext. 4325)
  MIS Manager: George Ianello (ext. 4324)
Accounting: Paul McLaughlin, Controller (ext. 4323)
  Credit Manager: Randy Zeitlin (ext. 4322)
  Customer Service Manager: Lynda DiCaprio (ext. 4366)
  Inventory Control Manager: Holly Verrill (ext. 4306)
  Warehouse Operations Manager: Don Federico (ext. 4321)

Full Member
Established: 1534
American Branch: 1949   Admitted to AAUP: 1950
Title output 2002: 2,148   Title output 2003: 2,145
Titles currently in print: 14,000   Journals published: 186

Editorial Program
A broad range of academic titles in the humanities; social sciences; biological and physical sciences; mathematics; medicine; psychology; law; religious studies; reference works; and English as a second language.

The Press also publishes the following journals: *Abstracts of Working Papers in Economics; Acta Numerica; Ageing and Society; AIEDAM: Artificial Intelligence for Engineering Design, Analysis and Manufacturing; AJS; American Political Science Review; Ancient Mesoamerica; Anglo-Saxon England; Animal Conservation; Annual Review of Applied Linguistics; Antarctic Science; Applied Psycholinguistics; Arabic Sciences and Philosophy; Archeological Dialogues; arq: Architectural Research Quarterly; Behavioral and Brain Sciences; Behavioural and Cognitive Psychotherapy; Bilingualism: Language and Cognition; Biofilms; Biological Reviews of the Cambridge Philosophical Society; Bird Conservation International; The British Journal for the History of Science; British Journal of Anaesthetic and Recovery Nursing; British Journal of Music Education; British Journal of Political Science; Bulletin of the London Mathematical Society; Bulletin of the School of Oriental and African Studies; Cambridge Archaeological Journal; The Cambridge Law Journal; Cambridge Opera Journal; Cambridge Quarterly of Healthcare Ethics; Cardiology in the Young; The China Quarterly; Clinics in Developmental Medicine; Combinatorics, Probability and Computing; Comparative Studies in Society and History; Compositio*

Mathematica; Contemporary European History; Continuity and Change; Development and Psychopathology; Developmental Medicine and Child Neurology; Dubois Review; Early Music History; Econometric Theory; Economics and Philosophy; Edinburgh Journal of Botany; Eighteenth-Century Music; English Language and Linguistics; English Today; Environment and Development Economics; Environmental Conservation; Epidemiology and Infection; Ergodic Theory and Dynamical Systems; European Business Organization Law Review; European Journal of Anaesthesiology; European Journal of Applied Mathematics; European Journal of Sociology; European Review; European Review of Economic History; Experimental Agriculture; Expert Reviews in Molecular Medicine; Fetal and Maternal Medicine Review; Field Mycology; Financial History Review; Genetical Research; Geological Magazine; Glasgow Mathematical Journal; Harvard Theological Review; The Historical Journal; International Journal of Asian Studies; International Journal of Astrobiology; International Journal of Middle East Studies; The International Journal of Neuropsychopharmacology; International Journal of Technology Assessment in Health Care; International Labor and Working-Class History; IO: International Organization; International Psychogeriatrics; International Review of Social History; Japanese Journal of Political Science; Journal of Advertising Research; The Journal of African History; Journal of African Law; The Journal of Agricultural Science; Journal of American Studies; Journal of Biosocial Science; Journal of Child Language; Journal of Dairy Research; Journal of Diagnostic Radiography and Imaging; The Journal of Ecclesiastical History; The Journal of Economic History; Journal of Fluid Mechanics; Journal of French Language Studies; Journal of Functional Programming; Journal of Germanic Linguistics; Journal of Latin American Studies; Journal of Linguistics; The Journal of Modern African Studies; Journal of Navigation; Journal of Pension Economics and Finance; Journal of Plasma Physics; Journal of Psychiatric Intensive Care; Journal of Public Policy; Journal of Radiotherapy in Practice; Journal of Social Policy; Journal of Southeast Asian Studies; Journal of Systematic Paleontology; Journal of the Institute of Mathematics of Jussieu; Journal of the International Neuropsychological Society; Journal of the International Phonetic Association; Journal of the London Mathematical Society; Journal of the Marine Biological Association of the United Kingdom; Journal of the Royal Asiatic Society; Journal of Tropical Ecology; Journal of Zoology; The Knowledge Engineering Review; Language in Society; Language Teaching; Language Variation and Change; Laser and Particle Beams; Legal Information Management; Legal Theory; Leiden Journal of International Law; The Lichenologist; LMS Journal of Computation and Mathematics; Macroeconomic Dynamics; Mathematical Proceedings of the Cambridge Philosophical Society; Mathematical Structures in Computer Science; Meteorological Applications; Microscopy and Microanalysis; Modern Asian Studies; Modern Intellectual History; Mycological Research; Mycologist; Natural Language Engineering; Netherlands International Law Review; Neuron Glia Biology; New Testament Studies; New Theatre Quarterly; Nordic Journal of Linguistics; Organized Sound; Oryx; Palliative & Supportive Care; Parasitology; Perspectives on Politics; Philosophy; Phonology; Plainsong and Medieval Music; Polar and Glaciological Abstracts; Polar Record; Popular Music; Probability in the Engineering and Informational Sciences; Proceedings of the Edinburgh Mathematical Society; Proceedings of the London Mathematical Society; Prospects; PS: Political Science & Politics; Psychological Medicine; Quarterly Reviews of Biophysics; Recall; Religious Studies; Reproductive Medicine Review; Review of International Studies; Reviews in Clinical Gerontology; Robotica; Royal Historical Society Camden Fifth Series; Royal Historical Society Transactions; Rural History: Economy, Society, Culture; Science in Context; Scottish Journal of Theology; Social Anthropology; Social Philosophy and Policy; Social Policy and Society; Studies in American Political Development; Studies in Second Language Acquisition; Systematics and Biodiversity; Tempo; Theatre Research International; Theatre Survey; Theory and Practice of Logic Programming; Twentieth-Century Music;

Urban History; *Utilitas*; *Victorian Literature and Culture*; *Visual Neuroscience*; *World Trade Review*; *Zygote*.

Special series, joint imprints, and/or copublishing programs (partial list): Cambridge Companions to Philosophy; Cambridge Earth Science Series; Cambridge Edition of the Works of F. Scott Fitzgerald; Cambridge Edition of the Works of D. H. Lawrence; Cambridge Film Classics; Cambridge History of China; Cambridge History of Japan; Cambridge History of Science; Cambridge Medical Reviews; Cambridge Studies in Medieval Life and Thought; Cambridge Monographs on Mathematical Physics; Cambridge Opera Handbooks; Cambridge Studies in American Literature and Culture; Cambridge Studies in Ecology; Cambridge Studies in Mathematical Biology; Cambridge Studies in Publishing and Printing History; Cambridge Studies in Environment and History, Cambridge Tracts in Mathematics; Cambridge Texts in the History of Political Thought; Developmental and Cell Biology Series; Econometric Society Monographs; Hematological Oncology; Neurobiology and Psychiatry; New Directions in Language Teaching; Publications of the German Historical Institute; Studies in Natural Language Processing; SIGS (professional computing); Woodrow Wilson Center Press Series.

Carnegie Mellon University Press

5032 Forbes Avenue
Pittsburgh, PA 15289-1021

Order Fulfillment:
CUP Services

Phone: (412) 268-2861
Fax: (412) 268-8706
Web site: www.cmu.edu/universitypress

750 Cascadilla Street
Ithaca, NY 14850
Customer Service: (800) 666-2211
Fax: (800) 688-2877

Staff
Director: Gerald Costanzo (e-mail: gc3d@andrew.cmu.edu)
Senior Editor: Cynthia Lamb (e-mail: cynthial@andrew.cmu.edu)
Fiction Editor: Sharon Dilworth (e-mail: sd20@andrew.cmu.edu)
Accounts Administrator: Anna Houck

Affiliate Member
Established: 1972
Title output 2002: 17
Titles currently in print: 291

Admitted to AAUP: 1991
Title output 2003: 19
Journals published: 1

Editorial Program
Carnegie Mellon's particular strength lies in literary publishing: Carnegie Mellon Poetry Series, Carnegie Mellon Classic Contemporary Series (the reissuing of significant early books by important contemporary poets), and the Carnegie Mellon Short Fiction Series. The Press also publishes in art, literary criticism, music, the performing arts, and social history.

Journal: *Aris—The Journal of the Carnegie Mellon Department of Architecture*

The Catholic University of America Press

240 Leahy Hall
620 Michigan Avenue, N.E.
Washington, DC 20064

Phone: (202) 319-5052
Fax: (202) 319-4985
E-mail: (user I.D.)@cua.edu
Online catalog: cuapress.cua.edu

Warehouse (Returns only):
Hopkins Fulfillment Service
RETURNS
c/o Maple Press Co.
Lebanon Dist. Center
704 Legionnaire Dr.
Fredricksburg, PA 17026

Customer Service:
Hopkins Fulfillment Service
PO Box 50370
Baltimore, MD 21211
Phone: (800) 537-5487
Fax: (410) 516-6998

UK Representative:
Eurospan

Canadian Representative:
Scholarly Book Services

Staff
Director: David J. McGonagle (e-mail: mcgonagle)
 Administrative Assistant: Jessica Emanuel (e-mail: emanuel)
Acquisitions Editorial: Gregory F. LaNave (philosophy, theology) (e-mail: lanave); David J.
 McGonagle (all other fields)
Managing Editor: Theresa Walker (e-mail: walkert)
Marketing Manager: Elizabeth Benevides (e-mail: benevides)
Design and Production: Anne Theilgard (Kachergis Book Design, 14 Small Street North,
 Pittsboro, NC 27312)
Journals: Melisa Darby, Administrative Assistant (e-mail: darby)

Full Member
Established: 1939
Title output 2002: 31
Titles currently in print: 382

Admitted to AAUP: 1985
Title output 2003: 24
Journals published: 3

Editorial Program
American and European history (both ecclesiastical and secular); American and European literature; Irish studies; philosophy; political theory; theology. Periods covered range from late antiquity to modern times, with special interest in late antiquity, early Christianity, and the medieval period. Submissions are not invited in fiction, poetry, mathematics, the natural sciences and related professional fields.

 Special series: Catholic Moral Thought; The Fathers of the Church: A New Translation; Medieval Texts in Translation; Patristic Monograph Series of the North American Patristics Society; Publications of the American Maritain Association (distributed); Studies in Philosophy and the History of Philosophy; Thomas Aquinas in Translation.

 Journals: *The Americas*; *The Catholic Historical Review*; *Pierre d'Angle*.

The University of Chicago Press

1427 E. 60th Street
Chicago, IL 60637-2954

Phone (Books): (773) 702-7700
Phone (Journals): (773) 702-7600
Fax: (773) 702-2705 (Books Acquisitions)
   (773) 702-9756 (Books Marketing)
   (773) 702-0172 (Journals Marketing)
   (773) 702-0694 (Journals Production)
E-mail: (firstinitial)(lastname)@press.uchicago.edu
Web site and online catalog: www.press.uchicago.edu

Chicago Distribution Center:
11030 South Langley Avenue
Chicago, IL 60628
Phone: (773) 702-7000
Fax: (773) 702-7212

UK Representative:
University Press Marketing

Canadian Representative:
The University Press Group

Staff

Director: Paula Barker Duffy (773/702-8878)
   Assistant to the Director: Ellen M. Zalewski (773/702-8879)
   Deputy Director for Administration & Chief Financial Officer: Chris Heiser (773/702-2998)
   Director of Business Development and Planning: Mary Summerfield (773/702-2383)
   Contracts and Subsidiary Rights Manager: Perry Cartwright (773/702-6096)
   Foreign Rights Manager: Gretchen Linder (773/702-7741)
Books Division: Lain Adkins, Manager (773/702-3160)
   Editorial Coordinator: Rachel Chance (773/702-7631)
Acquisitions Editorial:
   Editorial Directors: Alan Thomas (humanities & sciences) (773/702-7644); John Tryneski (social sciences & paperbacks) (773/702-7648)
   Editors: Catherine Beebe (National Bureau of Economic Research volumes) (773/702-7643); Susan Bielstein (art, architecture, ancient archeology, film studies) (773/702-7633); T. David Brent (anthropology, philosophy, psychology, psychiatry) (773/702-7642); Robert P. Devens (American history, law, regional publishing) (773/702-0158); Kathleen Hansell (music) (773/702-0427); Christie Henry (biological and physical sciences, geography and cartography) (773/702-0468); Douglas Mitchell (history, sociology, sexuality studies, rhetoric) (773/702-7639); Randolph Petilos (medieval studies, poetry in translation) (773/702-7647); Catherine Rice (history, philosophy, science, earth science); J. Alex Schwartz (economics, business, law) (773/702-7638); Alan Thomas (literature, religion, classics) (773/702-7644); John Tryneski (political science, law and society, economics, education) (773/702-7648)
   Managing Editor, Phoenix Poets: Randolph Petilos (773/702-7647)
   Paperback Editor: Margaret Hivnor (773/702-7649)
   Assistant Paperback Editor: Janet Deckenbach (773/702-7034)
   Reference: Linda Halvorson, Editorial Director (303/331-6430; e-mail: lhalvorson9@ccs.com)
   Project Editor: Mary Laur (773/702-7326)

Manuscript Editorial: Anita Samen, Managing Editor (773/702-5081)
Marketing: Carol Kasper, Director (773/702-7733)
  Distributed Books Coordinator: Daniel Lee (773/702-4916)
  Marketing Systems Coordinator: Karen Choy (773/702-7490)
  Marketing Manager for Reference & Regional Projects: Ellen Gibson (773/702-3233)
Marketing Design Manager: Mary Shanahan (773/702-7697)
  Marketing. Designer: Alice Reimann (773/702-7849)
Sales: John Kessler, Associate Marketing Director/Sales Director (773/702-7248)
  Assistant Sales Manager: Jim McCoy (773/702-7723)
  Sales Assistant: Robert Hoffman (773/702-0340)
  International Sales Manager: Betsy Solaro (773/702-7898)
  E-commerce/E-marketing Manager: Dean Blobaum (773/702-7706)
  Sales Representatives: Bailey Walsh (Midwest); Blake De Lodder (East Coast); Gary Hart (West Coast)
  Sales Assistant: Vertelle Kanyama (773/702-7899)
Promotions: Levi Stahl, Advertising Manager (773/702-0289)
  Advertising, Marketing, Promotions Assistant: Beni Chhun (773/702-2945)
  Direct Marketing Manager: Joe Weintraub (773/702-0377)
  Associate Direct Marketing Manager: Stuart Kisilinsky (773/702-8924)
  Direct Mail Associate: Anne Osterman (773/702-7887)
  Exhibits Manager: Kimberly Singer (773/702-4216)
  Exhibits Associate: Jennifer Johnson (773/702-0285)
Publicity: Erin Hogan, Associate Marketing Director and Publicity Director (773/702-3714)
  Publicity Manager: Mark Heineke (773/702-7897)
  Promotions Managers: Peter Cavagnaro (773/702-0279); Ashley Cave (773/702-7490); Stephanie Hlywak (773/702-0376); Kimberly Singer (773/702-4216)
  Publicity Assistants: Harriett Green (773/702-4217); Karl Mueller (773/702-7740)
  Reviews Assistant: Fredrich Burich (773/702-4054)
Design and Production: Sylvia Hecimovich, Design and Production Director (773/702-7924)
  Design Manager: Jill Shimabukuro (773/702-7654)
  Production Managers: Siobhan Drummond (773/702-7650); Phyllis Kingsland (773/702-1673)
IT Manager Books: Alister Gibson (773/702-8521)
Journals: Robert Shirrell, Manager (773/702-7600)
  Associate Journals Manager and Director, Astronomy Journals: Julie Steffen (773/753-3372)
  Publications Manager: Kari Roane (773/702-7362)
  Associate Publications Manager: Katharine Duff (773/702-7688)
  Assistant Publications Manager: Andrew Bauman (773/753-4241)
  Publications Manager, Astronomy Journals: Kerry Kroffe (773/702-2621)
  Production Manager, Astronomy Journals: Carolyn Chmiel (773/753-3373)
  Chief Manuscript Editor, Astronomy Journals: Elizabeth Huyck (773/753-8021)
  Publications Manager, Medical Journals: Everett Conner (773/753-2669)
  Chief Manuscript Editor, Medical Journals: Margaret Perkins (773/753-8031)
  Production Manager, General Journals: Tess Mullen (773/702-7632)
  Chief Manuscript Editor, General Journals: Mary E. Leas (773/702-7961)
  Director of Marketing: June Ellen Groppi (773/753-7359)

Advertising Manager: Tim Hill (773/702-8187)
Advertising and List Rental: Cheryl Jones (773/702-7361)
Subscription and Fulfillment Manager: Don Pavoni (773/753-4243)
Information Technology Manager: Stephen Shew (773/702-7530)
Electronic Publishing Systems Manager: John Muenning (773/753-3376)
BiblioVault:
BiblioVault Operations and Web Coordinator: Kate Davey (773/834-4417)
  BiblioVault Lead Programmer: Eric Gamazon (773/503-8035)
Chicago Distribution Center Services:
President of Chicago Distribution Services: Donald A. Collins (773/702-7020)
  Administrator: Sharon Klausner (773/702-7010)
  Director of Business Development and Planning: Mary Summerfield (773/702-2383)
  Distribution Service Manager: Sam Giannakis (773/702-7240)
  M.I.S. Manager: Christopher Jones (773/702-7229)
  Director of Accounting: Bob Peterson (773/702-7036)
  Press Accountant: Ryan Knight (773/702-7024)
  Credit & Collections, A/R Manager: Nick Cole (773/702-7164)
  Customer Service Manager: Karen Hyzy (773/702-7109)
  Warehouse Distribution Manager: Willie Cameron (773/702-7080)
  Warehouse Office Manager: Gail Candreva-Szwet (773/702-7080)
  Royalty and Returns Manager: Cassandra Wisniewski (773/702-7062)
  Distribution Services Coordinator: Sue Tranchita (773/702-7014)
  Journals Warehouse Manager: Donald P. Collins (773/660-4830)
  Chicago Digital Distribution Center Manager: Jeanne Weinkle (773/702-7238)

Full Member

Established: 1891   Admitted to AAUP: 1957
Title output 2002: 247   Title output 2003: 204
Titles currently in print: 5,312   Journals published: 42

Editorial Program
Sociology; anthropology; political science; business and economics; history; English;
American and foreign literature; literary criticism; biological and physical sciences and
mathematics; conceptual studies of science; law; philosophy; linguistics; geography and
cartography; art history; classics; architecture; history of photography; education; psychiatry
and psychology; musicology. Submissions are not invited in fiction or poetry or in conven-
tional textbooks.
Journals (*journals available online): *American Art; American Journal of Education; The
American Journal of Human Genetics*; American Journal of Sociology*; The American Natural-
ist*; The Astronomical Journal*; The Astrophysical Journal*; The Astrophysical Journal Supple-
ment Series*; Classical Philology; Clinical Infectious Diseases*; Comparative Education Review*;
Critical Inquiry*; Current Anthropology*; Economic Development and Cultural Change*; The
Elementary School Journal; Ethics*; History of Religions*; International Journal of American
Linguistics*; International Journal of Plant Sciences*; Isis*; Journal of British Studies*; The
Journal of Business*; The Journal of Consumer Research*; The Journal of Geology*; The Journal of
Infectious Diseases*; Journal of Labor Economics*; The Journal of Law and Economics*; The
Journal of Legal Studies*; The Journal of Modern History*; Journal of Near Eastern Studies*;
Journal of Political Economy*; The Journal of Religion; Law and Social Inquiry*; The Library*

Quarterly*; *Modern Philology**; *Osiris*; *Philosophy of Science**; *Physiological and Biochemical Zoology**; *Publications of the Astronomical Society of the Pacific**; *The Quarterly Review of Biology**; *Signs**; *Social Service Review**; and *Winterthur Portfolio**. Annuals: *Crime and Justice*; *Ocean Yearbook*; *Supreme Court Economic Review*; *The Supreme Court Review*.

Special imprints: Phoenix Books (trade paperbacks); Midway Reprints (short-run paperback reprints)

The Chinese University Press

The Chinese University of Hong Kong
Shatin, New Territories, Hong Kong

Phone: +852 2609-6508
Fax: +852 2603-6692
E-mail: cup@cuhk.edu.hk
Indiv: (user I.D.)@cuhk.edu.hk
Web site: www.chineseupress.com

Staff
Director: Steven K. Luk (852 22 609-6460; e-mail: stavenkluk)
  Secretary to the Director: Tina Chan (852 2609-6460)
Manager, Editorial Division: Yat-kong Fung (852 2609-6543; e-mail: yatkongfung)
Business Manager: Angelina Wong (852 2609-6500; e-mail: laifunwong)
Production Manager: Kingsley K.H. Ma (852 2609-6467; e-mail: kwaihungma)
Manager, Audio-Visual Division: Winnie C. Lai (852 2609-8925)
Project Coordinator: Gloria Chiu
Accountant: Yvonne Tam (852 2609-6507; e-mail: yvonnetam)

International Member
Established: 1977
Title output 2002: 54
Titles currently in print: 887

Admitted to AAUP: 1981
Title output 2003: 45
Journals published: 6

Editorial Program
Bilingual publication of academic and general trade titles. Areas of interest include Chinese studies in literature, history, philosophy, languages, and the arts. The Press publishes books on business, government, medicine, and the natural sciences.

Journals: *Asian Anthropology*; *Asian Journal of English Language Teaching*; *The China Review*; *Hong Kong Journal of Sociology*; *Journal of Psychology in Chinese Societies*; *Journal of Translation*.

Special series: Hong Kong Taxation

Marketing, joint imprints, and/or copublishing programs: Ch'ien Mu Lecture in History and Culture; Institute of Chinese Studies Monograph Series; Bibliography and Index Series; Historical Material Series; Centre for Chinese Archaeology & Art Publication Series; Hong Kong Centre for Economic Research Series.

The Chinese University Press also publishes dictionaries and general books in both the English and Chinese languages as well as audiovisual products.

University Press of Colorado

5589 Arapahoe Avenue
Suite 206C
Boulder, CO 80303

Phone: (720) 406-8849
Fax: (720) 406-3443
E-mail: (user I.D)@upcolorado.com
Web site: www.upcolorado.com

European Representative:
Gazelle Book Services

Distributor:
University of Oklahoma Press
4100 28th Ave., N.W.
Norman, OK 73069-8218
Orders: (800) 627-7377
Fax: (800) 735-0476; (405) 364-5798

Staff
Director: Darrin Pratt (e-mail: darrin)
Acquisitions Editor: Sandy Crooms (e-mail: sandy)
Editorial & Production Manager: Laura Furney (e-mail: laura)
Marketing & Sales Coordinator: Ann Wendland (e-mail: ann)
Business Manager: Michelle McIrvin (e-mail: michelle)

Full Member
(Affiliate Member 1982-2000)
Established: 1965
Title output 2002: 35
Titles currently in print: 294

Admitted to AAUP: 1982
Title output 2003: 21
Journals published: 1

Editorial Program
Physical sciences; natural history; ecology; American history; Western history; anthropology; archaeology; regional titles; and the following journal: *Proceedings of the Western Society for French History.*

Special series: Atomic History & Culture; Mesoamerican Worlds; Mining the American West; Women's West.

The Press also copublishes with and distributes titles for the Denver Museum of Natural History, the Colorado Historical Society, and the Center for Literary Publishing.

Columbia University Press

61 West 62nd Street
New York, NY 10023

Phone: (212) 459-0600
Fax: (212) 459-3677
E-mail: (user I.D.)@columbia.edu
Web site: www..columbia.edu/cu/cup

Business Office & Warehouse:
136 South Broadway
Irvington-on-Hudson, NY 10533-2500

Phone: (914) 591-9111
Fax: (914) 591-9201

UK Office:
University Presses of California, Columbia, and Princeton, Ltd.
Southern Cross Trading Estate
1 Oldlands Way, Bognor Regis
West Sussex PO22 9SA
United Kingdom
Phone: +44 1243 842165
Fax: +44 1243 842167

Staff

New York City (212/459-0600):
President and Director: James D. Jordan (ext. 7118; e-mail: jj2143)
  Assistant to the Director: Suzanne Ryan (ext. 7117; e-mail: sr2054)
  Subsidiary Rights Director: Clare Wellnitz (ext. 7147; e-mail: cw270)
  Permissions Assistant: Stephanie Walker (ext. 7156; e-mail: sw2009)
Acquisitions Editorial: Jennifer Crewe, Editorial Director (Asian studies, film, literary and
  cultural studies, food and culture) (ext. 7145; e-mail: jc373)
  Senior Executive Editors: John L. Michel (social work, social welfare, media studies,
  journalism) (ext. 7137; e-mail: jlm58); Peter Dimock (political science, American history
  and American studies, Middle East history) (ext. 7119; e-mail: pd304); Robin Smith (earth
  science, conservation biology, environmental sciences, ecology, paleo-biology) (ext. 7161; e-
  mail: rs1218); Wendy Lochner (religion, anthropology, medieval studies, philosophy) (ext.
  7121; e-mail: wl2003)
  Associate Editor: Anne Routon (Asian history) (ext. 7116; e-mail: akr36)
  Senior Editor-at-Large in Reference Publishing: James Warren (e-mail: jw245)
Manuscript Editorial: Anne McCoy, Managing Editor (ext. 7111; e-mail: aam10)
  Electronic Manuscripts Administrator: Leslie Bialler (ext. 7109; e-mail: lb136)
Marketing: Helena Schwarz, Director of Marketing and Sales (ext. 7132; e-mail: hs340)
  Sales Manager: Brad Hebel (ext. 7130; e-mail: bh2106)
  Publicity Director: Meredith Howard (ext. 7126; e-mail: mh2306)
  Exhibits Manager & Webmaster: Steffen Mathis (ext. 7158; e-mail: sm2063)
  Advertising and Promotions Manager: Lori Wood (ext. 7152; e-mail: lw2142)
  Library Marketing Director: Nan Hudes (ext. 7125; e-mail: nh2010)
  East Coast Sales Representative: Catherine Hobbs (ext. 7809; e-mail:
  chobbs@sybercom.net)
  Mid-West Sales Representative: Kevin Kurtz (ext. 7806; e-mail: kkurtz5@earthlink.net)
  West Coast Sales Representative: William Gawronski (ext. 7807; e-mail:

wgawronski@earthlink.net)

Design and Production: Linda Secondari, Creative Director, Manufacturing and Technology (ext. 7102; e-mail: ls241)

Senior Book Designer: Liz Cosgrove (ext. 7103; e-mail: lc2166)

Production Manager: Jennifer Jerome (ext. 7177; e-mail: jj352)

Network Manager: Courtney Lew (ext. 7153; e-mail: cl800)

Assistant Network Manager: Joe Pagano (ext. 7106; e-mail: jp2299)

Irvington (914/591-9111):

Business: Rebecca Schrader, Chief Financial Officer (ext. 6211 / 7122; e-mail: rs2049)

Controller and Business Manager: Sarah Vanderbilt (ext. 6227; e-mail: scv12)

Assistant to the Financial Officer: Carol Kotash (ext. 6231; e-mail: ck360)

Benefits Administrator, Human Resources Manager: Toni Laich (ext. 6217; e-mail: trl2103)

Warehouse Manager: Thomas Lofgren (ext. 6218; e-mail: tl2147)

Royalty Coordinator: Louise Erickson (ext. 6229; e-mail: le66)

Customer Service Manager: Diane Pillinger (ext. 6240; e-mail: pd182)

Full Member

Established: 1893

Title output 2002: 153

Titles currently in print: 2,342

Admitted to AAUP: 1937

Title output 2003: 147

Editorial Program

General reference works in print and electronic formats.

Scholarly works, general interest books, professional books and upper-level textbooks in the humanities, social sciences, and earth and life sciences. Subjects include history; literary and cultural studies; Asian studies; American studies; film; media studies; gender studies; Middle East studies; medieval studies; religion; anthropology; social work; political science; international affairs; geology; geophysics; ecology; conservation and environmental science; botany; and evolutionary studies. The Press publishes poetry, fiction, and drama in translation only.

Special series, joint imprints, and/or copublishing programs: ACLS Lectures on the History of Religion; American Lectures on the History of Religion; American Museum of Natural History Series on Biodiversity; Arts and Traditions of the Table; Asia Perspectives; Bampton Lectures in America; Between Men — Between Women; Biology and Resource Management; CERI Series in Comparative Politics and International Studies; Columbia Guides to American History; Columbia Guides to Asian History; Columbia Lectures on American Culture; Columbia Series in Science and Religion; Columbia Studies in Contemporary American History; Complexity in Ecological Systems; Critical Moments and Perspectives in Earth History and Paleobiology; Cultures of History; Economics for a Sustainable Earth; Empowering the Powerless; European Perspectives; Film and Culture; Foundations of Social Work Knowledge; Gender and Culture; Harriman Lectures; Historical Ecology; History and Society of the Modern Middle East; History of Urban Life; Italian Academy in America Lectures; Issues, Cases, and Methods in Biodiversity Conservation; John Dewey Essays in Philosophy; Leonard Hastings Schoff Lectures; Modern Chinese Literature from Taiwan; Popular Cultures, Everyday Lives; Records of Western Civilization; Religion in American Culture; Revolutions in Science; Translations from the Asian Classics; Weatherhead Books on Asia; Wellek Library Lectures; Woodbridge Lectures.

Columbia University Press is the distributor in the United States, Canada, and Latin America for Edinburgh University Press, Kegan Paul, University of Tokyo Press, Wallflower Press, East European Monographs, and Chinese University Press of Hong Kong.

Copenhagen Business School Press

J. M. Thieles Vej 1A, st. tv.
DK-1961 Frederiksberg C
Denmark

Phone: +45 3815 3960
Fax: +45 3815 3962
E-mail: cbspress@cbs.dk
Online catalog & Web site: www.cbspress.dk

Scandinavian Distributor:
DBK
Mimersvej 4
DK-4600 Koge
Denmark
Tel: +45 3269 7788
Fax: +45 3269 7789

North American Distributor:
Copenhagen Business School Press
Books International Inc. P.O. Box 605
Herndon, VA 20172-0605
Phone: (703) 661-1500
Fax: (703) 661-1501

Distributor, Rest of the World:
Marston Book Services

Staff
Director: Axel Schultz-Nielsen
Acquisitions Editorial: Axel Schultz-Nielsen
Marketing: Hanne Thorninger Ipsen
Production Manager: Torben W. Nielsen

International Member
Admitted to AAUP: 1997
Title output 2002: 12
Titles currently in print: 91

Established: 1967
Title output 2003: 13

Editorial Program
Academic titles in management, business, economics, organization, and marketing.

Cork University Press

Crawford Business Park
Crosses Green
Cork, Ireland

Phone: +353 (21) 490 2980
Fax: + 353 (21) 431 5329
E-mail: corkunip@ucc.ie
Web site: www.corkuniversitypress.com

US Representative:
Stylus Publishing
22883 Quicksilver Drive
Sterling, VA 20166-2012
Phone: (703) 661-1504
Fax: (703) 661-1501
E-mail: stylusmail@presswarehouse.com

UK Representative:
Marston Book Services

Staff
Director: Mike Collins (e-mail: mike.collins@ucc.ie)
Production: Caroline Somers (e-mail: c.somers@ucc.ie)
Editorial: Tom Dunne (e-mail: t.dunne@ucc.ie)

International Member
Established: 1925
Title output 2002: 15
Titles currently in print: 176

Admitted to AAUP: 2002
Title output 2003: 14
Journals published: 1

Editorial Program
While the Press specializes in the broad field of Irish Cultural, its subject range extends across the fields of music, art history, literary criticism and poetry. However, the focus of our list is in the areas of Irish cultural history, archaeology and landscape studies.

Special Series: Cross Currents; Field Day Monographs; Ireland into Film; Irish Narratives.

Cornell University Press

Street Address:
Sage House
512 East State Street
Ithaca, NY 14850

Mailing Address:
P.O. Box 250
Ithaca, NY 14851

Phone: (607) 277-2338
Fax: (607) 277-2374
E-mail: (user I.D.)@cornell.edu
Web site: www.cornellpress.cornell.edu

Order Fulfillment:
CUP Services
750 Cascadilla Street
Ithaca, NY 14850
Orders/Customer Service:
Phone: (800) 666-2211
Fax: (800) 688-2877

UK Representative:
University Presses Marketing

UK and European Distributor:
NBN International

Canadian Representative:
Lexa Publishers' Representatives

Staff

Director: John G. Ackerman (ext. 209; e-mail: jga4)
  Assistant Director & CFO: Roger A. Hubbs (607/277-2696; e-mail: rah9)
  Personnel Manager: Sally McClure-Parshall (ext. 228; e-mail: sjm19)
  Assistant to the Director: Michael Morris (ext. 210; e-mail: mam278)
Acquisitions Editorial:
  Editorial Director, ILR Press: Frances Benson (labor studies and workplace issues, business) (ext. 222; e-mail: fgb2)
  Executive Editor: Bernhard Kendler (art, classics, literature) (ext. 229; e-mail: bk32)
  Editors: John G. Ackerman (European history, Medieval studies, Russian history); Roger Haydon (politics, international relations, philosophy, history of science, Slavic studies, Asian studies) (ext. 225; e-mail: rmh11)
Manuscript Editorial: Priscilla Hurdle, Managing Editor (ext. 244; e-mail plh9)
  Manuscript Editors: Teresa Jesionowski (ext. 249; e-mail: tj15); Ange Romeo-Hall (ext. 243; e-mail: asr8); Karen Hwa (ext. 245; e-mail: kth9); Karen Laun (ext. 236; e-mail: kml35)
Marketing: Mahinder Kingra, Marketing Manager (ext. 255; e-mail: msk55)
  Sales Manager: Nathan Gemignani (ext. 251; e-mail: ndg5)
  Publicity/Special Projects Manager: Heidi Lovette (ext. 230; e-mail: hsl22)
  Subsidiary Rights Manager: Tonya Cook (e-mail: cup-subrights)
  Advertising Manager: TBA
  Direct Mail/Electronic Marketing Manager: Betsy Martens (ext. 256; e-mail: bvm3)
  Exhibits Coordinator: David Mitchell (ext. 248; e-mail: dwm23)
  Copy Supervisor: Susan Barnett (ext. 259; e-mail: scb33)
  Permissions Coordinator: Stephanie Munson (ext. 231; e-mail: sm120)

Design and Production: Deborah Bruner, Production and Design Manager (ext. 235; e-mail: dnb5)
  Associate Production Manager: George Whipple (ext. 237; e-mail: gtw2)
  Senior Designers: Lou Robinson (ext. 262; e-mail: lr11); Scott Levine (ext. 263; e-mail: sel37)
  Senior Production Coordinator: Christopher Basso (ext. 240; e-mail: cmb224)
  Production Coordinator: Karen Beebe (ext. 239; e-mail: kjb5)
Business: Roger A. Hubbs, Chief Financial Officer (607/277-2696; e-mail: rah9)
  Accounting & Operations Coordinator: Cindy Snyder (607/277-2696; e-mail: chs6)
  Procurement, Disbursements & Title Accounting: Trudy Cism (607/277-2696; e-mail: tec7)
CUP Services Distribution Center:
  CUP Services Operations Manager: Christopher Quinlan (607/277-2211, ext. 125; e-mail: cq@cupserv.org)
  Client Services, Accounts Receivable: Christine Jolluck (607/277-2037, ext. 126; e-mail: cj@cupserv.org)
  MIS: Patrick Garrison (607/277-2969, ext. 149; e-mail: plg6@cupserv.org)
  Customer Service: Sheila Maleski (607/277-2211, ext. 137; e-mail: orderbook@cupserv.org)
  Warehouse and Shipping: Jon Austin (607/277-2827, ext. 151; e-mail: ja@cupserv.org)

Full Member

Established: 1869	Re-established in present form: 1930
Admitted to AAUP: 1937	
Title output 2002: 158	Title output 2003: 143
Titles currently in print: 2,500	

Editorial Program

Serious nonfiction, with particular strengths in anthropology; Asian studies; classics; history; industrial and labor relations; life science; literary criticism and theory; music; natural history; philosophy; politics and international relations; race studies; religion; Slavic studies; sociology; and women's studies.

Submissions are not invited in poetry or fiction.

  Special imprints: Comstock Publishing Associates; ILR Press.

  Special series, joint imprints, and/or copublishing programs: Agora Editions; Ancient Commentators on Aristotle; The Anthropology of Contemporary Issues; Collection on Technology and Work; Conjunctions of Religion and Power in the Medieval Past; Cornell Series in Arthropod Biology; Cornell Studies in Classical Philology/Townsend Lectures; Cornell Studies in the History of Psychiatry; Cornell Studies in Money; Cornell Studies in the Philosophy of Religion; Cornell Studies in Political Economy; Cornell Studies in Security Affairs; The Cornell Wordsworth; The Cornell Yeats; The Culture and Politics of Health Care Work; Culture and Society after Socialism; Cushwa Center Studies of Catholicism in Twentieth-Century America; Islandica; Literature of American Labor; Masters of Latin Literature; Myth and Poetics; Psychoanalysis and Social Theory.

Duke University Press

Street Address:
905 West Main Street
Suite 18-B
Durham, NC 27701

Mailing Address:
Box 90660
Durham, NC 27708-0660

Phone: (919) 687-3600
Faxes: (919) 688-4574 (Books)
(919) 688-3524 (Journals)
(919) 688-4391 (Marketing)
E-mail: info@dukeupress.edu
Indiv:
(first initial)(last name)@dukeupress.edu
(unless otherwise indicated)
Web site: www.dukeupress.edu

Orders and Customer Service:
Phone: (888) 651-0122; (888) 387-5687
Fax: (888) 651-0124; (919) 688-2615

Warehouse:
Duke University Press
Distribution Center
120 Golden Drive
Durham, NC 27705
Phone: (919) 384-0733

UK / European Representative:
Combined Academic Publishers

Canadian Representative:
Lexa Publishers' Representatives

Staff

Director: Stephen A. Cohn (919/687-3606)
  Assistant to the Director: Kirsten Bohl (919/687-3685)
  Manager, Central Administration: Robyn L. Miller (919/687-3633)
  Subsidiary Rights and Permissions: Tom Robinson (919/687-3616)
Acquisitions Editorial: Ken Wissoker, Editor-in-Chief (anthropology, cultural studies, post-colonial theory, lesbian and gay studies, construction of race, gender and national identity, literary criticism, film and television, popular music, visual studies) (919/687-3648; e-mail: kwiss@duke.edu)
  Executive Editor: J. Reynolds Smith (literary theory and history, cultural theory and practice, religion, American studies, Latin American studies, Asian studies, race and ethnicity, science and technology, sociology, contemporary music) (919/687-3637; e-mail: j.smith@duke.edu)
  Senior Editor: Valerie Millholland (Latin American history and politics, European history and politics, American history, women's history, environmental studies, labor history, political science, law) (919/687-3628; e-mail: vmill@duke.edu)
  Assistant Editors: Miriam Angress (religion, women's studies, history, humanities, cultural studies) (919/687-3601); Courtney Berger (political theory) (919/687-3652)
Manuscript Editorial: Fred Kameny, Managing Editor (919/687-3603)
  Assistant Managing Editors: Pamela Morrison (919/687-3630); Justin Faerber (919/687-3669); Kate Lothman (919/687-3681); Mark Mastromarino (919/687-3660)
Marketing: Emily Young, Associate Director and Marketing Manager (919/687-3654)
  Associate Marketing Manager: H. Lee Willoughby-Harris (919/687-3646; e-mail: hlwh)
  Sales Manager: Michael McCullough (919/687-3604)
  Publicist: Laura Sell (919/687-3639)
  Catolog/Copywriting Coordinator: Katie Courtland (919/687-3663)

Advertising Coordinator: Greta Strittmatter (919/687-3649)
Exhibits Coordinator: Erin Hathaway (919/687-3647)
Publicity Assistant: Dafina Blacksher Diabate (919/687-3650)
Design and Production: Deborah Wong, Design & Production Manager (919/687-3629)
Senior Book Designer: Cherie Westmoreland (919/687-3643)
Book Designers: Amy Buchanan (919/687-3651; e-mail: arbuchanan); Rebecca Gimenez (919/687-3658)
Senior Production Assistant: Katy Clove (919/ 687-3668)
Administrative Assistant: Patty Van Norman (919/687-3622)
Journals: Debra Kaufman, Editorial & Administrative Manager (919/687-3657)
Managing Editor: Rob Dilworth (919/687-3624)
Marketing Manager: Donna Blagdan (919/687-3631)
Assistant Marketing Manager: Cason Lynley (919/687-3653)
Advertising Coordinator: Mandy Dailey-Berman (919/687-3636)
Circulation Coordinator: Kim Steinle (919/687-3655)
Production & Finance Manager: Michael Brondoli (919/687-3605)
Art Director/Journals Designer: Sue Hall (919/687-3620; e-mail: suehall)
Assistant Designer: David Spratte (919/687-3618)
Production Supervisor: Allison Belan (919/687-3619)
Business Office and Distribution: Agnes Wong Nickerson, Chief Financial Officer (919/687-3684; e-mail: agnesw)
Distribution Manager: Julie Tyson (919/812-1443)
Warehouse Supervisor: Margie Clayton (919/384-0733)
Fulfillment – Journals: Lesley Tippett (919/687-3617)
Fulfillment – Books: Grace Ryan (919/687-3610
Fulfillment Manager: TBA
Accounts Payable and Royalty Supervisor: Deborah Houser (919/687-3614)
Information Systems: Pamela Spaulding, Manager (919/687-3641)
Assistant Manager: Martin Leppitsch (919/687-3662)
Database Administrator/Unison Programmer: Ling Mao (919/687-3665)
Network Administrator/Help Desk Manager: Matthew Paul (919/687-3679)

Full Member

Established: 1921 (as Trinity College Press)   Admitted to AAUP: 1937
Title output 2002: 107   Title output 2003: 112
Titles currently in print: 1,876   Journals published: 32

Editorial Program

Scholarly books in the humanities and social sciences, with lists in art criticism and history; cultural studies; literary theory and history; legal studies; gay and lesbian studies; gender studies; American studies; American history; African-American studies; Asian studies; Asian-American studies; Latin American anthropology, history, literature, and politics; Slavic studies; European history and politics; cultural anthropology; minority politics and post-colonial issues; music; film and TV; environmental studies; political science and political philosophy; religion; sociology; and science studies.

Journals (*journals available online): *American Literature**; *American Literary Scholarship**; *American Speech**; *boundary 2**; *Camera Obscura**; *The Collected Letters of Thomas and Jane Welsh Carlyle*; *Common Knowledge**; *Comparative Studies of South Asia, Africa and the Middle*

East; differences*; *Duke Gifted Letter; Duke Mathematical Journal**; *Eighteenth-Century Life**; *Ethnohistory**; *French Historical Studies**; *GLQ: A Journal of Lesbian and Gay Studies**; *Hispanic American Historical Review**; *History of Political Economy**; *Journal of Health Politics, Policy and Law**; *Journal of Medieval and Early Modern Studies*; *Labor: Studies in Working Class History of the Americas*; *Mediterranean Quarterly**; *Modern Language Quarterly**; *Neuro-Oncology**; *Pedagogy: Critical Approaches to Teaching Literature, Language, Culture, & Composition**; *Poetics Today**; *positions: east asia cultures critique**; *Public Culture**; *Radical History Review**; *SAQ: South Atlantic Quarterly**; *Social Science History**, *Social Text**; and *Theater**.

Special series, joint imprints and/or copublishing programs: American Encounters: Global Interactions; Asia-Pacific: Culture, Politics and Society; Bicentennial Reflections on the French Revolution; Collected Letters of Thomas and Jane Welsh Carlyle; Console-ing Passions; Constitutional Conflicts; Cultures of Authorship; Duke Monographs in Medieval and Renaissance Studies; Body/Commodity/Text; the C. Eric Lincoln Series on the Black Experience; Ecologies for the Twenty-First Century; International and Comparative Working-Class History; Latin America in Translation; Latin America Otherwise: Languages, Empires, Nations; Latin America Readers; Living with the Shore; New Americanists; Next Wave: New Directions in Women's Studies; Objects/Histories; Perverse Modernities; Politics, Culture, & History; Post-Contemporary Interventions; Public Planet; Radical Perspectives: A Radical History Review Book Series; The Roman Jakobson Series in Linguistics and Poetics; Science and Cultural Theory; Series Q: SIC; Social Studies Across the Borders.

Duquesne University Press

600 Forbes Avenue
Pittsburgh, PA 15282

Phone: (412) 396-6610
Fax: (412) 396-5984
Web site: www.dupress.duq.edu

UK Representative:
Drake International Services

Distribution:
CUP Services
Box 6525
750 Cascadilla Street
Ithaca, NY 14851-6525
Orders only: (800) 666-2211
Fax: (607) 272-6292
Customer Service: (607) 277-2211

Staff
Director: Susan Wadsworth-Booth (412/396-5684; e-mail: wadsworth@duq.edu)
Marketing & Business Manager: Lori R. Crosby (412/396-5732; e-mail: crosbyl@duq.edu)
Production Editor: Kathy Meyer (412/396-1166; e-mail: meyerk@duq.edu)
Editorial Assistant: Akiko Motomura (412/396-4866)
Promotions/Marketing Assistant: TBA (412/396-4863)

Affiliate Member
Established: 1927

Title output 2002: 8
Titles currently in print: 90

Admitted to AAUP: 1995
(Former membership: 1962-72)
Title output 2003: 9

Editorial Program
Literary studies, specifically of late medieval, Renaissance and seventeenth-century literature; ethics; philosophy; psychology; creative nonfiction. The Press does not publish fiction, poetry, or unrevised dissertations.

Special series: Emerging Writers in Creative Nonfiction; Medieval & Renaissance Literary Studies.

Edinburgh University Press

22 George Square
Edinburgh EH8 9LF
United Kingdom

Phone: +44 (131) 650 4218
Fax: +44 (131) 662 0053
E-mail: marketing@eup.ed.ac.uk
Indiv: (firstname.lastname)@eup.ed..ac.uk
Web site: www.eup.ed.ac.uk

UK and European Distributor:
Marston Book Services

US Distributor:
Columbia University Press
136 South Broadway
Irvington, NY 10533
Web site: www.columbia.edu/cu/cup/

Canadian Distributor:
University of British Columbia Press

Staff

Chief Executive and Head of Journals: Timothy Wright (131 650 4219)
Deputy CEO/Head of Book Publishing: Jackie Jones (131 650 4217)
Marketing: Douglas McNaughton (131 650 4220)
Sales Administrator and Assistant to CEO: Anna Skinner (131 650 4218)
Rights Manager: Alison Bowden (131 650 4213)
Head of Production: Ian Davidson (131 650 4221)
Head of Finance: Jan Thomson (131 650 4216)

International Member

Established: 1950
Title output 2002: 70
Titles currently in print: 500

Admitted to AAUP: 2004
Title output 2003: 77
Journals published: 29

Editorial Program

Academic titles in social science and humanities; Islamic studies, Classics and ancient history; literature; linguistics; philosophy; religious studies; film and media studies; American studies; politics; Scottish history, politics and culture; gender studies; history; African studies.

Journals: *Africa*; *Architectural Heritage*; *Botanical Journal of Scotland*; *Comparative Criticism*; *Dance Research*; *Edinburgh Law Review*; *Episteme*; *History and Computing*; *Holy Land Studies*; *Journal of Arabic and Islamic Studies*; *Journal of British Cinema and Television*; *Journal of Qur'anic Studies*; *Journal of Scottish Philosophy*; *Journal of Transatlantic Studies*; *Journal of Victorian Culture*; *Paragraph*; *Parliamentary History*; *Politics and Ethics Review*; *Romanticism*; *Scottish Archaeological Journal*; *Scottish Economic & Social History*; *Scottish Geographical Journal*; *Scottish Historical Review*; *Sports Biomechanics*; *The Surgeon*; *Studies in World Christianity*; *Translation and Literature*.

University Press of Florida

15 N. W. 15th Street
Gainesville, FL 32611-2079

Phone: (352) 392-1351
Acquisitions phone: (352) 392-9190
Fax: (352) 392-7302
E-mail: (user I.D.)@upf.com
Web site: www.upf.com

Orders:
Phone: (800) 226-3822
Fax: (800) 680-1955

UK Representative:
Eurospan

Staff

Director: Kenneth J. Scott (ext. 204; e-mail: ks)
  Assistant to the Director: Bennie Watson (ext. 201; e-mail: bw)
Acquisitions Editorial: John Byram, Associate Director & Editor-in-Chief (anthropology, archaeology, Caribbean studies) (352/392-9190, ext. 223; e-mail: john)
  Assistant Director and Assistant Editor-in-Chief: Meredith Morris-Babb (history, Floridiana, dance) (386/615-6726; e-mail: mb)
  Acquisitions Editor: Amy Gorelick (Middle East, Latin American studies, literature) (352/392-9190, ext. 225; e-mail: ag)
Prepress: Lynn Werts, Associate Director & Prepress Manager (ext. 222; e-mail: lw)
  Manuscript Editorial: Deidre Bryan, Assistant Director & Managing Editor (ext. 218; e-mail: db)
  Project Editors: Susan Albury (ext. 213; e-mail: sa); Gillian Hillis (ext. 212; e-mail: gh); Jacqueline Kinghorn Brown (ext. 217; e-mail: jb)
  Editorial Assistant: Michele Fiyak-Burkley (ext. 216; e-mail: mf)
  Design Manager: Larry Leshan (ext. 221; e-mail: LL)
  Production Manager: David Graham (ext. 220; e-mail: dg)
  Designer/Compositor: Robyn Taylor (ext. 219; e-mail: rt)
Marketing: Jim Denton, Associate Director & Marketing Manager (ext. 232; e-mail: jd)
  Advertising and Exhibits Manager: Jenny Ward (ext. 238; e-mail: jw)
  Production Coordinator: Nicole Sorenson (ext. 235; e-mail: ns)
Sales & Publicity: Andrea Dzavik, Assistant Director & Sales and Promotions Manager (ext. 234; e-mail: ad)
  Sales & Promotion Assistant: Romina Guttierrez (ext. 243; e-mail: rg)
Business: Ben Layfield, Associate Director & Business Manager (ext. 209; e-mail: bl)
  Accounting/Order-Fulfillment Manager: Sandra Dyson (ext. 210; e-mail: sd)
  Credit Manager: Kim Lake (ext. 211; e-mail: kl)
  Warehouse and Shipping Manager: Charles Hall (352/392-6867; e-mail: charles)
Information Technology: Bryan Lutz, Manager (ext. 215; e-mail: bryan)

Full Member

Established: 1945

Title output 2002: 87

Titles currently in print: 1,073

Admitted to AAUP: 1950

Title output 2003: 84

Editorial Program

Floridiana; New world archaeology; conservation biology; Latin American studies; Caribbean studies; Middle East studies; African-American studies; Southern history and culture; Native American studies; dance; natural history; humanities; maritime studies.

Submissions are not invited in prose fiction or poetry.

Fordham University Press

Street Address:
2546 Belmont Avenue
Bronx, NY 10458-5172

Phone: (718) 817-4795
Fax: (718) 817-4785
E-mail: (user I.D.)@fordham.edu
Web site: www.fordhampress.com

European Representative:
Eurospan

Mailing Address:
University Box L
Bronx, NY 10458-5172

Distribution Address:
Bookmasters Distribution Services
30 Amberwood Pkwy.
Ashland, OH 44805
Phone: (800) 247-6553; (419) 281-1802

Canadian Representative:
Scholarly Book Services

Staff

Director: Robert Oppedisano (718/817-4789; e-mail: roppedisano)
    Executive Secretary: Mary Lou Pena (718/817-4781; e-mail: pena)
Editorial Director: Helen Tartar (718/817-4787; e-mail: tartar)
Editor-at-Large: Saverio Procario (718/817-4790; e-mail: procario)
Managing Editor: Chris Mohney (718/817-4786; e-mail: mohney)
Marketing Manager: Kate O'Brien (718/817-4782; e-mail: bkaobrien)
Sales and Subsidiary Rights Manager: Jacky Philpotts (718/817-4791; e-mail: philpotts)
Production Editor: Loomis Mayer (718/817-4788; e-mail: lmayer)
Business Manager: Margaret M. Noonan (718/817-4780; e-mail: mnoonan)
    Assistant Business Manager: Anne Sheridan (718/817-4780)

Full Member

Established: 1907

Title output 2002: 29

Titles currently in print: 413

Admitted to AAUP: 1938

Title output 2003: 29

Journals published: 2

Editorial Program

Fordham University Press publishes primarily in the humanities and social sciences, with emphasis on the fields of philosophy, theology, history, classics, economics, sociology, business, political science, and law, as well as literature and the fine arts. Additionally, the Press publishes books focusing on the metropolitan New York region and books of interest to the general public.

Journals: *Dante Studies* and *Traditio: Studies in Ancient and Medieval History, Thought, and Religion.*

Special series, joint imprints, and/or copublishing programs: Abrahamic Dialogues; American Philosophy Series; Business, Economics, Legal Studies; Communications and Media Studies; Hudson Valley Heritage; International Humanitarian Affairs; The Irish in the Civil War; Medieval Studies; Moral Philosophy and Moral Theology; The North's Civil War; Perspectives in Continental Philosophy; Reconstructing America; Studies in Religion and Literature; and World War II.

The Press also distributes the publications of Creighton University Press; University of San Francisco Press; St. Louis University Press; St. Joseph's University Press; Rockhurst University Press; the Institution for Advanced Study in the Theater Arts (IASTA); The Reconstructionist Press; Little Room Press; and St. Bede's Publications.

Gallaudet University Press

800 Florida Avenue, N.E.
Washington, DC 20002-3695

Phone: (202) 651-5488
Fax: (202) 651-5489
E-mail: (user I.D.)@gallaudet.edu
Web site: gupress.gallaudet.edu

European Distributor:
Forest Book Services

Orders:
Gallaudet University Press
Chicago Distribution Center
11030 South Langley Avenue
Chicago, IL 60628
Phone: (800) 621-2736
TTY: (888) 630-9347
Fax: (800) 621-8476

Staff
Executive Director: John Vickrey Van Cleve (202/651-5488; e-mail: john.vancleve)
Editorial: Ivey Pittle Wallace, Assistant Director (202/651-5662; e-mail: ivey.wallace)
Managing Editor: Deirdre Mullervy (202/651-5967; e-mail: deirdre.mullervy)
Marketing: Dan Wallace, Assistant Director (202/651-5661; e-mail: daniel.wallace)
   Marketing Assistant: Valencia Simmons (202/651-5917; e-mail: valencia.simmons)
Production: Jill Hendricks Porco, Coordinator (202/651-5025; e-mail: jill.porco)
   Production Assistant: Sara Stallard (TTY: 202/448-6908; e-mail: sara.stallard)
Business: Frances W. Clark (202/651-5488; e-mail: frances.clark)

Affiliate Member
Established: 1980
Title output 2002: 12
Titles currently in print: 171

Admitted to AAUP: 1983
Title output 2003: 12
Journals published: 2

Editorial program
Scholarly books and serious nonfiction from all disciplines as they relate to the interests and culture of people who are deaf, hard of hearing, or experiencing hearing loss. Particular areas of emphasis include signed languages, linguistics, deaf culture, deaf history, biography and autobiography, parenting, and special education, as well as instructional works and children's literature with sign language or deafness themes.

   Special imprints: Kendall Green Publications (children's works) and Clerc Books (instructional materials).

   Special series: Sociolinguistics in Deaf Communities; Gallaudet Classics in Deaf Studies.

   The Press also distributes select titles from Signum Verlag (Hamburg, Germany) and publishes the journals *Sign Language Studies* and *American Annals of the Deaf.*

Georgetown University Press

3240 Prospect Street, N.W.
Washington, DC 20007

Phone: (202) 687-5889
Fax: (202) 687-6340
E-mail: (user I.D.)@georgetown.edu
Web site: www.press.georgetown.edu

Orders:
c/o Hopkins Fulfillment Service
P.O. Box 50370
Baltimore, MD 21211
Phone: (410) 516-6956; (800) 537-5487
Fax: (410) 516-6998

Staff
Director: Richard Brown (202/687-5912; e-mail: reb7)
Associate Director and Acquisitions Editor: Gail Grella (202/687-6263; e-mail: grellag1)
Director of Marketing and Sales: Gina Armento Lindquist (202/687-9856; e-mail: gla2)
  Marketing Coordinator: TBA
  Exhibits and Publicity Assistant: Jenni Brewer (202/687-9298; e-mail: jrb52)
Editorial and Production Manager: Deborah Weiner (202/687-6251; e-mail: weinerd)
  Editorial and Production Coordinator: Hope Smith (202/687-0159; e-mail: hjs6)
Business Manager: Gene Rhee (202/687-4704; e-mail: rheee)
Publishing Assistant and Rights Coordinator: Andrea Brusca (202/687-4462; e-mail: aab28)

Full Member
Established: 1964
Title output 2002: 39
Titles currently in print: 529

Admitted to AAUP: 1986
Title output 2003: 42
Journals published: 1

Editorial Program
Bioethics; international affairs; languages and linguistics; political science and public policy; and religion and ethics.

Special series: Advancing Human Rights; American Governance and Public Policy; Carnegie Council on Ethics and International Affairs; Hastings Center Studies in Ethics; Georgetown Classics in Arabic Language and Linguistics; Georgetown Studies in Spanish Linguistics; Moral Traditions; Public Management and Change; Religion and Politics.

The Press publishes *The Journal of the Society of Christian Ethics*.

University of Georgia Press

330 Research Drive, Suite B-100
Athens, GA 30602-4901

Phone: (706) 369-6130
Fax: (706) 369-6131
E-mail: books@ugapress.uga.edu
Indiv: (user I.D.)@ugapress.uga.edu
Web site: www.ugapress.org

UK Distributor:
Eurospan

Warehouse:
955 E. Whitehall Road
Athens, GA 30602-5427

Orders and Customer Service:
Phone: (800) 266-5842; (706) 369-6163

Canadian Distributor:
Cariad Services to Publishers International

Staff

Director: Nicole Mitchell (706/369-6143; e-mail: mitchell)
  Assistant to the Director and Contracts and Rights Manager: Jane Kobres (706/369-6140; e-mail: jkobres)
  Development Officer: Lane Stewart (706/369-6130; e-mail: lstewart@uga.edu)
Acquisitions Editorial: Nancy Grayson, Associate Director and Editor-in-Chief (706/369-6139; e-mail: ngrayson)
  Acquisitions Editors: Derek Krissoff (706/369-6141; e-mail: krissoff); Christa Frangiamore (706/369-6145; e-mail: cfrangiamore)
  Assistant Editor: Andrew Berzanskis (706/369-6135; e-mail: andrewb)
Manuscript Editorial: Jennifer L. Reichlin, Managing Editor (706/369-6136; e-mail: jlreichlin)
  Project Editor: Jon Davies (706/369-6138; e-mail: jdavies)
  Assistant Project Editor: Sarah McKee (706/369-6137; e-mail: semckee)
Marketing and Sales: Allison Reid, Assistant Director for Marketing and Sales (706/369-6158; e-mail: areid)
  Publicity Manager: John McLeod (706/369-6160; e-mail: jmcleod)
  Exhibits and Promotions Manager: David Des Jardines (706/369-6159; e-mail: ddesjard)
  Marketing Designer: Anne Richmond Boston (706/369-6150; e-mail: arb)
  Marketing and Sales Assistant: TBA
Design and Production: Sandra Strother Hudson, Assistant Director for Design and Production (706/369-6154; e-mail: shudson)
  Assistant Production Manager and Designer: Kathi Dailey Morgan (706/369-6152; e-mail: kdmorgan)
  Production Coordinator and Designer: Walton Harris (706/369-6155; e-mail: wwharris)
  Designers: Mindy Hill (706/369-6151; e-mail: mhill); Erin Kirk New (706/369-6154; e-mail: ekirknew)
Business and Order Fulfillment: Phyllis Wells, Assistant Director for Business (706/369-6134; e-mail: pwells)
  Accountant: Marena Smith (706/369-6133; e-mail: msmith)
  Permissions Manager and Accounting Assistant: Stacey Bone (706/369-6144; e-mail: sbone)

Customer Service Manager: Brenda Adams (706/369-6146; e-mail: badams)
Customer Service Representatives: Joelyn Heslep (706/369-6163; e-mail: jheslep); Betty
Downer (706/369-6148; e-mail: downer)
Accounts Receivable Representative: Janice Bell (706/369-6149; e-mail: jbell)
Warehouse Manager: Bobby Allen (706/542-9279)
Assistant Warehouse Manager: Matt Stewart (706/542-9279)
The New Georgia Encyclopedia Project: (www.georgiaencyclopedia.org)
Editor: John Inscoe (706/542-8848; e-mail: jinscoe@uga.edu)
Managing Editor: Kelly Caudle (706/583-0723; e-mail: kcaudle@uga.edu)
Associate Editor: Elisabeth Hughes (706/583-0600; e-mail: ehughes@uga.edu)
Electronic Editor: Erin Randall McLeod (706/583-8065; e-mail: erandall@uga.edu)
Media Editor: Melinda G. Smith Mullikin (706/583-0438; e-mail: mgsmith)

Full Member

Established: 1938

Admitted to AAUP: 1940

Title output 2002: 68

Title output 2003: 68

Titles currently in print: 900

Editorial Program

Humanities and social sciences with particular interests in American and southern history;
American and southern literature; African-American studies; American studies; civil rights
history; legal history; environmental history; ecology and environmental studies; ecocriticism
and nature writing; landscape studies; life sciences and natural history; Appalachian studies;
folklore; anthropology; gender studies; popular culture; cinema and media studies; music;
urban studies; literary nonfiction; photography; and regional trade titles.

Special series: The Chaucer Library; Economy and Society in the Modern South; Publications of the Southern Texts Society; Southern Anthropological Society Proceedings; Southern
Environments; Studies in the Legal History of the South; The United States and the Americas; The Works of Tobias Smollett.

Literary competitions: Flannery O'Connor Award for Short Fiction; The Contemporary
Poetry Series; The Association of Writers and Writing Programs Award for Creative Nonfiction; Cave Canem Poetry Prize.

Lecture series: Mercer University Lamar Memorial Lectures; Georgia Southern University
Jack N. and Addie D. Averitt Lectures; George H. Shriver Lecture Series in Religion in
American History.

Getty Publications

Street Address:
2700 Colorado Avenue
Suite 500
Los Angeles, CA 90049-1682

Phone: (310) 440-7365
Fax: (310) 440-7758
E-mail: pubsinfo@getty.edu
Indiv: (user I.D.)@getty.edu
Web site: www.getty.edu/bookstore

Mailing Address:
1200 Getty Center Drive
Suite 500
Santa Monica, CA 90404

Warehouse Address:
Getty Publications Book Dist. Center
PO Box 49659
Los Angeles, CA 90049-0659

Customer Service/Order Fulfillment:
Phone: (310) 440-7333; (800) 223-3431
Fax: (818) 779-0051

UK and European Distributor:
Windsor Books International

Canadian Distributor:
Canadian Manda Group

Staff
Publisher: Chris Hudson (310/440-7095; e-mail: chudson)
  General Manager: Kara Kirk (310/440-6506; e-mail: kkirk)
  Rights Manager: Leslie Rollins (310/440-7102; e-mail: lrollins)
Acquisitions Editorial: Mark Greenberg, Editor-in-Chief (310/440-7097; e-mail: mgreenberg)
  Head of Publications, The Getty Research Institute: Julia Bloomfield (310/440-7446; e-mail: jbloomfield)
Manuscript Editorial: Ann Lucke, Managing Editor (310/440-6525; e-mail: alucke)
Marketing and Sales: Patrick Callahan, Marketing Manager (310/440-6536; e-mail: pcallahan)
  Sales Manager: Rob Flynn (310/440-6486; e-mail: rflynn)
Design and Production: Deenie Yudell, Design Manager (310/440-6508; e-mail: dyudell)
  Production Manager: Karen Schmidt (310/440-6504; e-mail: kschmidt)
Business and Warehouse: Jeff Wiebe, Distribution Center Manager (310/440-6602; e-mail: jwiebe)

Associate Member
Established: 1982
Title output 2002: 29
Distributed titles 2002: 5
Titles currently in print: 434

Admitted to AAUP: 1989
Title output 2003: 35
Distributed titles 2003: 1
Journals published: 1

Editorial Program
Scholarly and general interest publications on the visual arts: architecture, conservation, the history of art and the humanities; art related titles for children; and areas related to the collections of the Getty Museum: antiquities, decorative arts, drawings, manuscripts, paintings, photographs, and sculpture.
  Journal: *Sculpture Journal*

Harvard University Press

79 Garden Street
Cambridge, MA 02138-1499

Phone: (617) 495-2600
Faxes: (617) 495-5898 (General)
(617) 496-4677 (Editorial & Dir. Off.)
(617) 496-2550 (Marketing)
E-mail: (firstname_lastname)@harvard.edu
Web site: www.hup.harvard.edu

Customer Service:
(800) 405-1619 (US & Canada)
(401) 531-2800 (all others)
Faxes: (800) 406-9145 (US & Canada)
(401) 531-2801 (International)

London Office:
Harvard University Press
Fitzroy House
11 Chenies Street
London WC1E 7ET
United Kingdom
Phone: +44 171 306 0603
Fax: +44 171 306 0604
E-mail: info@hup-mitpress.co.uk

Staff

Director: William P. Sisler (617/495-2601)
  Executive Administrator, Office of the Director and Human Resources: Susan J. Seymour (617/495-2602)
  Director of Intellectual Property: Melinda Koyanis (617/495-2619)
  Subsidiary Rights Manager: Stephanie Vyce (617/495-2603)
Acquisitions Editorial:
  Executive Editors: Lindsay Waters (humanities, esp. literary criticism, philosophy) (617/495-2835); Michael G. Fisher (science and medicine) (617/495-2674); Joyce Seltzer (history and contemporary affairs) (212/337-0280; Fax: 212/337-0259)
  Acquisitions Editors: Michael Aronson (social sciences, esp. law and economics) (617/495-1837); Margaretta L. Fulton (humanities) (617/495-8122); Elizabeth Knoll (behavioral science and neuroscience); Kathleen McDermott (history) (617/495-4703); Ann Downer-Hazell (science and medicine) (617/496-1311)
Manuscript Editorial: Mary Ann Lane, Managing Editor (617/495-1846)
Marketing: Paul Adams, Marketing Director (617/495-4710)
  Advertising Director & Web Administrator: Denise Waddington (617/495-4712)
  Promotion Director: Sheila Barrett (617/495-2618)
  Publicity, Trade: Mary Kate Maco (617/495-4713)
  Publicity, Academic: Colleen Lanick (617/495-1284); Rose Ann Miller (617/495-4714); Megan Adams (617/496-1340)
Sales: Susan Donnelly, Sales Director (617/495-2606)
  Assistant Sales Director and Internet Retail Sales: Vanessa Vinarub (617/495-2650)
  Exhibits Manager: Gilly Parker (617/384-7515)

Design and Production: John Walsh, Assistant Director for Design and Production
(617/495-2623)
  Art Director: Marianne Perlak (617/495-2667)
Business: William A. Lindsay, Assistant Director & Chief Financial Officer (617/495-2613)
  Accountant: Fred Waters (617/495-4868)
  Customer Services Manager: Joan O'Donnell (617/495-2661)
London Office: Ann Sexsmith, Manager (e-mail: asexsmith@hup-mitpress.co.uk)

Full Member

Established: 1913   Admitted to AAUP: 1937
Title output 2002: 138   Title output 2003: 137
Distributed titles 2003: 30
Titles currently in print: 2,800

Editorial Program

Scholarly books and serious works of general interest in the humanities, the social and
behavioral sciences, the natural sciences, and medicine. The Press does not normally publish
poetry, fiction, festschriften, memoirs, symposia, or unrevised doctoral dissertations.
    Special imprints: The Belknap Press.
    Special series, joint imprints, and/or copublishing programs: The Adams Papers; Carl
Newell Jackson Lectures; Charles Eliot Norton Lectures; Cognitive Science Series;
Convergences; Developing Child Series; Godkin Lectures; Harvard Armenian Texts and
Studies; Harvard Books in Biophysics; Harvard East Asian Series; Harvard Economic
Studies; Harvard English Studies; Harvard Film Studies; Harvard Historical Monographs;
Harvard Historical Studies; Harvard Judaic Monographs; Harvard Studies in Business
History; Interpretations of Asia Series; John Harvard Library; Language and Thought Series;
Loeb Classical Library; Loeb Classical Monographs; Martin Classical Lectures; Oliver
Wendell Holmes Lectures; Paperbacks in Art History; Publications of the Joint Center for
Urban Studies; Questions of Science; Revealing Antiquity Series; Russian Research Center
Studies; Studies in Cultural History; Twentieth Century Fund Books/Reports; W.E.B.
DuBois Lectures; William E. Massey Sr. Lectures in the History of American Civilization;
and William James Lectures.
    The Press distributes publications for a number of Harvard University departments and
affiliates: Asia Center; Archaeological Exploration of Sardis; Department of The Classics;
Department of Comparative Literature; Francis A. Countway Library of Medicine;
Dumbarton Oaks Research Library and Collection; Houghton Library and the Judaica
Division of the Harvard College Library; Center for Hellenic Studies, Trustees for Harvard
University; Center for Middle Eastern Studies; Center for Jewish Studies; Harvard-Yenching
Institute; John F. Kennedy School of Government; Korea Institute; Milman Parry Collection;
Center for Population and Development; Peabody Museum of Archaeology and Ethnology;
David Rockefeller Center for Latin American Studies; Department of Sanskrit and Indian
Studies; School of Public Health's Global Burden of Disease Unit; Ukrainian Research
Institute; and the Wertheim Committee.

University of Hawai'i Press

2840 Kolowalu Street
Honolulu, HI 96822-1888

Phone: (808) 956-8257
Fax: (808) 988-6052
E-mail: (user I.D.)@hawaii.edu
Web site: www.uhpress.hawaii.edu

Order Fulfillment:
Phone: (888) UHPRESS; (808) 956-8255
Fax: (800) 650-7811; (808) 988-6052

European Distributor:
Eurospan

Staff

Director: William H. Hamilton (808/956-8257; e-mail: hamilton)
  Secretary to the Director: Agnes Hiramoto (808/956-8257; e-mail: hiramoto)
Acquisitions Editorial: Patricia Crosby, Executive Editor (808/956-6209; e-mail: pcrosby)
  Editors: Pamela Kelley, (808/956-6207; e-mail: pkelley); Keith Leber (808/956-6208;
  e-mail: kleber); Masako Ikeda (808/956-8696; e-mail: masakoi)
Manuscript Editorial: Cheri Dunn, Managing Editor (808/956-6210; e-mail: cheri)
  Managing Editor: Ann Ludeman (808/956-8695; e-mail: aludeman)
Marketing and Sales: Colins Kawai, Manager (808/956-6417; e-mail: ckawai)
  Sales Manager: Royden Muranaka (808/956-8830; e-mail: royden)
  Direct Mail Manager/Copywriter: Stephanie Chun (808/956-6426; e-mail: chuns)
  Publicity and Advertising Manager: Steven Hirashima (808/956-8698; e-mail: stevehir)
  Promotion Manager: Carol Abe (808/956-8697; e-mail: abec)
Design and Production: JoAnn Tenorio, Manager (808/956-8873; e-mail: tenorio)
  Assistant Production Manager: Paul Herr (808/956-8276; e-mail: herr)
  Designer: Santos Barbasa (808/956-8277; e-mail: barbasa)
  Production Editors: Lucille Aono (808/956-6328; e-mail: lucille); Brad Barrett (808/956-
  6318; e-mail: bradb)
  Fiscal Support Specialist: Terri Miyasato (808/956-8275; e-mail: terrimiy)
Journals: Joel Bradshaw, Manager (808/956-6790; e-mail: bradshaw)
  Production Editor: Cindy Chun (808/956-8834; e-mail: cindychu)
  Administrative Assistant: Norman Kaneshiro (808/956-8833; e-mail: uhpjourn)
East-West Export Books: Royden Muranaka, International Sales Manager (808/956-8830;
  e-mail: royden)
  Assistant: Kiera Nishimoto (808/956-8830; e-mail: kiera)
Business: Rosalyn Carr, Manager (808/956-6292; e-mail: rcarr)
  Credit Manager: Elyse Matsumoto (808/956-6228; e-mail: okido)
  Order Processing: Sandra Sedler, Cindy Yen
  Warehouse: Kyle Nakata, Clifford Newalu
Information Systems: Wanda China, Computer Operations Manager (808/956-6227; e-mail:
  wchina)

Full Member

Established: 1947

Title output 2002: 93

Distributed titles 2002: 140

Titles currently in print: 1,113

Admitted to AAUP: 1951

Title output 2003: 85

Distributed titles 2003: 48

Journals published: 16

Editorial Program

Asian, Pacific, and Asian American studies in history; art; anthropology; architecture; economics; sociology; philosophy and religion; languages and linguistics; law; literature; performing arts; political science; physical and natural sciences; regional studies.

The Press publishes the following journals: *Asian Perspectives*; *Asian Theatre Journal*; *Biography*; *Buddhist-Christian Studies*; *China Review International*; *The Contemporary Pacific*; *Journal of Modern Literature in Chinese*; *Journal of World History*; *Ka Ho'oilina: The Legacy*; *Korean Studies*; *Manoa*; *Oceanic Linguistics*; *Pacific Science*; *Philosophy East and West*; *Yearbook of the Association of Pacific Coast Geographers*; and *Yishu: Journal of Contemporary Art*.

Special Series, Joint Imprints, and/or Copublishing Programs: Asian Interactions and Comparisons (Association for Asian Studies); Center for Southeast Asian Studies (Kyoto University); Dimensions of Asian Spirituality; Extraordinary Lives: The Experience of Hawai'i Nisei; Harold Lyon Arboretum; Hawai'i Chinese History Center; Intersections: Asian and Pacific American Transcultural Studies; Korean Studies; Kolowalu Books; Kuroda Institute Studies in East Asian Buddhism; Latitude 20 Books; Nanzan Institute for Religion and Culture; Oceanic Linguistics Special Publications; PALI Language Texts; Pacific Islands Monographs; Perspectives on the Global Past; Society of Asian Comparative Philosophy Series; Studies in the Buddhist Tradition (University of Michigan); Talanoa: Contemporary Pacific Literature; Topics in Contemporary Buddhism.

Howard University Press

2225 Georgia Avenue, N.W.
Suite 718
Washington, DC 20059

Phone: (202) 238-2570
Fax: (202) 588-9849
E-mail: howardupress@howard.edu
Web site: www.founders.howard.edu/HUpress

Book Distribution Center:
Howard Univ. Press c/o Maple Press Co.
Lebanon Distribution Center
Fredericksburg, PA 17026
Customer service: (800) 537-5487
Fax: (410) 516-6998

Staff
Director: D. Kamili Anderson (202/238-2575; e-mail: danderson@howard.edu)
  Assistant to the Director: Anita L. Rice (202/238-2570; e-mail: arice@howard.edu)
Editorial Manager: Lenda P. Hill (202/238-2579; e-mail: lphill@howard.edu)
Sales and Marketing Manager: Michael L. Nelson (202/238-2571; e-mail:
  mnelson@howard.edu)
Design and Production Manager: TBA
Business Manager: Patricia A. Harris (202/238-2572; e-mail: paharris@howard.edu)

Affiliate Member
Established: 1972
Title output 2002: 2
Titles currently in print: 113

Admitted to AAUP: 1979
Title output 2003: 1

Editorial Program
Scholarly research addressing the contributions, conditions, and concerns of African-Americans, other people of African descent throughout the Diaspora, and people of color around the world in a broad range of disciplines: politics, economics, the social sciences, history, health and medicine, education, communications, fine arts and photography, science/technology, literature, literary criticism, drama studies, and more.
  Special series: Moorland-Spingarn Series.

University of Idaho Press

Book Orders:
Caxton Press
312 Main Street
Caldwell, ID 83605

Phone: (800) 657-5465; (208) 459-7421
Web site: www.caxtonpress.com/contacts.htm

Editorial Offices:
TBA

Staff
Director: TBA

Full Member
Established: 1972
Title output 2002: 7
Titles currently in print: 84

Admitted to AAUP: 1990
Title output 2003: NR

Editorial Program
History of the West with an emphasis on the northern Rockies and Idaho; natural history with an emphasis on the northern Rockies, native plants, and threatened species; literatures of the Northwest and mountain states; Native American studies; literary criticism with an emphasis on Hemingway, Steinbeck, and ecocriticism; and regional studies.

Special series, joint imprints, and/or copublishing programs: Idaho Yesterdays, with the Idaho State Historical Society.

University of Illinois Press

1325 S. Oak Street
Champaign, IL 61820-6903

Phone: (217) 333-0950
Fax: (217) 244-8082
E-mail: uipress@uillinois.edu
Journals: journals@uillinois.edu
Indiv: (user I.D.) @uillinois.edu
Web site: www.press.uillinois.edu

European Representative:
Combined Academic Publishers

Warehouse Address and Orders:
University of Illinois Press
c/o Hopkins Fulfillment Center
P.O. Box 50370
Baltimore, MD 21211
Orders: (Books) (800) 537-5487
(Journals) (866) 244-0626

Staff

Director: Willis G. Regier (217/244-0728; e-mail: wregier)
  Associate Director and Editor-in-Chief: Joan Catapano (217/265-0490; e-mail: jcatapan)
  Assistant to the Director: Mary Wolfe (217/244-4691; e-mail: mwolfe)
  Rights and Permissions: Heather Munson (217/244-6488; e-mail: uip-rights)
Acquisitions Editorial: Joan Catapano, Editor-in-Chief (history, feminist studies, African-American studies, film, anthropology) (217/265-0490; e-mail: jcatapan)
  Acquisitions Editors: Kerry Callahan (Asian studies, criminology, communications, philosophy, politics) (217/244-5182; e-mail: kerrypc); Elizabeth G. Dulany (Western history, Mormon history, American religion, animal studies) (217/244-0158; e-mail: edulany); Laurie C. Matheson (American history, Asian-American studies, labor history, sociology) (217/244-4685; e-mail: lmatheso); Judith M. McCulloh (music, folklore, Appalachian studies) (217/244-4681; e-mail: jmmccull); Willis G. Regier (classics, literature, religion, food studies, translations) (217/244-0728; e-mail: wregier); Richard L. Wentworth (sports history) (217/244-4680; e-mail: rwentwor)
Manuscript Editorial: Rebecca Crist, Managing Editor (217/244-3279; e-mail: rcrist)
  Assistant Managing Editors: Angela Burton (217/244-6579; e-mail: alburton); Jennifer Clark (217/244-8041; e-mail: jsclark1)
Marketing: Patricia Hoefling, Marketing Director (217/244-4683; e-mail: phoefling)
  Assistant Marketing Director/Web and Direct Mail Promotions: Barbara Horne (217/244-4686; e-mail: bhorne)
  Publicity Manager: Danielle Wilberg (217/244-4689; e-mail: dwilberg)
Sales Manager: Lynda Schuh (217/333-9071; e-mail: lschuh)
  Assistant Sales Manager: Susie Dueringer (217/244-4703; e-mail: sdueringer)
  Exhibits and Awards Manager: Margo Chaney (217/244-6491; e-mail: mechaney)
  Advertising Manager: Denise Peeler (217/244-4690; e-mail: dpeeler)
Production: Kristina Ding, Production Manager (217/244-4701; e-mail: kding)
Design: Copenhaver Cumpston, Art Director (217/333-9227; e-mail: cumpston)
Journals: Ann Lowry, Assistant Director and Journals Manager (217/244-6856; e-mail: alowry)
  Assistant Journals Manager: Clydette Wantland (217/244-6496; e-mail: cwantlan)
  Journals Circulation Manager: Cheryl Jestis (866/244-0626; e-mail: jestis)

Chief Financial Officer: Lisa Emerson (217/244-0091; e-mail: lemerson)
  Assistant to CFO: Ahdieh Coleman (217/244-6479; e-mail: ahdiehkc)
Network Administrator: Louis W. Mesker (217/244-8025; e-mail: lmesker)
Electronic Publisher: Paul Arroyo (217/244-7147; e-mail: parroyo)

Full Member

Established: 1918	Admitted to AAUP: 1937
Title output 2002: 160	Title output 2003: 135
Titles currently in print: 1,610	Journals published: 27

Editorial Program

Scholarly books and serious nonfiction, with special interests in American history; American literature (especially twentieth century); critical theory; American music; African-American history and literature; sport history; religious studies; cultural studies; communications; cinema studies; law and society; regional photography and art; philosophy; architectural history; environmental studies; sociology; western history; women's studies; working-class history.

The Press also publishes poetry and the following journals: *American Journal of Psychology; American Literary Realism; American Music; American Philosophical Quarterly; Beethoven Forum; The Bulletin of the Center for Children's Books; Contours: A Journal of the African Diaspora; Ethnomusicology; Feminist Teacher; History of Philosophy Quarterly; Journal of the Abraham Lincoln Association; The Journal of Aesthetic Education; Journal of American Folklore; The Journal of Criminal Law and Criminology; Journal of Education Finance; Journal of English and Germanic Philology; Journal of Film & Video; Journal of Seventeenth-Century Music; Journal of Symbolic Logic; Law and History Review; Library Trends; Northwestern Journal of International Law & Business; Northwestern University Law Review; Perspectives on Work; Public Affairs Quarterly; State Politics and Policy Quarterly;* and *World History Connected.*

Special series, joint imprints, and/or copublishing programs: The Asian American Experience; Bach Perspectives; Blacks in the New World; Contemporary Film Directors; The Environment and the Human Condition; Folklore and Society; The Food Series; Great Arguments in the Supreme Court; Hispanisms; The History of Communication; International Nietzsche Studies; Music in American Life; Sport and Society; Statue of Liberty-Ellis Island Centennial Series; Theodore Dreiser Edition; Women in American History; Working Class in American History.

Indiana University Press

601 North Morton Street
Bloomington, IN 47404-3797

Phone: (812) 855-8817
Fax: (812) 855-8507
E-mail: iupress@indiana.edu
Indiv: (user I.D.)@indiana.edu
Web site: iupress.indiana.edu

Warehouse Address:
802 E. 13th Street
Bloomington, IN 47408-2101
Phone: (812) 855-4362

Orders:
Phone: (800) 842-6796
Fax: (812) 855-7931

UK Representative:
Baker & Taylor International

Staff

Director: Janet Rabinowitch (812/855-4773; e-mail: jrabinow)
   Assistant to the Director and Rights Manager: Alisa Alering (812/855-6314; e-mail: aalering)
Acquisitions Editorial:
   Editorial Director: Robert Sloan (812/855-7561; e-mail: rjsloan)
   Sponsoring Editors: Michael Lundell (812/855-6803; e-mail: mlundell); Dee Mortensen (812/855-0268; e-mail: mortense); Gayle Sherwood (812/855-5261; e-mail: gsherwoo)
   Assistant Sponsoring Editors: Jane Quinet (812/855-5262; e-mail: jquinet); Donna Wilson (812/855-5063; e-mail: domheld); Rebecca Tolen (812/ 855-2756; e-mail: retolen); Linda Oblack (812/855-2175; e-mail: loblack); Elizabeth Marsh (812/856-0097; e-mail: elihill)
Manuscript Editorial: Jane Lyle, Managing Editor (812/855-9686; e-mail: jlyle)
   Assistant Managing Editor/Production Editor: Miki Bird (812/855-4645; e-mail: msbird)
   Assistant Managing Editors: Elizabeth Garman (812/855-5428; e-mail: egarman); Dawn Ollila (812/855-5064; e-mail: dollila)
Marketing and Sales: Bryan Gambrel, Marketing and Sales Director (812/855-6553; e-mail: bpgambre)
   Marketing Manager: Marilyn Breiter (812/855-5429; e-mail: mbreiter)
   Direct Marketing Manager: Deborah Rush (812/855-4415; e-mail: drush)
   Direct Marketing Coordinator: Laura Baich (812/855-8287; e-mail: lbaich)
   Advertising and Exhibit Assistant: Brigitta Powers (812/855-4522; e-mail: powersbr)
   Publicity Assistant: Theresa Halter (812/855-8054; e-mail: thalter)
   Text Promotion Manager: Jennifer Stuart (812/855-9137; e-mail: jjstuart)
Sales: Mary Beth Haas, Sales Manager (812/855-9440; e-mail: mbhaas)
   Assistant Sales Manager: Kim Johnson (812/855-5366; e-mail: kimkijoh)
   Sales Assistant: Rhonda Van Der Dussen (812/855-6657; e-mail: rdussen)
Production and Design: Emmy Ezzell, Production Director (812/855-5563; e-mail: ezzell)
   Production Manager: Bernadette Zoss (812/856-5233; e-mail: bzoss)
   Book Designer: Pam Rude (812/855-0264; e-mail: psrude)
   Senior Artists and Book Designers: Sharon Sklar (812/855-9640; e-mail: ssklar); Matt Williamson (812/855-8778; e-mail: mswillia)
   Production Support Assistant: Dan Pyle (812/855-6777; e-mail: dapyle)

Journals, Electronic, and Serials Publishing: Kathryn Caras, Director of Electronic and Serials Publishing (812/855-3830; e-mail: kcaras)
    Assistant Journals Manager: Pam Wilson (812/856-5218; e-mail: pjwilson)
    Journals Assistant (812/855-9449)
    Journals Marketing & Production Coordinator: Amy Shock (812/856-0582; e-mail: ashock)
    Electronic Information Specialist (Database Specialist): Joy Andreakis (812/856-0210; e-mail: jandreak)
Business and Operations: Jan Jenkins, Director of Operations (812/855-4901; e-mail: janjenki)
    Senior Accounting Coordinator: Kathy Whaley (812/855-2726; e-mail: kwhaley)
    Assistant Business Manager for Network Systems and Order Processing: Janie Pearson (812/855-1588; e-mail: cjfender)
    Assistant Business Manager for Accounts Receivable & Customer Service: Kim Childers (812/855-4134; e-mail: kchilder)
    Senior Customer Service Representative: Mary Lou Shelly (812/855-8818; e-mail: mlshelly)
    Customer Service Representatives: Candace Tarry (812/855-1519; e-mail: ctarry); Jessica Droppo (812/855-0263; e-mail: jdroppo)
    Warehouse Manager: Mark Kelly (812/855-4362; e-mail: markkell)
Network & Systems Administrator: David Cooley (812/855-6468; e-mail: drcooley)

Full Member

Established: 1950	Admitted to AAUP: 1952
Title output 2002: 138	Title output 2003: 130
Titles currently in print: 2,261	Journals published: 22

Editorial Program

African studies; African-American studies; anthropology; Asian and South Asian studies; art; classics; bioethics; cultural and critical theory; film and media studies; folklore; gardening; history; international studies; Jewish studies; ethics; medieval and Renaissance studies; Middle East studies; military history; music; paleontology; philanthropy; philosophy; railroads; religion; Russian and East European studies; state and regional studies; women's and gender studies

    Journals: *Africa Today*; *ALEPH*; *e-Service Journal*; *Ethics & the Environment*; *Film History*; *History & Memory*; *Hypatia: A Journal of Feminist Philosophy*; *Indiana Journal of Global Legal Studies*; *Israel Studies*; *Jewish Social Studies*; *Journal of Early Modern Cultural Studies*; *Journal of Feminist Studies in Religion*; *Journal of Folklore Research*; *Journal of Modern Literature*; *Meridians*; *Nashim*; *NWSA Journal*; *Philosophy of Music Education Review*; *Prooftexts: A Journal of Jewish Literary History*; *Research in African Literatures*; *Small Axe: A Journal of Caribbean Studies*; *Victorian Studies*.

    Special series: Advances in Semiotics; African Epic; African Expressive Cultures; African Issues; African Systems of Thought; American West in the Twentieth Century; Animal Communication; Arts and Politics of the Everyday; Blacks in the Diaspora; Books from differences; Caribbean and Latin American Studies; Chinese Literature in Translation; Counterpoints: Music and Education; Drama and Performance Studies; The Early Music Institute; Essential Asia; Everywoman: Studies in History, Literature, and Culture; Excavations at Franchthi Cave, Greece; Folklore Studies in Translation; Folklore Today;

Folkloristics, The Helen and Martin Schwartz Lectures in Jewish Studies; A History of the Trans-Appalachian Frontier; Hypatia Books; Indiana Masterpiece Editions; Indiana Series in Arab and Islamic Studies; Indiana Series in Middle East Studies; Indiana Series in the Philosophy of Religion; Indiana Series in the Philosophy of Technology; Indiana Studies in Biblical Literature; Indiana University Center on Philanthropy Series in Governance; Indiana-Michigan Series in Russian and East European Studies; Interdisciplinary Studies in History; Jewish Literature and Culture; Jewish Political and Social Studies; Key Women Writers; Kinsey Institute Series; Library of Indiana Classics; Life of the Past; Material Culture; Medical Ethics; Midwestern History and Culture; The Modern Jewish Experience; Music: Scholarship and Performance; Perspectives; Philanthropic and Nonprofit Studies (formerly Philanthropic Studies); Public Affairs; Race, Gender, and Science; Railroads Past and Present; Religion in Asia and Africa; Religion in North America; Restoring Women to History; Russian Music Studies; Science, Technology, and Society; The Second World; A Selected Edition of W. D. Howells; Society for Cinema Studies in Translation; Studies in Ancient Folklore and Popular Culture; Studies in Continental Thought; Studies in Phenomenology and Existential Philosophy; Theories of Representation and Difference; Traditional Arts of Africa; United Nations Intellectual History Project; Unnatural Acts: Theorizing the Performative; The Variorum Edition of the Poetry of John Donne; Vietnam War Era Classics Series; Voices in Performance and Text; Women Artists in Film; Women of Letters.

University of Iowa Press

Editorial Office:
119 West Park Road
100 Kuhl House
Iowa City, IA 52242-1000

Phone: (319) 335-2000
Fax: (319) 335-2055
E-mail: (user I.D.)@uiowa.edu
Web site and online catalog: www.uiowapress.org

Order Fulfillment:
University of Iowa Press
c/o Chicago Distribution Center
11030 South Langley Avenue
Chicago, IL 60628
Phone: (800) 621-2736
Fax: (800) 621-8476

UK/European Representative:
Eurospan

Canadian Representative:
Scholarly Book Services

Staff

Director: Holly Carver (319/335-2013; e-mail: holly-carver)
  Assistant to the Director/Rights and Permissions: Rhonda Wetjen (319/335-3424; e-mail: rhonda-wetjen)
Editorial: Holly Carver (natural history, regional history, anthropology/archaeology)
  Acquisitions Editor: Prasenjit R. Gupta (literary criticism and history, creative nonfiction, letters and diaries) (319/335-3440; e-mail: prasenjit-gupta)
Managing Editor: Charlotte Wright (319/335-2011; e-mail: charlotte-wright)
Marketing: TBA, Manager
  Promotions Manager: Sara T. Sauers (319/335-2015; e-mail: sara-sauers)
  Interim Publicist: Deidre Woods (319/335-2008; e-mail: deidre-woods)
Design and Production: Karen Copp, Associate Director and Design and Production Manager (319/335-2014; e-mail: karen-copp)

Full Member

Established: 1969
Title output 2002: 37
Titles currently in print: 500

Admitted to AAUP: 1982
Title output 2003: 32

Editorial Program

American literary criticism and history, particularly children's literature, biography, and women's studies; letters, diaries, and memoirs; short fiction (award winners only); poetry (single-author titles and anthologies); creative nonfiction; regional studies; regional natural history; archaeology/anthropology; theatre history; American studies.

Series: American Land and Life Series; Bur Oak Books and Bur Oak Guides; Iowa Poetry Prize; Iowa Short Fiction Award and John Simmons Short Fiction Award; Iowa Szathmáry Culinary Arts Series; Iowa Whitman Series; Kuhl House Poets; Sightline Books: The Iowa Series in Literary Nonfiction; Singular Lives: The Iowa Series in North American Autobiography; Studies in Theatre History and Culture; Writers in Their Own Time.

Island Press

Editorial/Administration:
1718 Connecticut Avenue, N.W. Suite 300
Washington, DC 20009

Phone: (202) 232-7933
Fax: (202) 234-1328
E-mail: (firstinitial)(lastname)@islandpress.org
Web site: www.islandpress.org

Customer Service/Distribution:
Chicago Distribution Center
11003 South Langley Avenue
Chicago, IL 60628
Phone: (800) 621-2736
Fax: (800) 621-8476

UK Representative:
The Eurospan Group

Canadian Representative:
Broadview Press

Staff
President: Charles C. Savitt
Executive Assistant: Kathy Dismukes (ext. 27)
Acquisitions/Editorial: Dan Sayre, Vice President and Publisher (ext. 12)
Business & Admin: Ken Hartzell, Vice President and Chief Financial Officer (ext. 29)
Vice President for Programs: Kristy Manning (919/967-1553)
Permissions: Angela Osborn (ext. 35)
Director of Marketing: TBA
Director of Production: Anna Nunan (ext. 45)
Director of New Media & IT: Alphonse MacDonald (ext. 44)

Associate Member

Established: 1984	Admitted to AAUP: 1999
Title output 2002: 41	Title output 2003: 46
Distributed titles 2002: 250	Distributed titles 2003: 243
Titles currently in print: 532	

Editorial Program
Scholarly and professional titles in environmental studies and natural resource management; nonfiction literary trade titles (through Shearwater Books imprint) on nature and the environment; biweekly electronic publishing on environmental topics and news (through Web site Eco-Compass). Subject areas include ecosystems management, protection of biodiversity and human health, environmentally responsible land use planning, sustainable design, marine science and policy, climate and energy, and economics and policy.

Special Series, joint imprints and/or co-publishing programs: Case Studies in Land and Community Design (with the Landscape Architecture Foundation); Conservation Directory annual (with the National Wildlife Federation); Ecoregions of the World: A Conservation Assessment (with The World Wildlife Fund); Frontier Issues in Economic Thought (with The Global Development and Environment Institute); The Millennium Ecosystem Assessment; The Science and Practice of Ecological Restoration (with the Society for Ecological Restoration International); State of the Hotspots (with Conservation International); The State of the World's Oceans Series; SCOPE Monograph Series (with The Scientific Committee on Problems of the Environment); The World's Water (with The Pacific Institute for Studies in Development, Environment, and Security).

The Jewish Publication Society

2100 Arch Street, 2nd Floor
Philadelphia, PA 19103

Orders:
Phone: (800) 355-1165

Phone: (215) 832-0600
Fax: (215) 568-2017
E-mail: (user I.D.)@jewishpub.org
Web site: www.jewishpub.org

UK Representative:
Eurospan

Canadian Representative:
Georgetown Publications, Inc.

Staff

Director: Ellen Frankel (215/832-0607; e-mail: ellenjps@aol.com)
   Assistant to the Director: Toby Meersand (215/832-0609; e-mail: meersand)
Publishing Director and Managing Editor: Carol Hupping (215/832-0605; e-mail: chupping)
Acquisitions: Eunice Smith (215/832-0618; e-mail: esmith)
Production: Robin Norman (215/832-0606; e-mail: rnorman)
Sales and Marketing: Laurie Schlesinger (215/832-0613; e-mail: lschlesinger)
Finance: Nyles Cole (215/832-0602; e-mail: ncole)

Associate Member

Established: 1888

Admitted to AAUP: 2004
(Former membership: 1993-2001)

Title output 2002: 15
Titles currently in print: 175

Title output 2003: 15

Editorial Program

Nonfiction trade titles and serious works of nonfiction, all with Jewish content, particularly in Bible studies, Jewish ethics, contemporary issues, philosophy, midrash and folktales, history, holidays and customs, women's studies, theology, biography, classic texts, and reference. JPS publishes the NJPS Bible and Bible commentaries, as well as children's books; story collections; and young adult novels, biographies, and nonfiction.

   Special series: JPS Kids Catalog; JPS Bible Commentary; and JPS Desk Reference Collection.

The Johns Hopkins University Press

2715 N. Charles Street
Baltimore, MD 21218-4363

Phone: (410) 516-6900
Fax: (410) 516-6998/6968
E-mail: (user I.D.)@press.jhu.edu
Web site: www.press.jhu.edu/

Distribution Center:
704 Legionaire Drive
Fredericksburg, PA 17026

UK Representative:
Yale Representation Ltd.

Staff
Director: Kathleen Keane (410/516-6971; e-mail: kk)
   Assistant to the Director: Karen Reider (410/516-6971; e-mail: kar)
   Rights and Permissions: Heather Lengyel (410/516-6063; e-mail: hlengyel)
   Office and Facilities Coordinator: Nora Reedy (410/516-7035; e-mail: nreedy)
   Director, Finance and Administration: Catherine Millar (410/516-6941; e-mail: cam)
   Director of Development: Jack Holmes (410/516-6928; e-mail: jholmes)
Acquisitions Editorial: Trevor Lipscombe, Editor-in-Chief (mathematics, physics, astronomy) (410/516-6909; e-mail: tcl)
   Executive Editors: Henry Y. K. Tom (European history, political science, sociology, religious studies) (410/516-6908; e-mail: htom); Jacqueline C. Wehmueller (consumer health, history of medicine, higher education) (410/516-6904; e-mail: jwehmueller)
   Senior Editors: Robert J. Brugger (American history, history of science and technology, regional books) (410/516-6909; e-mail: rbrugger); Wendy Harris (genetics, psychiatry, gerontology, bioethics) (410/516-6907; e-mail: wharris)
   Editors: Michael Lonegro (humanities, classics, ancient Near Eastern studies) (410/516-6917; e-mail: mlonegro); Vincent Burke (life sciences) (410/576-6999; e-mail: vjb)
Manuscript Editorial: Juliana M. McCarthy, Managing Editor (410/516-6912; e-mail: jmm)
   Assistant Managing Editor: Linda E. Forlifer (410/516-6911; e-mail: lef)
   Manuscript Editor: Anne M. Whitmore (410/516-6916; e-mail: awhitmore)
   Production Editors: Kimberly F. Johnson (410/516-6915; e-mail: kjohnson); Carol Zimmerman (410/516-6914; e-mail: czimmerman); Courtney Bond (410/516-6901; e-mail: cbond); Andre M. Barnett (410/516-6995; e-mail: amb)
Marketing: Becky Brasington Clark, Director (410/516-6931; e-mail: rbc)
   Sales Director: TBA
   Advertising: Karen Willmes (410/516-6932; e-mail: kwillmes)
   Publicist: Kathy Alexander (410/516-4162; e-mail: ka)
   Exhibits and Awards: Margaret Galambos (410/516-6937; e-mail: mgalambos)
   Electronic and Web Promotions: Colleen Condon (410/516-6972; e-mail: cc)
   Direct Mail Coordinator: Casey Schmidt (410/516-6930; e-mail: ccs)
Design and Production: Kenneth Sabol, Production Manager (410/516-6922; e-mail: ksabol)
   Art Director: Martha Sewall (410/516-6921; e-mail: mds)

Senior Art Designers: Glen Burris (410/516-6924; e-mail: gburris); Wilma Rosenberger (410/516-6925; e-mail: wrosenberger)

Journals: William M. Breichner, Publisher (410/516-6985; e-mail: wbreichner)
  Journals Marketing Manager: Kristen Luby (410/516-6983; e-mail: kel)
  Journals Production Supervisor: Carol Hamblen (410/516-6986; e-mail: chamblen)
  Journals Subscription Manager: Alta Anthony (410/516-6938; e-mail: aanthony)
  Journals Subscription Supervisor: Carla Hubbard (410/516-6964; e-mail: chubbard)
  Journals Advertising Coordinator: Monica Queen (410/516-6984; e-mail: mqueen)

Electronic Publishing: Aileen McHugh, Director, Project Muse and Electronic Publishing (410/516-6981; e-mail: amchugh)
  Marketing and Sales Manager, Online Products: Melanie B. Schaffner (410/516-3846; e-mail: mbs)
  International Sales Coordinator, Project MUSE: Ana Snoeyenbos (410/516-9992; e-mail: asnoeyenbos)
  Subscription Support Specialist: Lora Czarnowsky (410/516-6989; e-mail: llc)
  Electronic Projects Manager: Wendy Queen (410/516-3845; e-mail: wendy@chaos.press.jhu.edu)
  Metadata Coordinator: Elizabeth W. Brown (410/516-6834; e-mail: ebrown)
  Authorities Librarian: William Kulp (410/516-8968; e-mail: bkulp)
  Authorities Librarian/Indexer: Elisa Tan (410/516-6496; e-mail: etan)

Business: Beth Corrigan, Accounting Manager (410/516-6974; e-mail: mcorrigan)
  Customer Service Supervisor: Grace Wilson (410/516-6960; e-mail: gwilson)
  Credit & Collection: Carolyn Frazier (410/516-3854; e-mail: cfrazier)
  Manager, Fulfillment Operations: William F. Bishop (410/516-6961; e-mail: bbishop)

Information Systems: Stacey L. Armstead, Manager (410/516-6979; e-mail: sarmstead)
  Information Systems Analyst: Gilbert Seiler (410/516-6977; e-mail: gseiler)
  Database Administrator/Programmer: Robert Oeste (410/516-6933; e-mail: roeste)

Full Member

Established: 1878

Admitted to AAUP: 1937

Title output 2002: 228

Title output 2003: 224

Titles currently in print: 2,500

Journals published: 57

Editorial Program

History (American, European, ancient, history of science, technology, and medicine); humanities (literary and cultural studies, classics); medicine and health (consumer health, human genetics, gerontology and geriatrics, clinical psychology and psychiatry); natural sciences (biology, physical sciences, mathematics, natural history); political science (US government, international relations and comparative politics); economics; geography and environmental studies; higher education; reference books; regional books; and the following journals: *American Imago; American Jewish History; American Journal of Philology; American Journal of Mathematics; American Quarterly; Arethusa; Bulletin of the History of Medicine; Callaloo; Children's Literature; Children's Literature Association Quarterly; Comparative Technology Transfer and Society; Configurations; Diacritics; ELH; Eighteenth-Century Studies; The Emily Dickinson Journal; The Henry James Review; Human Rights Quarterly; ICSID Review; Journal of Asian American Studies; Journal of Colonialism and Colonial History; Journal of Democracy; Journal of Early Christian Studies; Journal of Health Care for the Poor and Underserved; Journal of Modern Greek Studies; Journal of the History of Ideas; Journal of the*

History of Philosophy; Journal of Women's History; Kennedy Institute of Ethics Journal; Late Imperial China; The Lion and the Unicorn; Literature and Medicine; MLN; Modern Fiction Studies; Modernism/Modernity; New Literary History; Perspectives in Biology & Medicine; Philosophy and Literature; Philosophy, Psychiatry, and Psychology; portal: Libraries and the Academy; Postmodern Culture; Reviews in American History; Reviews in Higher Education; SAIS Review; Shakespeare Quarterly; South Central Review; Studies in English Literature; Technology & Culture; Theatre Journal; Theatre Topics; Theory and Event; Transactions of the American Philological Association; World Politics; World Shakespeare Bibliography Online; and *The Yale Journals of Criticism.* The Press publishes three online-only journals, *Postmodern Culture; Theory and Event;* and *Journal of Colonialism and Colonial History.*

The Press also handles subscription fulfillment for publications of the Interamerican Development Bank and the United Nations, *Development Business, Monthly Operational Summary;* for Princeton University Press's journal, *Annals of Mathematics.* The Press now handles customer service and fulfillment for journals published by The Penn State University Press, and for *Imagine,* a publication of the Center for Talented Youth of The Johns Hopkins University.

Special series, joint imprints, and/or co publishing programs: The American Moment; Ancient Society and History; Documentary History of the First Federal Congress; Early America: History, Context, Culture; Johns Hopkins: Poetry and Fiction; The Johns Hopkins Series in the Mathematical Sciences; The Johns Hopkins Studies in the History of Technology; The Johns Hopkins Symposia in Comparative History; The Johns Hopkins University Studies in History and Political Science; New Studies in American Intellectual and Cultural History; The Papers of Dwight David Eisenhower; The Papers of George Catlett Marshall; The Papers of Frederick Law Olmsted; The Papers of Thomas A. Edison; Parallax: Re-visions of Culture and Society; New Series in NASA History; Reconfiguring American Political History; Revisiting Rural America; Studies in Industry and Society.

The Press is publisher for the International Food Policy Research Institute; is co publisher with the Woodrow Wilson Center Press; and is distributor for Resources for the Future, Inc. and the New York Academy of Sciences.

University Press of Kansas

2501 Bob Billings Parkway
Lawrence, KS 66049-3905

Phone: (785) 864-4154
Fax: (785) 864-4586
E-mail: upress@ku.edu
Indiv: (user I.D.)@ku.edu
Web site: www.kansaspress.ku.edu

Warehouse Address:
2425-B Bob Billings Parkway
Lawrence, KS 66049-3903
Phone: (785) 864-4156

Orders:
Phone: (785) 864-4155

UK/European Representative:
Eurospan

Canadian Representative:
Scholarly Book Services

Staff
Director: Fred Woodward (785/864-4667; e-mail: fwoodward)
  Assistant Director: Susan Schott (785/864-9165; e-mail: sschott)
  Assistant to the Director: Sara Henderson White (785/864-9125; e-mail: shwhite)
Editorial: Michael Briggs, Editor-in-Chief (political science, military history, law) (785/864-9162; e-mail: mbriggs)
  Acquisitions Editors: Nancy Scott Jackson (American history, American studies, Native American studies, women's studies) (785/864-9160; e-mail: njackson); Fred Woodward (political science, presidential studies, US political history, American political thought, regional studies) (785/864-4667; e-mail: fwoodward)
  Editorial Assistant: Hilary Lowe (785/864-9161; e-mail: edassist)
Manuscript Editorial, Design and Production: Susan McRory, Senior Production Editor (785/864-9185; e-mail: smcrory)
  Production Editor: Larisa Martin (785/864-9169; e-mail: lmartin)
  Production Specialist: Jan Butin (785/864-9123; e-mail: jbutin)
Marketing: Susan Schott, Marketing Manager (785/864-9165; e-mail: sschott)
  Publicity Manager: Ranjit Arab (785/864-9170; e-mail: rarab)
  Direct Mail & Exhibits Manager: Debra Diehl (785/864-9166; e-mail: ddiehl)
  Advertising Coordinator/Marketing Designer: Karl Janssen (785/864-9164; e-mail: kjanssen)
  Marketing Assistant: Suzanne Galle (785/864-9167; e-mail: sgalle)
Business: Conrad Roberts, Business Manager (785/864-9158; e-mail: ceroberts)
  Accounting Manager: Britt DeTienne (785/864-9159; e-mail: bdetienne)
  Warehouse Manager: Alex Kaufman (785/864-4156)

Full Member
Established: 1946
Title output 2002: 59
Titles currently in print: 684

Admitted to AAUP: 1946
Title output 2003: 58

Editorial Program

American history; military and intelligence studies; Western history and Native American studies; American government and public policy; presidential studies; law; ethics and political philosophy; American studies; women's studies; Kansas, the Great Plains, and the Midwest. The Press does not consider fiction, poetry, or festschriften for publication.

Special series, joint imprints, and/or copublishing programs: American Political Thought; American Presidency Series; CultureAmerica; Development of Western Resources; Feminist Ethics; Kansas Nature Guides; Landmark Law Cases and American Society; Modern First Ladies; Modern War Studies; Studies in Government and Public Policy; US Army War College Guides to Civil War Battles.

The Press distributes a series of natural history handbooks for the University of Kansas Natural History Museum.

The Kent State University Press

Street Address:
307 Lowry Hall
Kent State University
Kent, OH 44242-0001

Mailing Address:
P.O. Box 5190
Kent, OH 44242-0001

Phone: (330) 672-7913
Fax: (330) 672-3104
E-mail: (user I.D.)@kent.edu
Web site: www.kentstateuniversitypress.com

Orders:
Phone: (419) 281-1802
Fax: (419) 281-6883

UK/European Representative:
Eurospan

Canadian Representative:
Scholarly Book Services

Staff

Director: Will Underwood (330/672-8094; e-mail: wunderwo)
Editorial: Joanna Hildebrand Craig, Assistant Director and Acquiring Editor (330/672-8099; e-mail: jhildebr)
Managing Editor: Kathy Method (330/672-8095; e-mail: kmethod)
Marketing: Susan L. Cash, Manager (330/672-8097; e-mail: scash)
 Marketing Assistant: Melissa K. Edler (330/672-8098; e-mail: medler)
Design and Production: Christine A. Brooks, Manager (330/672-8092; e-mail: cbrooks)
 Assistant Design and Production Manager: Saul Flanner (330/672-8091; e-mail: sflanner)
Journals Circulation/Secretary: Sandra D. Clark (330/672-8090; e-mail: sclark1)
Bookkeeper: Norma E. Hubbell (330/672-8096; e-mail: nhubbell)

Full Member

Established: 1966
Title output 2002: 27
Titles currently in print: 327

Admitted to AAUP: 1970
Title output 2003: 30
Journals published: 2

Editorial Program

History: Civil War era; US military, cultural/social, and diplomatic; Ohio/Midwestern studies; true crime; fashion/costume; material culture. Literature: US (to ca. 1950); regional/ Midwestern. Regional literary nonfiction; poetry only through Wick Poetry Program; no fiction.

Series: Civil War in the North; Cleveland Theater; Literature and Medicine; New Studies in US Foreign Relations; Reading Hemingway; Teaching Hemingway; Translation Studies; True Crime; Voices of Diversity: Narratives of the Immigrant Experience; Wick Poetry Program.

Imprints: Black Squirrel Books (Ohio reprints); journals *Civil War History* and *Ohio History*.

The University Press of Kentucky

663 South Limestone Street
Lexington, KY 40508-4008

Phone: (859) 257-4249
Fax: (859) 323-1873
E-mail: (user I.D.)@uky.edu
Web site: www.kentuckypress.com

Warehouse Address:
2100 Capstone Drive
Suite 101
Lexington, KY 40511

Orders:
Phone: (859) 257-8400;
(800) 839-6855
Fax: (859) 257-8481

UK and European Representative:
Eurospan

Canadian Representative:
Scholarly Book Services

Staff

Director: Stephen M. Wrinn (859/257-8432; e-mail: smwrin2)
  Assistant to the Director & Editorial Assistant: Anne Dean Watkins (e-mail: adwatk0)
Acquisitions Editorial: Joyce Harrison, Editor-in-Chief (American and Southern history, Civil War, religion in the south, African-American studies, Appalachian studies, folklore, popular and material culture) (859/257-8434; e-mail: jharr4)
  Acquisitions Editors: Stephen M. Wrinn (American history and American studies, world history, military history, political science, political theory, public policy, international studies); Gena Henry (Kentuckiana and regional studies) (859/257-8150; e-mail: gena.henry)
  Editorial Assistant: Ann Malcolm (859/257-9492; e-mail: ann.malcolm)
Editing, Design & Production: Melinda Wirkus, Director of Editing, Design & Production (859/257-8438)
  Production Manager: Richard E. Farkas (859/257-8435; e-mail: rfark1)
  Assistant Production Managers: Pat Gonzales (859/257-4669; e-mail: pagonz0); Danielle Dove (859/257-8439; e-mail: dmdove0)
  Manuscript Editors: David Cobb (859/257-4252; e-mail: dlcobb); Nichole Lainhart (859/ 257-8433; e-mail: dnstew00)
Marketing: Leila Salisbury, Marketing Director (859/257-8442; e-mail: leilas)

Sales Manager: Wyn Morris (859/257-8761; e-mail: lemorr2)
Exhibits and Direct Mail Manager: Allison Webster (859/257-2817; e-mail: abwebs0)
Advertising & Rights Manager: Mack McCormick (859/257-5200; e-mail: fmmcco0)
Grantwriter/Publicity Assistant: Kristin Barras (859/257-6855; e-mail: kabarr2)
Finance and Administration: Craig R. Wilkie, Assistant Director & CFO (859/257-8436;
e-mail: crwilk00)
Administrative Assistant and Technology Support: Tim Elam (859/257-8761; e-mail:
taelam2)
Warehouse and Distribution: Teresa W. Collins, Warehouse Manager (859/257-8405;
e-mail: twell1)
Credit Manager: Scot Skidmore (859/257-8445; e-mail: jsskid2)
Customer Service Representative: Robert Brandon (859/257-8400, 800/839-6855; e-mail:
rbrandon)
Shipping Manager: Karen Wahler (e-mail: kywahl2)
Shipping Clerk: Carol Nevil (e-mail: carol.nevil)

Full Member

Established: 1943   Admitted to AAUP: 1947
Title output 2002: 54   Title output 2003: 68
Titles currently in print: 917

Editorial Program

Scholarly books in the fields of American history; military history; film studies; political
science; international studies; folklore and material culture; African-American studies; serious
nonfiction of general interest. Regionally, the Press maintains an interest in Kentucky and
the Ohio Valley, Appalachia, and the upper South. Submissions are not invited in fiction,
drama, or poetry.

Special series: Civil Rights and the Struggle for Black Equality in America; Culture of the
Land: A Series in the New Agrarianism; Eighteenth-Century Novels by Women; Kentucky
Voices; Material Worlds; New Books for New Readers; New Directions in Southern History;
The Ohio River Valley Series; Political Thought and Contemporary Issues; Public Papers of
the Governors of Kentucky; Religion in the South; Studies in Romance Languages; Topics in
Kentucky History; Women and Southern Culture.

Louisiana State University Press

P.O. Box 25053
Baton Rouge, LA 70894-5053

Phone: (225) 578-6294
Fax: (225) 578-6461
E-mail: lsupress@lsu.edu
Indiv: (user I.D.) @lsu.edu
Web site: www.lsu.edu/lsupress

Warehouse:
Printing Building
3555 River Road
Baton Rouge, LA 70803

UK Distributor:
Eurospan

Canadian Distributor:
Scholarly Book Services

Staff

Director: MaryKatherine Callaway (225/578-6295; e-mail: mkc)
  Assistant to the Director: Erica Bossier (e-mail: ebossie)
Acquisitions Editorial: TBA, Editor-in-Chief (225/578-6618)
  Executive Editor: John Easterly (e-mail: jeaster)
  Editors: Rand Dotson (history) (e-mail: pdotso1); Candis LaPrade (literary studies)
  (e-mail: claprade); Michael Steinberg (geography) (e-mail: mstein5)
  Permissions and Copyright: Deborah Carter (e-mail: dcarte8)
Manuscript Editorial: Lee Sioles, Manuscript Editor Manager (e-mail: lsioles)
  Editors: George Roupe (e-mail: groupe1); Cynthia Williams (e-mail: cynthiaw)
Marketing: Margaret Hart, Manager (225/578-6666; e-mail: mhart)
  Senior Publicist and Assistant Marketing Manager: Barbara Outland (e-mail: boutlan)
  Promotions Coordinator: Shelly Ortiz (e-mail: sbrizz2)
  Advertising and Direct Mail Coordinator: Lauren Cavanaugh (e-mail: rcavan1)
  Marketing Designer: Michelle Garrod (e-mail: mgarro1)
Sales: Rebekah Brown, Manager (225/578-8650; e-mail: rbrown1)
  Events and Exhibits Coordinator: Loris Moise (e-mail: lmoise2)
Design and Production: Laura Gleason, Assistant Director and Production Manager (225/
  578-5912; e-mail: lgleasn)
  Assistant Production Manager: Amanda Scallan (e-mail: amandas)
  Designers: Barbara Neely Bourgoyne (e-mail: bnbourg); Andrew Shurtz (e-mail: ashurt1)
  Production Assistant: Melanie Samaha (e-mail: msamaha)
Business: William Bossier, Associate Director and Business Manager (225/578-8271; e-mail:
  wbossie)
  Assistant Business Manager: Patrick Reynolds (e-mail: preynolds)
Subsidiary Rights: McIntosh & Otis, Inc., 353 Lexington Ave., New York, NY 10016
  (212/687-7400)

Full Member

Established: 1935
Title output 2002: 68
Titles currently in print: 1,159

Admitted to AAUP: unknown
Title output 2003: 61

Editorial Program

Humanities and social sciences, with special emphasis on Southern history and literature; Southern studies; geography and environmental studies; poetry; and jazz.

Special series, joint imprints and/or copublishing programs: Antislavery, Abolition, and the Atlantic World; Conflicting Worlds; Eisenhower Center Studies on War and Peace; A History of the South; Library of Southern Civilization; The Miller Center Series on American Presidency; Papers of Jefferson Davis; The Pegasus Prize for Literature; Pennington Center Nutrition Series; politics@media; Political Traditions in Foreign Policy; Southern Biography; Southern Literary Studies; Southern Messenger Poets; T. Harry Williams Center for Oral History; Voices of the South; W.L. Fleming Lectures in Southern History.

McGill-Queens University Press

Montreal Office:
3430 McTavish Street
Montreal, QC H3A 1X9
Canada

Phone: (514) 398-3750
Fax: (514) 398-4333
E-mail: mqup@mqup.ca
Indiv: (user I.D.)@mcgill.ca
Web site: www.mqup.ca

Canadian Distributor:
Georgetown Terminal Warehouses
34 Armstrong Avenue
Georgetown, ON L7G 4R9
Canada
Phone: (905) 873-9781
Fax: (905) 873-6170
E-mail: orders@gtwcanada.com

Kingston Office:
Queen's University
Kingston, ON K7L 3N6
Canada

Phone: (613) 533-2155
Fax: (613) 533-6822
E-mail: mqup@post.queensu.ca

US Distributor:
CUP Services
P.O. Box 6525
Ithaca, NY 14851-6525
Phone: (800) 666-2211
Fax: (800) 688-2877
E-mail: orderbook@cupserv.org;
Pubnet@2021862

UK & European Distributor:
Marston Books Services Ltd

Staff

Executive Director: Philip J. Cercone (Montreal, 514/398-2910; e-mail: philip.cercone)
Editorial, Montreal Office:
   Editor-in-Chief: Philip J. Cercone
   Editors: John Zucchi (514/398-3750; e-mail: john.zucchi); Aurèle Parisien (514/398-5336; e-mail: aurele.parisien)
   Manuscript Editor: Joan V. McGilvray (514/398-3922; e-mail: joan.mcgilvray)
   Editorial Assistants: Joanne Pisano (514/398-2068; e-mail: joanne.pisano); Brenda Prince (514/398-3279; e-mail: brenda.prince)
Editorial, Kingston Office:
Senior Editor: Donald H. Akenson (613/533-2155; e-mail: mqup@post.queensu.ca)

Editors: Joan Harcourt (613/533-2155; e-mail: bjh@post.queensu.ca); Roger Martin (613/533-2155; e-mail: mqup@post.queensu.ca); Kyla Madden (613/533-2155; e-mail: 6kmm3@post.queensu.ca)
Marketing, Montreal Office:
Marketing Manager: Roy Ward (514/398-6306; e-mail: roy.ward)
  Sales & Advertising Manager: Pierre Roy (514/398-5165; e-mail: pierre.roy)
  Direct Mail & Exhibits Coordinator: Filomena Falocco (514/398-2912; e-mail: filomena.falocco)
  Electronic Marketing Coordinator: Sylvie O'Halloran (514/398-1343; e-mail: sylvie.ohalloran)
  Marketing Assistant: Sandra Lynch (514/398-2914; e-mail: marketing.mqup)
  Publicist: Francesca LoDico (514/398-2555; e-mail: francesca.lodico)
Design & Production, Montreal Office:
Production Manager: Susanne McAdam (514/398-6996; e-mail: susanne.mcadam)
  Production Coordinator: Elena Goranescu (514/398-7395; e-mail: elena.goranescu)
  Production Assistant: Carmen Yu (514/398-1342; e-mail: production.mqup)
Business, Montreal Office:
Business Manager: Arden Ford (514/398-8390; e-mail: arden.ford)
Administrative Coordinator: Dorothy Beaven (514/398-2911; e-mail: dorothy.beaven)
  Administrative Clerk: Carol Cardinal (514/398-2056; e-mail: carol.cardinal)
  Clerk/Receptionist: Carmie Vacca (514/398-3750; e-mail: carmie.vacca)

Full Member
Established: 1969 as a joint press
Admitted to AAUP: 1963 (as McGill University Press)
Title output 2002: 129   Title output 2003: 132
Titles currently in print: c. 2,100

Editorial Program
Scholarly books and well-researched studies of general interest in the humanities and social sciences, including anthropology, especially North American native peoples; architecture; Arctic and northern studies; art history, Canadian studies; Canadian literature; classics; communication and media studies; cultural studies; economics; education; environmental studies; ethnic studies; film studies; folklore and material culture; geography; health and society; history; Irish and Gaelic studies; law; linguistics; literary criticism; medieval and renaissance studies; military history; native studies; philosophy; poetry; photography; political economy; political science; public administration; Quebec studies; religious studies; Slavic and Eastern European studies; sociology; theatre; and women's studies.
    Special series, joint imprints, and/or copublishing programs:
CHORA, Intervals in the Philosophy of Architecture; Canada-United Kingdom Colloquia; Canadian Association of Geographers Series in Canadian Geography; Canadian Public Administration; Carleton Contemporary; Carleton Library; Central Problems of Philosophy; Centre for Editing Early Canadian Texts; Changing American; Comparative Charting of Social Change; Continental European Philosophy; Critical Perspectives on Public Affairs; Fontanus Monograph; Foreign Policy, Security and Strategic Studies; Fundamentals of Philosophy; Governance and Public Management; Harbinger Poetry; Hugh MacLennan Poetry; International Informatics; International Social Survey Programme; McGill-Queen's Native and Northern; McGill-Queen's Studies in Ethnic History; McGill-Queen's Studies in

the History of Ideas; McGill-Queen's Studies in the History of Religion; McGill-Queen's/ Associated Medical Services Studies in the History of Medicine, Health, and Society; Nordic Voices; Public Policy; Public Policy and the Third Sector; Rupert's Land Record Society; Social Union; Studies on the History of Quebec/Études d'histoire du Québec; Textual Analysis, Discourse and Culture; War and European Society; and Women's Experience.

Marquette University Press

1415 West Wisconsin Avenue
Box 3141
Milwaukee, WI 53211-3141

Phone: (414) 288-1564
Fax: (414) 288-7813
E-mail: (user I.D.)@marquette.edu
Online catalog: marquette.edu/mupress/

Warehouse Address:
30 Amberwood Parkway, P.O. Box 388
Ashland, OH 44805

Orders and Customer Service:
Phone: (800) 247-6553; (419) 281-1802
Fax: (419) 281-6883

Canadian Representative:
Scholarly Book Services

Staff
Director: Andrew Tallon (414/288-7298; e-mail: andrew.tallon)
Editorial, Marketing, Design and Production: Andrew Tallon
Business: Maureen Kondrick (414/288-1564; e-mail: maureen.kondrick)
Journals: Andrew Tallon
    Journals Marketing: Pamela K. Swope (800/444-2419, ext. 1; e-mail: pkswope@pdcnet.org)

Affiliate Member
Established: 1916
Title output 2002: 14
Titles currently in print: 265

Admitted to AAUP: 1998
Title output 2003: 15
Journals published: 2

Editorial Program
Philosophy; theology; history; urban studies; journalism; education; and mediæval history.
    Philosophy Series: Aquinas Lecture; Mediæval Philosophical Texts in Translation; Marquette Studies in Philosophy.
    Theology Series: Marquette Studies in Theology; Père Marquette Lecture; Reformation Texts with Translation: Series 1, Biblical Studies; Series 2, Women in the Reformation; Series 3, Late Reformation.
    History Series: Klement Lecture (Civil War); Urban Studies Series.
    Journal: *Philosophy & Theology*.

University of Massachusetts Press

Street Address:
671 North Pleasant Street
Amherst, MA 01002

Mailing Address:
P.O. Box 429
Amherst, MA 01004

Phone: (413) 545-2217
Fax: (413) 545-1226
E-mail: (user I.D.)@umpress.umass.edu
(unless otherwise indicated)
Web site: www.umass.edu/umpress

Boston Office:
Paul Wright
c/o Graduate Studies
U. of Mass. Boston
Boston, MA 02125
Phone: (617) 287-5710
Fax: (617) 287-5699

Orders:
c/o Hopkins Fulfillment Services
P.O. Box 50370
Baltimore, MD 21211
Phone: (800) 537-5487
Fax: (410) 516-6998

Canadian Representative:
Scholarly Book Services

UK & European Representative:
Eurospan

Staff

Director: Bruce Wilcox (e-mail: wilcox)
Acquisitions Editorial: Clark Dougan, Senior Editor (e-mail: cdougan)
    Boston Editor: Paul Wright (e-mail: paul.wright@umb.edu)
Manuscript Editorial: Carol Betsch, Managing Editor (e-mail: betsch)
Web and Promotion Manager: Alice Maldonado (e-mail: maldonado)
Design and Production: Jack Harrison, Manager (e-mail: harrison)
    Designer & Associate Production Manager: Sally Nichols (e-mail: snichols)
Business and Marketing: Richard Lozier, CFO & Business Manager (e-mail: rlozier)

Full Member

Established: 1963
Title output 2002: 40
Titles currently in print: 950

Admitted to AAUP: 1966
Title output 2003: 44

Editorial Program

Scholarly books and serious nonfiction, with special interests in African American studies; American studies, history, and literature; architecture and landscape design; biography; cultural studies; environmental studies; ethnic studies; history of the book; intellectual history; politics; women's and gender studies; and books of regional interest.

Special series, joint imprints and/or copublishing programs: American Popular Music; AWP Award Series in Short Fiction; Critical Perspectives on Modern Culture; Culture, Politics, and the Cold War; Juniper Prizes (poetry and fiction); Massachusetts Studies in Early Modern Culture; Native Americans of the Northeast; Political Development of the American Nation; Studies in Print Culture and the History of the Book.

The MIT Press

5 Cambridge Ctr., 4th floor
Cambridge, MA 02142-1493

Phone: (617) 253-5646 (main)
(617) 253-5641 (marketing)
Fax: (617) 258-6779
E-mail: (user I.D.)@mit.edu
Web site: mitpress.mit.edu

London Office:
The MIT Press, Ltd.
Fitzroy House
11 Chenies Street
London WC1E 7EY
United Kingdom
Phone: +44 (20) 7306 0603
Fax: +44 (20) 7306 0604
E-mail: info@hup-mitpress.co.uk

Book Orders:
Phone: (800) 405-1619 (US/Can);
(401) 658-4226 (International)
Fax: (800) 406-9145 (US/Can);
(401) 531-2801 (International)
E-mail: mitpress-orders@mit.edu

Customer Service:
Phone: (401) 658-4226
E-mail: mitpress-order-inq@mit.edu

Warehouse Address:
Triliteral
100 Maple Ridge Drive
Cumberland, RI 02864
E-mail: sheila.lilja@triliteral.org

Staff

Director: Ellen Faran (617/253-4078; e-mail: ewfaran)
  Assistant to the Director: Mary-Frances Gydus (617/253-5255; e-mail: mfgydus)
  Associate Director for Operations: Michael Leonard (617/253-5250; e-mail: leonardm)
Acquisitions Editorial: Ellen Faran, Editor-in-Chief (acting) (617/253-4078; e-mail:
  ewfaran)
  Editors: Roger Conover (art, architecture, design, photography, cultural studies, critical
  theory) (617/253-1677; e-mail: conover); John S. Covell (economics, business & finance)
  (617/253-3757; e-mail: jcovell); Clay Morgan (environmental sciences & bioethics) (617/
  253-4113; e-mail: claym); Barbara Murphy (neuroscience and biology) (617/253-1558;
  e-mail: murphyb); Elizabeth Murry (economics, business & finance) (617/253-1605; e-
  mail: elizm); Robert Prior (computer science) (617/253-1584; e-mail: prior); Doug Sery
  (computer science) (617/253-5187; e-mail: dsery); Tom Stone (cognitive science, psychology & linguistics) (617/252-1636; e-mail: tstone)
Manuscript Editorial: Michael Sims, Managing Editor (617/253-2080; e-mail: msims)
Marketing and Sales: Gita Manaktala, Director of Marketing (617/253-3172;
  e-mail: manak)
  Domestic Sales & Marketing Manager: Anne Bunn (617/253-8838; e-mail: annebunn)
  International Sales & Marketing Manager: Tom Clerkin (617/253-2887; e-mail: clerkin)
  Subsidiary Rights Manager: Cristina Sanmartín (617/253-0629; e-mail: csan)
  Publicity Manager: Kerry Murphy (acting) (617/258-0564; e-mail: kerrym)
  Internet Marketing Manager: Eric Maki (617/258-0583; e-mail: emaki)
  Direct Mail Manager: Astrid Baehrecke (617/253-7297; e-mail: baehreck)
  Advertising Manager: Vinnie Scorziello (617/253-3516; e-mail: gigivida)

Textbook Manager: Michelle Pullano (617/253-3620; e-mail: mpullano)
Exhibits Manager: John Costello (617/258-5764; e-mail: jcostell)
Design and Production: Yasuyo Iguchi, Design Manager (617/253-1961; e-mail: iguchi)
   Production Manager: Terry Lamoureux (617/253-2881; e-mail: terryl)
Journals: Rebecca McLeod, Journals Manager (617/258-0596; e-mail: mcleod)
   Journals Business Manager: June McCaull (617/253-2864; e-mail: jmccaull)
   Journals Circulation Manager: Abbie Hiscox (617/253-3765; e-mail: hiscox)
   Journals Editorial & Production Manager: Rachel Besen (617/258-0585; e-mail: rbesen)
   Journals Marketing Manager: Sarah Muzzy (617/452-3712; e-mail: smuzzy)
   Journals Internet Marketing Manager: Philip Cadigan (617/258-0598; e-mail: pcadigan)
   Journals Subsidiary Rights Manager: Christina Ellas (617/258-0591; e-mail: cellas)
Warehouse: Sheila Lilja, General Manager (e-mail: shiela.lilja@triliteral.org)
   Customer Service Manager: Cathy Morrone (401/531-2800; e-mail:
   cathy.morrone@triliteral.org)
Information Systems: Paul Dzus, IT Manager (617/258-6783; e-mail: pdzus)

Full Member

Established: 1961

Admitted to AAUP: 1961

Title output 2002: 300

Title output 2003: 278

Titles currently in print: 3,400

Journals published: 34

Editorial Program

Contemporary art; architecture/design arts; photography; critical theory; computer science and artificial intelligence; new media studies; cognitive science; neuroscience; psychology; philosophy; linguistics; energy, environment, and ecology; economics, finance and business; environmental studies; science, technology, and society (STS); natural history; social theory; and the following journals: *African Arts*; *Asian Economic Papers*; *Artificial Life*; *Computational Linguistics*; *Computer Music Journal*; *Daedalus*; *Design Issues*; *Education Finance and Policy*; *Evolutionary Computation*; *Global Environmental Politics*; *Grey Room*; *Information Technologies and International Development*; *International Security*; *Journal of Architectural Education*; *Journal of Cognitive Neuroscience*; *Journal of Cold War Studies*; *Journal of Economics and Management Strategy*; *Journal of Industrial Ecology*; *Journal of Interdisciplinary History*; *Journal of the European Economic Association*; *Leonardo*; *Leonardo Electronic Almanac*; *Leonardo Music Journal*; *Linguistic Inquiry*; *Molecular Imaging*; *Neural Computation*; *October*; *PAJ: A Journal of Performing Arts*; *Perspectives on Science: Historical, Philosophical, Social*; *Presence: Teleoperators and Virtual Environments*; *Quarterly Journal of Economics*; *Review of Economics and Statistics*; *TDR: The Drama Review*; and *Washington Quarterly*.

Special Series: Artificial Intelligence; Bradford Books; Cellular and Molecular Neuroscience; Cognitive Neuroscience; Complex Adaptive Systems; Contemporary German Social Thought; Computational Models of Cognition and Perception; Computational Neuroscience; Computer Systems; CSIA Studies in International Security; Current Studies in Linguistics; Dynamical Economic Science; Foundations of Computing; Global Environmental Accords; Graham Foundation Books; History of Computing; Information Systems; Inside Technology; Issues in the Biology of Language and Cognition; Jean Nicod Series; Language, Speech, and Communication; Learning, Development and Conceptual Change; Leonardo Books; Linguistic Inquiry Monographs; Logic Programming; Neural Network Modeling and Connectionism; October Books; Organization Studies; Representation and Mind; Scientific and Engineering Computation; Technical Communication, Multimedia, and Information Systems; Writing Architecture. Copublishing and distribution programs: AAAI Press; Canadian Centre for Architecture; Zone Books.

Mercer University Press

1400 Coleman Avenue
Macon, GA 31207

Phone: (478) 301-2880
Fax: (478) 301-2585
E-mail: (user I.D.)@mercer.edu
Web site: www.mupress.org

<u>UK Representative:</u>
Gracewing Publishing

Orders:
Phone: (800) 637-2378, ext. 2880
(800) 342-0841, ext. 2880

Staff
Publisher and Acquisitions: Marc A. Jolley (e-mail: jolley_ma)
   Assistant to the Publisher: Amelia Barclay (e-mail: barclay_ah)
Acquisitions Editorial: Edd Rowell, Senior Editor (e-mail: rowell_el)
Manuscript Editorial: Kevin Manus, Associate Editor (e-mail: manus_kc)
Marketing: Barbara Keene, Director of Marketing (e-mail: keene_b)
   Marketing Assistant: Jenny Toole (e-mail: toole_rw)
Production: Marsha Luttrell, Production Assistant (e-mail: luttrell_mm)
Business: James Golden, Business Manager (e-mail: golden_jw)
   Customer Service: Rhett Green (e-mail: green_hw)

Full Member
Established: 1979
Title output 2002: 41
Titles currently in print: 588

Admitted to AAUP: 2000
Title output 2003: 45

Editorial Program
Regional trade titles and serious works of nonfiction in history, particularly in the history of the United States (with an emphasis on the American South), the history of religion, and the history of literature; Southern regional studies; literature and literary criticism; Southern literary fiction; African-American studies; political science; philosophy of religion; theology and biblical studies; Jewish studies; art and art criticism; natural history.

   Special series: Baptists; Civil War Georgia; the International Kierkegaard Commentary; Mercer Classics in Biblical Studies; the Mercer Commentary on the Bible; the Melungeons; Music and the American South; Sports and Religion; and Voices of the African Diaspora.

The University of Michigan Press

839 Greene Street
Ann Arbor, MI 48104-3209

Phone: (734) 764-4388
Fax: (734) 615-1540
E-mail: um.press@umich.edu
Indiv: (user I.D.)@umich.edu
Web site: www.press.umich.edu

Orders:
University of Michigan Press
c/o Chicago Distribution Center
11030 South Langley Avenue
Chicago, IL 60628
Phone: (800) 621-2736 (US customers)
(773) 568-1550 (Int'l customers)
Faxes: (800) 621-8476 (US customers)
(773) 660-2235 (Int'l customers)

UK Representatives:
University Presses Marketing,
NBN International

Staff

Director: Philip Pochoda (734/936-0452; e-mail: pochoda)
  Assistant Director: Mary Erwin (734/763-4134; e-mail: merwin)
  Assistant to the Director: Yune Tran (734/615-6478; e-mail: ytran)
  Permissions: Sarah Murphy (734/647-0068; e-mail: semurphy)
Acquisitions Editorial:
  Executive Editor: LeAnn Fields (literature, performance studies, disability studies, gender studies, women's studies) (734/647-2463; e-mail: lfields)
  Editors: Jim Reische (political science, law) (734/763-6419; e-mail: jreische); Chris Hebert (music, fiction, distributed titles) (734/615-6479; e-mail: hebertc); Mary Erwin (regional) (734/763-4134; e-mail: merwin); Kelly Sippell (applied linguistics) (734/764-4447; e-mail: ksippell); TBA (classical studies, archaeology, medieval history, Renaissance studies, German studies); Raphael Allen (economics, anthropology, and medical health) (734/936-8889; e-mail: allenrc)
  Editorial Assistants: Rebecca Mostov (734/647-2463; e-mail: rmostov); Amy Anderson (734/936-2841)
English as a Second Language: Kelly Sippell, Manager (734/764-4447; e-mail: ksippell)
  Marketing Coordinator: Giles Brown (734/763-3237; e-mail: agbrown)
  Acquisitions Associate: Debra Shafer (734/763-1018; e-mail: dshafer)
  Senior Copyediting Coordinator: Deborah Kopka (734/936-0459; e-mail: dkopka)
Manuscript Editorial: Christina Milton, Managing Editor (734/764-4390; e-mail: cmilton)
  Senior Copyediting Coordinators: Marcia LaBrenz (734/647-4480; e-mail: mlabrenz); Kevin Rennells (734/763-1526; e-mail: rennells)
  Copyediting Coordinator: Mary Hashman (734/936-0461; e-mail mhashman)
  Assistant Editor: Alma Reising (734/764-4387; e-mail: amacr)
  Associate Editors: Andrea Olson (734/936-0394; e-mail: ajolson); Ellen McCarthy (e-mail: emcc)
  Editorial Assistant: Rosemary Bush (734/763-0170; e-mail: rabush)
Marketing and Sales: Michael Kehoe, Sales Manager (734/936-0388; e-mail: mkehoe)
  Marketing Director: Pete Sickman-Garner (734/763-0163; e-mail: pgarner)
  Direct Advertising Supervisor: Margaret Haas (734/936-0389; e-mail: mhaas)

Publicist: Mary Bisbee-Beek (734/764-4330; e-mail: bisbeeb)
Marketing Graphic Artist: Carrie Davis (734/763-6737; e-mail: carrieed)
Marketing Exhibits: Kristin Thomas (734/763-0163; e-mail: krthomas)
Webmaster: Melissa Baker-Young (734/764-6802; e-mail: mbakeryo)
Design and Production: John Grucelski, Production Manager (734/764-4391; e-mail: jgrucel)
Senior Production Coordinators: Mary Meade (734/763-1525; e-mail: mmeade); Jillian Downey (734/615-8114; e-mail: jilliand)
Production Coordinators: Michael Landauer (734/764-4391; e-mail: landauer); Felice Lau (734/763-6417; e-mail: ftebbe)
Designer: Heidi Dailey (734/764-4128; e-mail: hdailey)
Business: Gabriela Beres, Business Manager (734/936-2227; e-mail: gsberes)
Accountant: Karyn McIntire (734/763-0146; e-mail: klydic)
Accounts Payable: Linda Rowley (734/647-9083; e-mail: lrowley)
Accounts Receivable: Amy Oliver (734/936-0396; e-mail: amyjo)
Facilities: Larry Gable (734/764-2468; e-mail: lgable)
Mail: Will Lovick (e-mail: willski)
Data Systems Administrator: Kerri Kijewski (734/936-3636; e-mail: kijewski)

Full Member

Established: 1930   Admitted to AAUP: 1963
Title output 2002: 160   Title output 2003: 137
Titles currently in print: 2,198

Editorial Program

Scholarly and trade works in African-American studies; American studies; American history; anthropology; cultural studies; disability studies; economics; English as a second language; environmental studies; gay and lesbian studies; German studies; law; literature; literary criticism and theory; media studies and film; Michigan and Great Lakes; music; Native American studies; political science; theater and performance; and women and gender studies; fiction; sports.

Special series: Advances in Heterodox Economics; Amherst Series in Law; Jurisprudence and Social Thought; Analytical Perspectives on Politics; Ann Arbor Paperbacks; Bibliotheca Teubneriana; The Body, in Theory: Histories of Cultural Materialism; The Comparative Studies in Society and History Book; Conversations in Medicine and Society; Corporealities: Discourses of Disability; Critical Perspectives on Women and Gender; Development and Inequality in the Market Economy; Economics, Cognition, and Society; Economics of Education; Editorial Theory and Literary Criticism; English for Academic & Professional Purposes; Evolving Values for a Capitalist World; Great Lakes Environment; History, Languages, and Cultures of the Spanish and Portuguese Worlds; Human-Environment Interaction; Intensive Course in English; Interests, Identities and Institutions in Comparative Politics; International Series on the Research of Learning and Instruction of Writing; Jazz Perspectives; Kelsey Museum Studies; Law, Meaning, and Violence; The Memoirs of the American Academy in Rome; Michigan Series in English for Academic and Professional Purposes; The Michigan Series on Teaching Multilingual Writers; Michigan Studies in International Political Economy; Michigan Studies in Political Analysis; Middle English Dictionary; Monumenta Chartae Papyraceae; The Paper and Monographs of the American Academy in Rome; Pew Studies in Economics and Security; Pitt Series in English as a Second

Language; Poets on Poetry; Political Analysis; The Politics of Race and Ethnicity; Recentiores: Later Latin Texts and Contexts; Selected Tanner Lectures in Human Values; Social History, Popular Culture, and Politics in Germany; Studies in International Economics; Studies in International Trade Policy; Studies in Literature and Science; Stylus: Studies in Medieval Culture; Supplements to the Memoirs of the American Academy in Rome; Sweetwater Fiction; TEXT: An Interdisciplinary Annual of Textual Studies; The Thackeray Edition; Theater: Theory/Text/Performance; Thomas Spencer Jerome Lectures; Triangulations: Lesbian/Gay/Queer/Theater/Drama/Performance; Under Discussion.

The Press distributes works of Pluto Press, K.G. Saur Verlag, the Center for Chinese Studies, and the Center for South and Southeast Asian Studies.

Michigan State University Press

1405 South Harrison Road, Suite 25
Manly Miles Building
East Lansing, MI 48823-5202

Phone: (517) 355-9543
Fax: (517) 353-6766
E-mail: msupress@msu.edu
Indiv: (user I.D.)@msu.edu
Web site and online catalog: msupress.msu.edu

<u>Customer Service:</u>
Phone: (517) 355-9543, ext. 100
Fax: (517) 432-2611;
(800) 678-2120

<u>UK/European Distributor:</u>
Eurospan

<u>Canadian Distributor:</u>
University of British Columbia
Georgetown Terminal Warehouse

Staff
Director: Fredric C. Bohm (ext. 115; e-mail: bohm)
Editorial: Julie L. Loehr, Editor-in-Chief/Assistant Director (ext. 103; e-mail: loehr)
  Acquisitions Editor: Martha A. Bates (ext. 104; e-mail: batesmar)
Editor: Kristine Blakslee (ext. 131; e-mail: blakes17)
Marketing & Sales: Julie Reaume (ext. 109; e-mail: reaumej)
  Marketing Specialist: Justin Cox (ext. 113; e-mail: coxju)
  Web Site Coordinator: Dawn Martin (ext. 108; e-mail: marti778)
Production: Annette Tanner, Manager (ext. 114; e-mail: tanneran)
Journals: Margot Kielhorn, Manager (ext. 102; e-mail: kielhor5)
  Editor: Carol Cole (ext. 111; e-mail: colec)
Business Manager: Laura Carantza (ext. 116; e-mail: carantza)
  Fulfillment Manager: Julie Wrzesinski (ext. 101; e-mail: wrzesin2)
Information Systems: Jesse W. Howard, Manager (ext. 106; e-mail: howard10)
  IT Administrator: Peter Cole (ext. 111; e-mail: colepet)

Full Member

Established: 1947

Title output 2002: 38

Titles currently in print: 525

Admitted to AAUP: 1992

Title output 2003: 41

Journals published: 8

Editorial Program

Scholarly books and general nonfiction with areas of special interest in agriculture; African Studies; African-American studies; American studies; business; Canadian studies; creative nonfiction; Great Lakes regional studies; Native American studies; books relating to the state of Michigan; poetry; the social and environmental sciences; US history; urban studies; women's studies; and the following journals: *Fourth Genre; French Colonial History; Italian Culture; The New Centennial Review; Northeast African Studies; Real Analysis Exchange; Red Cedar Review;* and *Rhetoric of Public Affairs.*

Special series: Black American and Diasporic Studies; Canadian Series; Native American Series; North American Fur Trade Conference, Selected Papers; Red Cedar Classics; Rhetoric and Public Affairs Series; and Schoolcraft Series.

The Press distributes publications for African Books Collective; University of Alberta Press; University of Calgary Press; University of Manitoba Press; Colleagues Press; Grand Valley State University; Kresge Art Museum; Lynx House Press; Mackinac Island Historic Parks; Michigan State University African Studies Center; the Michigan State University Museum; National Railway Museum, UK; National Museum of Photography; Film and Television, UK; and the Science Museum, London.

Minnesota Historical Society Press

345 Kellogg Blvd. West
Saint Paul, MN 55102

Orders:
Phone: (800) 621-2736

Phone: (651) 297-2221
Fax: (651) 297-1345
E-mail: (user I.D.)@mnhs.org
Web site: www.mnhs.org/mhspress

Staff
Director: Gregory M. Britton (651/297-4463; e-mail: greg.britton)
Acquisitions: Gregory M. Britton
Editorial: Ann Regan (651/297-4457; e-mail: ann.regan)
Marketing and Sales: Alison Vandenberg (651/296-2939; e-mail: alison.vandenberg)
Design and Production: Will Powers (651/296-1448; e-mail: william.powers)
Rights and Permissions: Sarah Rubinstein (651/297-4459; e-mail: sally.rubinstein)
Journals: Anne Kaplan (651/297-4462; e-mail: anne.kaplan)

Associate Member
Established: 1859
Title output 2002: 22
Titles currently in print: 265

Admitted to AAUP: 2001
Title output 2003: 23
Journals published: 1

Editorial Program
The Minnesota Historical Society Press publishes books on the history and culture of the Upper Midwest. Specific list strengths include regional studies, memoir and literary nonfiction, ethnic studies, travel and adventure, military history, African-American history, Native American studies, architectural history, and photography.

The Press maintains Borealis Books as a separate trade imprint. It also publishes the quarterly journal, *Minnesota History.*

Special series: Native Voices; People of Minnesota.

University of Minnesota Press

111 Third Avenue South
Suite 290
Minneapolis, MN 55401-2552

Orders:
Phone: (773) 702-7109

Phone: (612) 627-1970
Fax: (612) 627-1980
E-mail: (user I.D.)@umn.edu
Web site: www.upress.umn.edu

UK Representative:
University Presses Marketing

Staff
Director: Douglas Armato (612/627-1972; e-mail: armat001)
  Associate Director and Test Division Manager: Beverly Kaemmer (612/627-1963; e-mail: kaemm002)

Assistant to the Director: Gretchen Asmussen (612/627-1972; e-mail: asmus001)

Rights and Permissions: Jeffery Moen (612/627-1978; e-mail: moenx017)

Acquisitions Editorial: Carrie Mullen, Executive Editor (anthropology, geography, sociology, political science) (612/627-1979; e-mail: mulle016)

Editors: Richard Morrison (literary and cultural studies, American studies) (612/627-1974; e-mail: morri094); Todd Orjala (regional, Scandinavian studies) (612/627-1973; e-mail: t-orja)

Associate Editors: Andrea Kleinhuber (cinema, media, and visual studies) (612/627-1977; e-mail: klein111); Pieter Martin (architecture, public art) (612/627-1976; e-mail: marti190)

Managing Editor: Laura Westlund (612/627-1985; e-mail: westl003)

Marketing and Sales: Mary Poggione, Director of Marketing and Sales (612/627-1931; e-mail: poggi001)

Publicist: Patricia McFadden (612/627-1932; e-mail: mcfa0029)

Direct Marketing Manager: Stacy Zellmann (612/627-1934; e-mail: zellm003)

Exhibits and Sales Assistant: Katie Houlihan (612/627-1938; e-mail: houli011)

Trade Advertising and Journals Manager: Emily Hamilton (612/627-1936; e-mail: eph)

Design and Production: Adam Grafa, Manager (612/627-1981; e-mail: grafa001)

Business: Michelle Prytz, Fiscal Manager (612/627-1941; e-mail: prytz)

Computer Operations: Robin Moir, Electronic Publishing Coordinator (612/627-1944; e-mail: moirx001)

Full Member

Established: 1925	Admitted to AAUP: 1937
Title output 2002: 105	Title output 2003: 105
Titles currently in print: 1,100	Journals published: 3

Editorial Program

Literary and cultural studies; social and political theory; cinema and media studies; art and visual studies; digital culture; feminist studies; gay and lesbian studies; anthropology; architecture; geography; international relations; Native American studies; personality assessment, clinical psychology and psychiatry; philosophy; Upper Midwest studies; and the journals (* available online) *Cultural Critique**, *The Moving Image**, and *Wicazo Sa Review**.

Special series, joint imprints, and/or copublishing programs: Borderlines; Commerce and Mass Culture; Contradictions of Modernity; Critical American Studies; Cultural Studies of the Americas; Electronic Mediations; Fesler-Lampert Minnesota Heritage Book Series; Globalization and Community; Minnesota Studies in the Philosophy of Science; MMPI-2 Monographs; MMPI-A Monographs; Native American Studies; Public Worlds; Social Movements, Protest, and Contention; Sport and Culture; Theory and History of Literature; Visible Evidence.

University Press of Mississippi

3825 Ridgewood Road
Jackson, MS 39211-6492

Phone: (601) 432-6205
Fax: (601) 432-6217
E-mail: press@ihl.state.ms.us
Indiv: (user I.D)@ihl.state.ms.us
Web site: www.upress.state.ms.us

Canadian Representative:
Scholarly Book Services

Warehouse Address:
Lebanon Distribution Center
704 Legionnaire Drive
Fredricksburg, PA 17026

Orders:
(800) 737-7788; (601) 432-6246

UK Representative:
Roundhouse Publishing

Staff
Director: Seetha Srinivasan (601/432-6275; e-mail: seetha)
   Administrative Assistant: Cynthia Foster (601/432-6205; e-mail: cfoster)
   Development Assistant: Cynthia Ridler (601/432-6206; e-mail: bkfrds)
Acquisitions Editorial: Craig Gill, Editor-in-Chief (601/432-6371; e-mail: gill)
   Assistant Editor: Walter Biggins (601/432-6102; e-mail: wbiggins)
Manuscript Editorial: Anne Stascavage, Editor (601/432-6249; e-mail: anne)
Marketing and Sales: Steve Yates, Marketing Manager (601/432-6695; e-mail: syates)
   Assistant Marketing Manager: Ginger Tucker (601/432-6424; e-mail: ginger)
   Advertising and Marketing Services Manager: Kathy Burgess (601/432-6105; e-mail: kerr)
   Marketing Assistant for Publicity and Sales: Cliff Prince (601/432-6459; e-mail: cprince)
Design and Production: John A. Langston, Art Director (601/432-6554; e-mail: john)
   Designer: Todd Lape (601/432-6274; e-mail: toddl)
   Production Coordinator: Shane Gong (601/432-6795; e-mail: gong)
   Production Assistant: Pete Halverson (601/432-6274; e-mail: peteh)
Busines: Isabel Metz, Associate Director and Business Manager (601/432-6551;
   e-mail: isabel)
   Customer Service and Order Supervisor: Sandra Alexander (601/432-6272; e-mail: sandy)
   Customer Service Representative and Business Assistant: Joy Thompson (601/432-6246;
   e-mail: thompson)

Full Member
Established 1970
Title output 2002: 66
Distributed titles 2002: 6
Titles currently in print: 725

Admitted to AAUP: 1976
Title output 2003: 58
Distributed titles 2003: 2

Editorial Program
Scholarly and trade titles in African-American studies, American studies, literature, history, and culture; art and architecture; ethnic studies; fiction; folklife; health; music; natural sciences; performance; photography; popular culture; serious nonfiction of general interest; Southern studies; women's studies; other liberal arts.
   Special series: American Made Music; Chancellor's Symposium in Southern History;

Conversations with Comic Artists; Conversations with Filmmakers; Conversations with Public Intellectuals; Faulkner and Yoknapatawpha; Hollywood Legends; Literary Conversations; Margaret Walker Alexander Series in African-American Studies; Southern Icons; Studies in Popular Culture; Understanding Health and Sickness; Willie Morris Books in Memoir and Biography; Writers and Their Work.

Imprints: Banner Books; Muscadine Books.

The Missouri Historical Society Press

Street Address:
225 S. Skinker Boulevard
St. Louis, MO 63105

Mailing Address:
P.O. Box 11940
St. Louis, MO 63112-0040

Phone: (314) 746-4557
Fax: (314) 746-4548
E-mail: (user I.D.)@mohistory.org
Web site: www.mohistory.org

Distributor:
University of Missouri Press
Orders: (800) 828-1894

Staff
Publications Manager and Acquisitions Editorial: Victoria W. Monks (314/746-4558; e-mail: vwmonks)
Manuscript Editorial: Lauren Mitchell (314/746-4556; e-mail: lmm)
Journals: Victoria Monks, Editor, *Gateway* (314/746-4558; e-mail: vwmonks)
Business: Carolyn Schmidt, Chief Financial Officer (314/454-3104; e-mail: cjs)

Associate Member
Established: 1991
Title output 2002: 3
Titles currently in print: 37

Admitted to AAUP: 1998
Title output 2003: 5
Journals published: 1

Editorial Program
Regional trade titles and serious works of nonfiction in history, particularly the history of St. Louis and Missouri, urban history, women's studies, African-American studies, photography, architectural history, biography, and regional literature.

Gateway welcomes submissions on regional topics that deal with persistent historical issues. Editorial guidelines available from Victoria Monks.

Special series: The Missouri Historical Society Guide Book, The Missouri Historical Society Reprint.

University of Missouri Press

2910 LeMone Boulevard
Columbia, MO 65201-8227

Phone: (573) 882-7641
Fax: (573) 884-4498
Indiv: (user I.D.)@umsystem.edu
Web site: www.system.missouri.edu/upress

Orders:
Phone: (800) 828-1894
E-mail: orders@umsystem.edu

UK Representative:
Eurospan

Canadian Representative:
Scholarly Book Service

Staff

Director: Beverly Jarrett (e-mail: jarrettb)
  Associate Director: Linda Frech (e-mail: frechl)
  Executive Staff Assistant: Barbara Corson (e-mail: corsonb)
  Editorial Assistant: Susan King (e-mail: kingsu)
Acquisitions Editorial: Beverly Jarrett, Editor-in-Chief
  Acquisitions Editors: Clair Willcox (e-mail: willcoxc); Gary Kass (e-mail: kassg)
Manuscript Editorial: Jane Lago, Managing Editor (e-mail: lagoj)
  Manuscript Editors: John Brenner (e-mail: brennerj); Julie Schroeder (e-mail: schroederjm); Sara Davis (e-mail: davissd); Gary Kass (e-mail: kassg)
Marketing: Karen Renner, Marketing Manager (e-mail: rennerk)
  Publicity/Exhibits Manager: Beth Chandler (e-mail: chandlerb)
  Advertising and Design Manager: Cathy Birk (e-mail: birkc)
  Advertising and Sales Assistant: Eve Kidd (e-mail: kidde)
Design and Production: Dwight Browne, Assistant Director and Production Manager (e-mail: browned)
  Assistant Production Manager: Nikki Waltz (e-mail: waltzn)
  Senior Designer: Kristie Lee (e-mail: leek)
  Designer: Jenny Cropp (e-mail: croppj)
Business: Linda Frech, Associate Director and Chief Financial Officer (e-mail: frechl)
  Business Manager: Tracy Martinez (e-mail: martinezt)
  Order Fulfillment Supervisor: Debbie Guilford (e-mail: guilfordd)
  Order Entry Clerk: Lyn Smith (e-mail: smithls)
  Warehouse Clerk: Tom Burns

Full Member

Established: 1958
Title output 2002: 57
Title currently in print: 626

Admitted to AAUP: 1960
Title output 2003: 66

Editorial Program

American and European history, including intellectual history and biography; African-American studies; women's studies; American and British literary criticism; journalism; political science, including foreign relations; political philosophy and ethics; regional studies of Missouri, the Midwest, and South Central United States; and creative non-fiction.

Special series: Afro-Romance Writers; Eric Voegelin Institute in Political Philosophy; Give 'Em Hell Harry; Mark Twain and His Circle; Missouri Biography; Missouri Heritage Readers; New Directions in the History of the Southern Economy; Shades of Blue and Gray; Southern Women; Sports and American Culture.

Modern Language Association of America

26 Broadway, 3rd floor
New York, NY 10004-1789

Phone: (646) 576-5000
Fax: (646) 458-0030
E-mail: info@mla.org
Indiv: (firstinitial)(lastname)@mla.org
Web site: www.mla.org

Book Orders:
Phone: (646) 576-5161
Fax: (646) 576-5160
E-mail: bookorders@mla.org

Staff
Executive Director: Rosemary G. Feal (646/576-5102)
  Associate Executive Director: Regina M. Vorbeck (646/576-5110)
  Director of Book Publications: David G. Nicholls (646/576-5040)
  Permissions and Contracts Manager: Marcia E. Henry (646/576-5042)
Acquisitions Editorial: Joseph Gibaldi, Director of Book Acquisitions & Development (646/576-5041)
  Acquisitions Editor: Sonia Kane (646/576-5043)
Manuscript Editorial (includes journals): Judy Goulding, Director of Publishing Operations and Managing Editor of MLA Publications (646/576-5015)
  Associate Managing Editor for Book Publications: Elizabeth Holland (646/576-5020)
Marketing and Sales: Kathleen Hansen, Marketing Director (646/576-5018)
Design and Production: Judith Altreuter, Production Director and Supervisor of Electronic Production Services (646/576-5010)
Director of Financial Operations: Amilde Hadden (646/576-5170)
Information Technology Center Manager: Kinglen Wang (646/576-5200)

Associate Member
Established: 1883
Title output 2002: 13
Titles currently in print: 246

Admitted to AAUP: 1992
Title output 2003: 11
Journals published: 4

Editorial program
Scholarly, pedagogical, and professional books on language and literature, and *ADE and ADFL Bulletins*; *MLA International Bibliography*; *MLA Newsletter*; *PMLA*; *Profession*.

  Book Series: Approaches to Teaching World Literature; New Variorum Edition of Shakespeare; Options for Teaching; Teaching Languages, Literatures, and Cultures; Text and Translations.

The National Academies Press

500 Fifth Street, N.W.
Washington, DC 20001

Bookstore phone: (202) 334-2612
Fax: (202) 334-2793
E-mail: (user I.D.)@nas.edu
Web site: www.nap.edu

Orders (US and Canada):
Phone: (800) 624-6242; (202) 334-3313
Fax: (202) 334-2451
E-mail: zjones@nas.edu

UK Distributor:
Marston Book Services, Ltd.

Staff
Director: Barbara Kline Pope (202/334-3328; e-mail: bkline)
  Assistant to the Director: Olive Schwarzschild (202/334-3038; e-mail: oschwarz)
Director of Operations: Sandy Adams (202/334-3157; e-mail: sadams)
Executive Editor and Acquisitions Editor: Stephen M. Mautner (202/334-3336; e-mail: smautner)
  Senior Editor, Joseph Henry Press: Jeffrey Robbins (e-mail: jrobbins)
Director of Outreach and Marketing: Ann Merchant (202/334-3117; e-mail: amerchan)
  Sales and Marketing Manager: Stanley Cohen (202/334-3037; e-mail: scohen)
  Sales Representatives: Natalie Jones (London) (2082 924400; e-mail: njones4748@aol.com); David Smith (South East & East Anglia) (1279-437979; e-mail: djsmith@aptresource.free-online.co.uk); James Benson (Northern England & North Wales) (1524-222512; e-mail: quantumjames@btopenworld.com); Mark Latcham (South & East Midlands, Mid and South Wales, Dorset, Hampshire & Herefordshire) (1778 423672; e-mail: quantummark@btopenworld.com); Barbara Martin (South West, West Midlands & Buckinghamshire) (1908 660560; e-mail: barbaramartin@barbaramartin.plus.com); Jim Chalmers (Scotland & Cumbria) (1418 841398; e-mail: quantumjim@btopenworld.com)
Production Manager: Dorothy Lewis (202/334-2409; e-mail: dlewis)
Director, Composition, Graphics and Design: Jim Gormley (202/334-3325; e-mail: jgormley)
Business Manager: Rachel Levy (202/334-3329; e-mail: rlevy)
  Customer Service: Zina Jones (202/334-3116; e-mail: zjones)
  Warehouse: Tim Murphy (202/334-2625; e-mail: tmurphy)
Permissions Editor: Erin Burkert (202/334-3180; e-mail: eburkert)
Director of Publishing Technologies: Michael Jensen (202/334-2403; e-mail: mjensen)

Associate Member
Established: 1864
Title output 2002: 204
Titles currently in print: 1,664

Admitted to AAUP: 1988
Title output 2003: 181

Editorial Program
Primarily professional-level, policy-oriented titles in agricultural sciences; behavioral and social sciences; biology; chemistry; computer sciences; earth sciences; economics; education; energy; engineering; environmental issues; industry; international issues; materials science;

medicine; natural resources; nutrition; physical sciences; public policy issues; statistics; transportation; and urban and rural development. The scholarly list emanates from studies from the National Academies; the trade list is acquired from scientists and science writers.

Joseph Henry Press (imprint): Independently acquired titles in all areas of sciences, technology, and health.

National Gallery of Art

Street Address:
Sixth Street and Constitution Avenue NW
Washington, DC 20565

Mailing Address:
2000B South Club Drive
Landover, MD 20785

Phone: (202) 842-6200
Fax: (202) 408-8530
E-mail: j-metro@nga.gov
Web site: www.nga.gov

Customer Service/Order Fulfillment:
Phone: (202) 842-6465

Staff
Deputy Director: Alan Shestack
Editor-in-Chief: Judy Metro
Manuscript Editorial: Gail Spilsbury, Acting Manager, Systematic Catalogue
  Senior Editor: Karen Sagstetter
  Managing Editor (CASVA): Carol Eron
  Editors: Ulrike Mills, Julie Warnement
  Editorial Assistants: Amanda Sparrow, Caroline Weaver
Design: Margaret Bauer, Manager
  Designer: Wendy Schleicher Smith
Production: Chris Vogel, Production Manager
  Production Editor: Mariah Shay
  Production Assistant: Rio DeNaro
Web Site Manager: Phyllis Hecht
  Web Site Designers: Guillermo Saenz, Suzy Sarraf, Dan Trachtman
Business: Linda Mosley, Budget Coordinator
Permissions Coordinator: Sara Sanders-Buell

Associate Member
Established: 1941
Title output 2002: 12
Titles currently in print: 104

Admitted to AAUP: 1992
Title output 2003: 12

Editorial Program
The National Gallery publishes exhibition catalogues on all subjects and permanent collection catalogues (including Western art of the early Renaissance through the contemporary era); a symposium series, Studies in the History of Art, in conjunction with the Center for Advanced Study in the Visual Arts; educational online programs and catalogues; scholarly and popular publications based on objects in the museum's collections; scholarly publications on conservation; educational materials and guides for use by the public and by teachers and schools; and the Gallery's annual report, calendar of events, and bulletins. Unsolicited manuscripts are not invited at this time.

Naval Institute Press

291 Wood Road
Annapolis MD 21402-5034

Orders:
Phone: (800) 233-8764

Phone: (410) 268-6110
Fax: (410) 295-1084/5
E-mail: (firstinitial)(lastname)@navalinstitute.org
Web site: www.navalinstitute.org

Staff

Press Director: Mark Gatlin (410/295-1031)
  Senior Administrative Assistant: Eve Secunda (410/295-1030)
  Subsidiary Rights and Electronic Publications Manager: Susan Todd Brook (410/295-1037)
  Import Book Coordinator and Permissions Editor: Peggy Wooldridge (410/295-1042)
Executive Editor: Paul W. Wilderson (410/295-1046)
  Senior Acquisitions Editor: Thomas J. Cutler (410/295-1038)
  Acquisitions Editor: Eric Mills (410/295-1034)
Editorial Manager: Linda O'Doughda (410/295-1041)
  Production Editors: Patti Bower (410/295-1039); Kristin Wye Rodney (410/295-1086)
Marketing Director: Tom Harnish (410/295-1025)
  Publicity/Copy Manager: Susan Artigiani (410/295-1081)
  Exhibits and Special Sales Manager: Brian Walker (410/295-1082)
  Direct Mail/Marketing Coordinator: Janice Smith (410/295-1080)
  Administrative and Promotion Assistant: Judy Heise (410/295-1028)
  Bookstore Manager: Virginia Schultz (410/295-3754)
Design and Production Manager: James Bricker (410/295-1045)
  Senior Designer: Donna Doyle (410/295-1040)
  Manufacturing Supervisor: Eddie Vance (410/295-1044)
Journals: Fred H. Rainbow, Editor-in-Chief, Proceedings (410/295-1077)
  Managing Editor, *Proceedings*: Julianne Olver (410/295-1072)
  Editor-in-Chief, *Naval History*: Fred L. Schultz (410/295-1079)
Business: Mary Kay Meilunas, Chief Financial Officer (410/571-1738)
  Customer Service Manager: Debbie Wienecke (410/571-1712)

Full Member

Established: 1899
Title output 2002: 90
Titles currently in print: 950

Admitted to AAUP: 1949
Title output 2003: 85
Journals published: 2

Editorial Program

Joint and general military subjects; naval biography; naval history and literature; naval and military reference; oceanography; navigation; military law; naval science textbooks; sea power; shipbuilding; professional guides; nautical arts and lore; technical guides; fiction; and the journals *Proceedings* and *Naval History*.

Special series: Bluejacket Books (paperback series); Classics of Naval Literature; Classics of Sea Power; Fundamentals of Naval Science; Library of Naval Biography; Naval Institute

Special Warfare; Now Hear This (audio book series).

Joint imprints and copublishing programs: Anatomy of the Ship Series; History of the Ship Series.

University of Nebraska Press

233 North 8th Street
Lincoln, NE 68588-0255

Phone: (402) 472-3581
Fax: (402) 472-0308 (Editorial)
E-mail: (user I.D.)@unl.edu
Web site and online catalog: www.nebraskapress.unl.edu; bisonbooks.com

Orders:
Phone: (402) 472-3584; (800) 755-1105
Fax: (402) 472-6214; (800) 526-2617

UK Distributor:
Combined Academic Publishers

Staff

Interim Director: Gary Dunham (402/472-4452; e-mail: gdunham1)
 Rights and Permissions: Elaine Maruhn (402/472-7702; e-mail: emaruhn1)
 Subsidiary Rights: (402/474-1660)
Acquisitions Editorial: Elizabeth Demers, Interim Editor-in-Chief and History Editor (402/472-5945; e-mail: edemers2)
 Associate Director & Humanities Editor: Ladette Randolph (402/472-2861; e-mail: lrandolph1)
 Sports Editor: Rob Taylor (402/472-0325; e-mail: rtaylor3)
Manuscript Editorial: Beth Ina, Managing Editor (402/472-7709; e-mail: bina2)
 Assistant Managing Editor: Linnea Fredrickson (402/472-0011; e-mail: lfredrickson2)
 Project Editor: Renae Carlson (402/472-4008; e-mail: rcarlson2)
 Assistant Project Editors: Joeth Zucco (402/472-0199; e-mail: jzucco2); Ann Baker (402/472-0095; e-mail: abaker2)
Marketing and Sales: Sandra Johnson, Marketing Manager (402/472-5937; e-mail: sjohnson3)
 Sales Manager: Kathryn Kelley (402/472-5949; e-mail: kkelley1)
 Publicity Manager: Erika Kuebler Rippeteau (402/472-5938; e-mail: erippeteau1)
 Advertising Manager: Amy Dolton Feriozzi (402/472-3888; e-mail: aferiozzi)
 Direct Mail Manager: Tish Fobben (402/472-4627; e-mail: pmockler1)
 Database and Web Manager: TBA (402/472-0890)
Design and Production: Debra Turner, Assistant Director and Production Manager (402/472-5944; e-mail: dturner1)
 Assistant Production Manager: Alison Rold (402/472-7706; e-mail: arold1)
 Designers: Richard Eckersley (402/472-5943; e-mail: reckersley1); Dika Eckersley (402/472-0317; deckersley1); Andrea Shahan (402/472-7718; e-mail: ashahan1); Raymond Boeche (402/472-0318; e-mail: rboeche1); Roger Buchholz (402/472-7713; e-mail: rbuchholz1)
 Art Researcher: Carolyn Einspahr (402/472-7704; e-mail: ceinspahr1)
Journals: Manjit Kaur, Manager (402/472-7703; e-mail: mkaur2)

Journals Assistant Project Editor: Sabrina Stellrecht (402/472-2292; e-mail: sstellrecht2)
Journals Marketing Manager: Joyce Gettman (402/472-8330; e-mail: jgettman2)
Journals Circulation Assistant: Erin Trummer (402/472-8536; e-mail: etrummer2)
Business Services: Kandra Hahn, Assistant Director for Business Operations (402/472-4922;
e-mail: khahn2)
Accountant: Deborah Kohl (402/472-9202; e-mail: dkohl2)
Customer Service: TBA (402/472-3584)
Shipping & Warehouse Supervisor: John Hernandez (402/472-2656; e-mail: jhernandez2)

Full Member

Established: 1941	Admitted to AAUP: Unknown
Title output 2002: 157	Title output 2003: 195
Distributed titles 2002: 31	Distributed titles 2003: 15
Titles currently in print: 2,184	Journals published: 11

Editorial Program

Subject areas: agriculture; African-American studies; American literature; American studies; the American West; anthropology and ethnology; creative nonfiction; environmental studies; history; the Great Plains; Jewish studies and Judaica; Latin American studies; military history; music; Native Americans and First Nations; natural history; Nebraskiana; philosophy and religion; photography; science fiction; sports history; translations; women's studies. Submissions are not invited in original poetry or fiction.

Journals: *American Indian Quarterly; Black Scholar: Journal of Black Studies and Research; French Forum; Frontiers: A Journal of Women's Studies; Legacy: A Journal of American Women Writers; Nebraska Review; NINE: A Journal of Baseball History & Culture; Nineteenth-Century French Studies; Prairie Schooner; River Teeth: A Journal of Nonfiction Narrative; Studies in American Indian Literatures; Studies in American Jewish Literature; symploke: A Journal for the Intermingling of Literary, Cultural, and Theoretical Scholarship; Women and Music: A Journal of Gender and Culture.*

Imprints: Bison Books

Book series: American Lives; American Indian Lives; Bach Perspectives; Bison Frontiers of Imagination; Blacks in the American West; Brahms Studies; Cather Studies; Complete Letters of Henry James; Critical Studies in the History of Anthropology; Engendering Latin America; European Women Writers; Fourth World Rising; French Modernist Library; Frontiers of Narrative; Great Campaigns of the Civil War; Great Plains Photography; Histories of Scandinavian Literature; History of the American West; Human Rights in International Perspective; Indians of the Southeast; Iroquoians and Their World; Jerry Malloy Book Prize; Jewish Writing in the Contemporary World; Journals of the Lewis and Clark Expedition; Key Issues of the Civil War Era; Latin American Women Writers; Law in the American West; Latin American Women Writers; Nebraska Symposium on Motivation; North American Beethoven Studies; North American Indian Prose Award; Our Sustainable Future; Politics and Governments of the American States; Post-Western Horizons; Publications of the Center for the History of Music Theory and Literature; Sources of American Indian Oral Literature; Stages; Studies in Jewish Civilization (for Creighton University Press); Studies in the Anthropology of North American Indians; Studies in the Native Languages of the Americas; Studies in War, Society, and the Military; Texts and Contexts; This Hallowed Ground: Guides to Civil War Battlefields; Vidal Sassoon International Center Studies in Antisemitism; Willa Cather Scholarly Edition; Women in German Yearbook; Women in the West.

Distributors for the Buros Institute of Mental Measurement, Dalkey Archive Press, Gordian Knot Books, the Kentucky Quilt Project, Lewis and Clark College, the Society for American Baseball Research, and Zoo Press.

University of Nevada Press

Reno Office:
Morrill Hall, Mail Stop 166
Reno, NV 89557-0076

Phone: (775) 784-6573
Fax: (775) 784-6200
Web site: www.nvbooks.nevada.edu

Canadian Representative:
Scholarly Book Services

Orders:
Phone: (877) NVBOOKS

Warehouse Address:
Terrawatt Facility
5625 Fox Avenue, Rm. 120
Reno, NV 89506

UK Representative:
Eurospan

Staff
Director: Joanne O'Hare (ext. 228; e-mail: johare@unr.edu)
Editorial: Joanne O'Hare
Managing Editor & Basque Acquisitions Editor: Sara Vélez Mallea (ext. 226; e-mail: velez@unr.edu)
  Project Editor: Michelle Filippini (ext. 234; e-mail: filippin@unr.edu)
Marketing Manager: Victoria Davies (ext. 232; e-mail: vickid@unr.nevada.edu)
Production Manager: TBA
Business: Sheryl Laguna (ext. 224; e-mail: sll@scs.unr.edu)
  Customer Service/Office Manager: Charlotte Eberhard Heatherly (ext. 222; e-mail: ceh@unr.edu)
  Warehouse Manager: Michael Jackson (e-mail: jackson@scs.unr.edu)

Full Member
Established: 1961
Title output 2002: 24
Titles currently in print: 283

Admitted to AAUP: 1982
Title output 2003: 30

Editorial Program
Scholarly books and serious fiction and nonfiction, with special interests in the history, literature, biography, anthropology, and natural history of Nevada, the Great Basin, and the West, and books dealing with the Basque peoples of Europe and the Americas. Additional interests include Native American studies; geography, natural resources, ethnic studies, and gambling.

Special series: Basque Studies; Environmental Arts and Humanities; The Gambling Studies; Great Basin Natural History; The Urban West; Western Literature; Wilbur S. Shepperson Series in Nevada History.

University Press of New England

Administrative, Editorial, Marketing
and Production Offices:
1 Court Street, Suite 250
Lebanon, NH 03766-1358

Phone: (603) 448-1533
Fax: (603) 448-7006
E-mail: university.press@dartmouth.edu
Indiv: (firstname.lastname)@dartmouth.edu
Web site: www.upne.com

Canadian Representative:
University of British Columbia Press/
Unipresses

Customer Service/Order Fulfillment
Phone: (800) 421-1561
(603) 643-5585 exts. 103 & 104

Customer Service, Sales, Business Office
and Warehouse/Distribution Center:
UPNE Centerra Distribution Center
37 Lafayette Street
Lebanon, NH 03766-1446
Phone: (603) 643-5585
Fax: (603) 643-1540

European Representative:
Eurospan

Staff

Director: Richard M. Abel (603/448-1533, ext. 211)
  Assistant to the Director, Editorial Assistant, & Permissions Manager: Susanna French
  (603/448-1533, ext. 201)
  Associate Director, Operations: Thomas Johnson (603/643-5585, ext. 202)
  Systems Administrator: David Bellows (603/643-5585, ext. 101)
Executive Editor: Phyllis Deutsch (603/448-1533, ext. 222)
  Acquisitions Editors: John Landrigan (603/448-1533, ext. 221); Ellen Wicklum (603/448-
  1533, ext. 225)
  Assistant Editor: Richard Pult (603/448-1533, ext. 226)
Manuscript Editorial: Mary Crittendon, Managing Editor (603/448-1533, ext. 243)
  Production Editors: Ann Brash (603/448-1533, ext. 244); Jessica Stevens (603/448-1533,
  ext. 217); Elizabeth Rawitsch (603/448-1533, ext. 235)
Marketing: Sarah L. Welsch, Associate Director, Marketing & Sales (603/643-5585, ext.
  203, or 603/448-1533, ext. 234)
  Sales and Trade Exhibits Manager: Sherri Strickland (603/643-5585, ext. 106)
  Publicity and Subsidiary Rights Manager: Barbara Briggs (603/448-1533, ext. 233)
  Direct Marketing, Advertising & Academic Exhibits Manager: TBA
  (603/448-1533, ext. 232)
  Marketing Associate: Sara J. Carpenter (603/448-1533, ext. 231)
Design and Production: Michael Burton, Assist. Director, Design and Production (603/448-
  1533, ext. 241)
  Designer: Katherine B. Kimball (603/448-1533, ext. 246)
  Production Coordinator: Douglas Tifft (603/448-1533, ext. 245)
Business (Centerra Offices): Thomas Johnson, Associate Director, Operations
  (603/643-5585, ext. 202)
  Accounting Supervisor: Sondra Farnham (603/643-5585, ext. 201)
  Accounting Associate: Timothy Semple (603/643-5585, ext. 102)

Customer Service Representatives: Barbara Benson (603/643-5585, ext. 103); Deborah Forward (603/643-5585, ext. 104)
Warehouse/Distribution: Anne Demers (603/643-5585, ext. 204); Ginger Harrington (603/643-5585, ext. 206); Jeffrey Gould; Michael Hoover (603/643-5585, ext. 205)

Full Member

Established: 1970   Admitted to AAUP: 1975
Title output 2002: 87   Title output 2003: 88
Titles currently in print: 900

Publishes books under the consortium member imprints of Brandeis University Press, Dartmouth College Press, University of New Hampshire Press, Tufts University Press, and University of Vermont Press, and University Press of New England.

Editorial Program

General trade, scholarly, instructional, and reference works for scholars, teachers, students, and the public. The Press concentrates in American studies, literature, history, religion, and cultural studies; art, architecture, photography, and material culture; ethics; ethnic studies (including African-American, Jewish, Native American, and Shaker studies); fiction; interdisciplinary studies; folklore, music, and popular culture; languages; nature and the environment; natural sciences; New England studies; social issues/social sciences; and Trans-Atlantic and cross-cultural studies. Special series feature such topics as civil society, modernism, and visual culture.

Special series: Becoming Modern: New Nineteenth-Century Studies; Brandeis Series in American Jewish History, Culture and Life; Brandeis Series on Jewish Women; Bread Loaf Anthologies; Civil Society: Historical and Contemporary Perspectives; Collected Writings of Rousseau; Hardscrabble Books: Fiction of New England; Interfaces: Studies in Visual Culture; Menahem Stern Jerusalem Lectures: Brandeis University/Historical Society of Israel; New England Health Books; Reencounters with Colonialism: New Perspectives on the Americas; Revisiting New England: The New Regionalism; Series in Environmental Studies; Tauber Institute for the Study of European Jewry Series; Understanding Science and Technology; Vermont Folklife Center's Children's Book Series.

The Press also distributes publications of Wesleyan University Press; Beinecke Rare Book and Manuscript Library of Yale University; Bibliopola Press; Chipstone Foundation; Connecticut Historical Society; Farnsworth Museum; Fence Books; Four Way Books; Israel Museum, Jerusalem; Library of Congress; Peabody Essex Museum; Peter E. Randall Publisher; Society for the Preservation of New England Antiquities; Sheep Meadow Press; Thistle Hill Publications; Vermont Folklife Center; Winterthur; and others.

University of New Mexico Press

MSCO1 01-1200
1720 Lomas Boulevard N.E.
Albuquerque, NM 87131-0001

Phone: (505) 277-2346
Fax: (505) 277-9270
E-mail: unmpress@unm.edu
Indiv: (user I.D.)@unm.edu
(unless otherwise indicated)
Web site: www.unmpress.com

Customer Service and Warehouse:
3721 Spirit Drive S.E.
Albuquerque, NM 87106
Phone: (505) 277-4810
Faxes: (505) 277-3350,
(800) 622-8667 (orders);
(505) 277-3350 (customer service)

UK and European Representative:
Gazelle Book Services

Staff

Director: Luther Wilson (e-mail: lwilson)
  Assistant to Director and Rights and Permissions: Sandi Keeton (e-mail: sandi@upress.unm.edu)
Associate Director and Editor-in-Chief: David V. Holtby (e-mail: dholtby)
  Acquisitions Editors: Elizabeth Hadas (e-mail: ehadas); David Holtby (e-mail: dholtby); Luther Wilson (e-mail: lwilson)
Managing Editor: Maya Allen-Gallegos (e-mail: mayag@upress.unm.edu)
Sales and Marketing: Glenda Madden, Manager (e-mail: gmadden)
  Advertising and Exhibits: Erica Martinez (e-mail: erica@upress.unm.edu)
  Promotion and Publicity: Nancy Woodard (e-mail: nwoodard)
  Publicist: Amanda Sutton (e-mail: amanda@upress.unm.edu)
  Sales/Remainder Manager: Sheri Hozier (e-mail: sherih)
Senior Graphic Designers: Melissa Tandysh (e-mail: melissat); Mina Yamashita (e-mail: minay@upress.unm.edu)
Business Manager: Richard Schuetz (e-mail: rschuetz@upress.unm.edu)
  Manager, Business Services: Ernest Earick (e-mail: earick)
  Accounting Tech: Lyudmila Markova (e-mail: milam)
  Customer Service and Credit Manager: Stewart Marshall (e-mail: smarshal)
  Customer Service Assistants: Cecilia Campos (e-mail: ccampos); Judy Kepler (e-mail: jkepler@upress.unm.edu); Nancy Wilson (e-mail: nwilson)
  Warehouse Manager: Rick Hays (e-mail: rickh@upress.unm.edu)
Network Manager: Mike Ritthaler (e-mail: mritthaler@upress.unm.edu)

Full Member

Established: 1929
Title output 2002: 67
Titles currently in print: 590

Admitted to AAUP: 1937
Title output 2003: 76

Editorial Program
Scholarly books and serious fiction, poetry, and nonfiction, with special interests in social and cultural anthropology; ethnic studies; archaeology; American frontier history; Western American literature; Latin American history; history of photography; art and photography; and books that deal with important aspects of Southwest or Rocky Mountain states, including natural history and land grant studies.

Special series, joint imprints and/or copublishing programs: Calvin P. Horn Lectures in Western History and Culture; Coyote Books; Dialogos Series; Historians of the Frontier and American West; Historical Society of New Mexico Publications; Histories of the American Frontier; Jewish Latin America; The Journals of Don Diego de Vargas; New American West; New Mexico Land Grant; Pasó por Aquí Series on the Nuevomexicano Literary Heritage; School of American Research Southwest Indian Arts; Tamarind Papers; University of Arizona Southwest Center; University of New Mexico Public Policy.

New York University Press

838 Broadway, 3rd Floor
New York, NY 10003-4812

Phone: (212) 998-2575
Fax: (212) 995-3833
E-mail: orders@nyupress.edu
Indiv: (firstname.lastname)@nyu.edu
Web site: www.nyupress.org

UK and European Representative:
Eurospan

Orders and Customer Service:
Phone: (800) 996-6987
Fax: (212) 995-4798

Warehouse:
The Maple Press
Lebanon Distribution Center
704 Legionnaire Drive
Fredricksburg, PA 17026

Staff
Director: Steve Maikowski (212/998-2573)
  Assistant to the Director and Subsidiary Rights Coordinator: Emily Turner (212/998-2571)
Acquisitions Editorial: Eric Zinner, Editor-in-Chief (cultural and literary studies, American studies, media studies, Latino studies; Asian-American studies) (212/998-2544)
  Editors: Ilene Kalish, Executive Editor (sociology, anthropology, politics, social science) (212/998-2556); Deborah Gershenowitz (American history, law) (212/998-2570); Jennifer Hammer (religion, Jewish studies, psychology) (212/998-2491)
  Assistant Editor: Emily Park (212/998-2426)
  Editorial Assistant: Salwa Jadabo (212/992-9995)
Manuscript Editorial/Design and Production: Despina P. Gimbel, Managing Editor (212/998-2572)
  Production Manager: Charles Hames (212/998-2628)
  Production Coordinator: Jonathan Bowen (212/998-2578)
  Production Assistant/Permissions Coordinator: Nicholas Taylor (212/992-9998)
Marketing and Sales: Fredric Nachbaur, Marketing and Sales Manager (212/998-2588)

Direct Mail Coordinator: Matthew Bucher (212/998-2558)
Publicist: Amanda Davis (212/992-9991)
Exhibits Coordinator/Sales Assistant: Erin McElroy (212/998-2547)
Business: Carline Yup, Business Manager (212/998-2569)
  Accounts Receivable Coordinator: Nadine Rached (212/992-9987)
  Sales Coordinator: Jesse Henderson (212/998-2546)
Computer and Information Systems: Stephen Kaldon, Information Systems Specialist
(212/998-2536)

Full Member

Established: 1916   Admitted to AAUP: 1937
Title output 2002:110   Title output 2003: 88
Titles currently in print: 1,600

Editorial Program

History; law; sociology; Asian-American studies; African-American studies; Latino/a studies,
political science; criminology; psychology; gender studies; cultural studies; media; literature
and literary criticism; urban studies; Jewish studies; anthropology; religion; reference; Balkan,
Middle Eastern, and Central Asian studies; American business; New York regional interest.

Special series: Alternative Criminology; American History and Culture; Critical America;
Clay Sanskrit Series; Cultural Front; Ex Machina: Law, Technology, and Society; Historic
Lives; The History of Disability; Nation of Newcomers: Immigrant History as American
History; Overcoming Series; Qualitative Studies in Psychology; Religion, Race, and
Ethnicity; Qualitative Studies in Religion: Main Trends of the Modern World; Sexual
Cultures.

NYU Press is the exclusive North American distributor for Monthly Review Press.

The University of North Carolina Press

116 South Boundary Street
Chapel Hill, NC 27514-3808

Phone: (919) 966-3561
Fax: (919) 966-3829
E-mail: uncpress@unc.edu
Indiv: (user I.D.)@unc.edu
Web site: www.uncpress.unc.edu

UK & European Representative:
Eurospan

Warehouse:
925 Branch Street
Chapel Hill, NC 27516-1417
Phone: (919) 942-5341

Orders:
Phone: (800) 848-6224
Fax: (800) 272-6817

Canadian Representative:
Scholarly Book Services

Staff

Director: Kate Douglas Torrey (ext. 223; e-mail: Kate_Torrey)
  Assistant to the Director: Catherine Fagan (ext. 223; e-mail: Catherine_Fagan)
Acquisitions Editorial: David Perry, Assistant Director and Editor-in-Chief (regional trade, Civil War) (ext. 240; e-mail: David_Perry)
  Assistant to the Editor-in-Chief: Katy O'Brien (ext. 238; e-mail: Katy_OBrien)
  Assistant Director and Senior Editor: Charles Grench (history, classics, political science) (ext. 242; e-mail: Charles_Grench)
  Assistant Editor and Assistant to Senior Editor: Amanda McMillan (ext. 246; e-mail: Amanda_McMillan)
  Editors: Elaine Maisner (religious studies, Latin American studies, anthropology, regional trade) (ext. 237; e-mail: Elaine_Maisner); Sian Hunter (literary studies, American studies, social medicine, gender studies) (ext. 239; e-mail: Sian_Hunter); Mark Simpson-Vos (special projects, regional reference, Native American studies, electronic projects) (ext. 238; e-mail: Mark_Simpson-Vos)
  Editorial Assistant: David Hines (ext. 265; e-mail: David_Hines)
Manuscript Editorial: Ron Maner, Managing Editor and Assistant Director (ext. 236; e-mail: Ron_Maner)
  Assistant Managing Editor/Electronic Manuscript Specialist: Pamela Upton (ext. 241; e-mail: Pam_Upton)
  Assistant Managing Editor: Paula Wald (ext. 229; e-mail: Paula_Wald)
  Editors: Mary Caviness (ext. 264; e-mail: Mary_Caviness); Paul Betz (ext. 228; e-mail: Paul_Betz); Stephanie Wenzel (ext. 247; e-mail: Stephanie_Wenzel)
  Assistant Editor: Brian Frazelle (ext. 266; e-mail: Brian_Frazelle)
Marketing: Kathleen Ketterman, Assistant Director and Marketing Manager (ext. 263; e-mail: Kathleen_Ketterman)
  Sales Director: Michael Donatelli (ext. 232; e-mail: Michael_Donatelli)
  Director of Publicity: Gina Mahalek (ext. 234; e-mail: Gina_Mahalek)
  Chief Copywriter and Catalog Coordinator: Ellen Bush (ext. 233; e-mail: Ellen_Bush)
  Director of Advertising and Electronic Marketing: Christine Egan (ext. 231; e-mail: Chris_Egan)
  Direct Marketing Manager and Restocks Coordinator: Laura Gribbon (ext. 230; e-mail: Laura_Gribbon)

Exhibits Manager and Awards Coordinator: Ivis Bohlen (ext. 235; e-mail: Ivis_Bohlen)
Publicity Assistant: Amy McDonald (ext. 244; e-mail: Amy_McDonald)
Sales and Marketing Assistant and Metadata Manager: Lori Burek (ext. 268; e-mail: Lori_Burek)
Marketing Designer: Catherine Brutvan (ext. 267; e-mail: Cat_Brutvan)
Design and Production: Richard Hendel, Associate Director and Design/Production Manager (ext. 250; e-mail: Rich_Hendel)
Assistant Production Manager: Heidi Perov (ext. 249; e-mail: Heidi_Perov)
Reprints Controller: Jackie Johnson (ext. 251; e-mail: Jackie_Johnson)
Compositor: Eric Brooks (ext. 245; e-mail: Eric_Brooks)
Composition and Journals Production Controller: Kim Bryant (ext. 226; e-mail: Kim_Bryant)
Journals: Suzi Waters, Journals Manager (ext. 256; e-mail: Suzi_Waters)
Business: Robbie Dircks, Associate Director & CFO (ext. 224; e-mail: Robbie_Dircks)
Rights & Contracts Manager: Vicky Wells (ext. 225; e-mail: Vicky_Wells)
Accounting Manager: Roy Alexander (ext. 254; e-mail: Roy_Alexander)
Customer Service/Credit Manager: Teresa Shoffner (ext. 258; e-mail: Teresa_Shoffner)
Office Manager: Alison Kieber (ext. 221; e-mail: Alison_Kieber)
Electronic Projects Coordinator: Marjorie Fowler (ext. 248; e-mail: Marjorie_Fowler)
Database Administrator/Website Administrator: Marcus McKoy (ext. 262; email: Marcus_McKoy)
Warehouse Manager: Randy Shoffner (919/942-5341)

Full Member

Established: 1922

Title output 2002: 117

Titles currently in print: 1,384

Admitted to AAUP: 1937

Title output 2003: 100

Journals published: 7

Editorial Program

American and European history; American and English literature; American studies; African-American studies; Southern studies; political science; folklore; religious studies; legal history; classics; gender studies; media studies; Native American studies; rural studies; urban studies; public policy; Latin American studies; anthropology; business and economic history; social medicine; regional trade; North Caroliniana; and the following journals: *Early American Literature*; *The High School Journal*; *Social Forces*; *Southern Cultures*; *Southern Literary Journal*, *Studies in Philology*, and *Southeastern Geographer*. Submissions are not invited in fiction, poetry, or drama.

Special Series: Bettie Allison Rand Lectures in Art History; Blythe Family Fund Series; Chapel Hill Books; Civil War America; Cultural Studies of the United States; Dental Laboratory Technology Manuals; Dental Assisting Manuals; Envisioning Cuba; The Fred W. Morrison Series in Southern Studies; Gender and American Culture; H. Eugene and Lillian Youngs Lehman Series; Islamic Civilization and Muslim Networks; James Sprunt Studies in History and Political Science; The John Hope Franklin Series in African American History and Culture; Latin America in Translation/en Traducción/em Traducão; Luther H. Hodges Series in Business, Society, and the State; Military Campaigns of the Civil War; The New Cold War History; New Directions in Southern Studies; Richard Hampton Jenrette Series in Architecture and the Decorative Arts; Studies in Comparative Literature; Studies in Rural Culture; Studies in Social Medicine; Studies in Legal History; Studies in the Germanic

Languages and Literature; Studies in the History of Greece and Rome; Studies in the Romance Languages and Literatures; Thornton H. Brooks Series in American Law and Society.

Joint imprints: Omohundro Institute of Early American History and Culture, sponsored by Colonial Williamsburg and the College of William and Mary.

Copublication programs: Museum of Early Southern Decorative Arts, Winston-Salem.

The Press distributes titles published by the Thomas Jefferson Foundation.

The University of North Texas Press

Street Address:
1820 Highland Street
Bain Hall 101
Denton, TX 76201

Mailing Address:
P.O. Box 311336
Denton, TX 76203

Phone: (940) 565-2142
Fax: (940) 565-4590
E-mail: (user I.D.)@unt.edu
Web site: www.unt.edu/untpress

Orders:
Phone: (800) 826-8911

UK Representative:
Eurospan

Canadian Representative:
Cariad Services

Staff
Director: Ron Chrisman (e-mail: rchrisman)
  Assistant to the Director: Mary Young (e-mail: myoung)
Managing Editor: Karen DeVinney (e-mail: kdevinney)
Assistant Editor: Paula Oates (e-mail: poates)

Full Member
Established: 1988
Title output 2002: 14
Titles currently in print: 253

Admitted to AAUP: 2003
Title output 2003: 14

Editorial Program
Humanities and social sciences, with special emphasis on Texas history and culture, military history, western history, criminal justice, folklore, multi-cultural topics, music, natural and environmental history, culinary history, and women's studies. Submissions in poetry and fiction are invited only through the Vassar Millar and Katherine Anne Porter Prize competition.

Special series: A. C. Greene; Al Filo: Mexican American Studies; Contemporary Issues and Debates; Evelyn Oppenheimer; Frances B. Vick; Great American Cooking; Katherine Anne Porter Prize in Short Fiction; North Texas Crime and Criminal Justice; North Texas Military Biography and Memoir; Philosophy and the Environment; Practical Guide; Publications of the Texas Folklore Society; Temple Big Thicket; Texas Poets; Texas Writers; Vassar Miller Prize in Poetry; War and the Southwest; and Western Life.

Northeastern University Press

Street Address:
716 Columbus Avenue, Suite 416
Boston, MA 02120-2111

Mailing Address:
360 Huntington Avenue, 416CP
Boston, MA 02115-5096

Phone: (617) 373-5480
Fax: (617) 373-5483
E-mail: (user I.D)@neu.edu
Web site: www.nupress.neu.edu

Distribution Center:
Northeastern University Press
CUP Services
750 Cascadilla Street
Ithaca, NY 14850

UK and European Representative:
Eurospan

Orders/Customer Service:
Phone: (800) 666-2211; (607) 277-2211
Fax: (800) 688-2877

Staff
Acting Director: Jill Bahcall (617/373-5481; e-mail: j.bahcall)
Production Director: Ann Twombly (617/373-5477; e-mail: a.twombly)

Full Member
Established: 1977
Title output 2002: 35
Distributed titles 2003: 2

Admitted to AAUP: 1984
Title output 2003: 35
Titles currently in print: 422

Editorial Program
American history, American studies, criminal justice, ethnic and women's literature, law and society, literature, music, political science, women's studies, books of regional interest.

Special Series: Northeastern Classics Editions; The Northeastern Library of Black Literature; The Northeastern Series of Feminist Theory; The Samuel French Morse Poetry Prize; New England Studies; Women's Life Writings from Around the World; The Northeastern Series in Transnational Crime; The Northeastern Series in Criminal Behavior; The Northeastern Series on Gender, Crime, and Law.

The Press also distributes books from the Massachusetts Historical Society and selected titles from the National Museum of Women in the Arts.

Northern Illinois University Press

310 Fifth Street
DeKalb, IL 60115

Phone: (815) 753-1826
Fax: (815) 753-1845
E-mail: (user id)@niu.edu
Web site: www.niu.edu/univ_press

Customer Service:
Phone: (815) 753-1826

Order Fulfillment:
Phone: (815) 753-1075

UK Distributor:
Eurospan

Staff

Director: Mary Lincoln (815/753-1826; e-mail: mlincoln)
Acquisitions Editorial: Melody Herr (815/753-9907; e-mail: mherr)
Manuscript Editorial: Susan Bean, Managing Editor (815/753-9908; e-mail: sbean)
  Manuscript Editor: Kelly Parker (815/753-9906; e-mail: kparker)
Marketing and Sales: Sarah Atkinson, Marketing Manager (815/753-9905: e-mail: satkinson)
Design and Production Manager: Julie Fauci (815/753-9904; e-mail: jfauci)
Business and Warehouse: Barbara Berg, Business Manager (815/753-1826; e-mail: bberg)
  Order Processing: Pat Yenerich (815/753-1075; e-mail: pyenerich)

Full Member

Established: 1964
Title output 2002: 21
Titles currently in print: 285

Admitted to AAUP: 1972
Title output 2003: 18

Editorial Program

US history; US Civil War; European history; Russian history and culture; philosophy; political science; cultural studies; literary criticism, history, and theory; American literature; British literature; anthropology; transportation studies; ethnic studies; women's studies; studies on Chicago and the Midwest.

Special series, joint imprints, and/or copublishing programs: Russian Studies, Railroads in America.

Northwestern University Press

629 Noyes Street
Evanston, IL 60208-4210

Phone: (847) 491-2046
Fax: (847) 491-8150
E-mail: nupress@northwestern.edu
Indiv: (user I.D.)@northwestern.edu
Web site: www.nupress.northwestern.edu

Orders:
Northwestern University Press
Chicago Distribution Center
11030 South Langley Avenue
Chicago, IL 60628
Phone: (800) 621-2736; (773) 568-1550
Fax: (800) 621-8476; (773) 660-2235

UK Distributor:
Eurospan

Canadian Distributor:
Cariad, Ltd.

Staff

Director: Donna Shear (847/491-8111; e-mail: d-shear)
  Rights and Permissions Manager/Assistant Acquisitions Editor: Rachel Zonderman
  Delaney (847/491-7384; e-mail: rdelaney)
Editor-in-Chief: Susan Betz (847/491-8112; e-mail: s-betz)
  Senior Project Editor: Amy Schroeder (847/467-7362; e-mail: a-schroeder)
  Project Editor: Collette Stockton (847/491-8116; e-mail: c-stockton)
Electronic Manuscript Editor: Serena Roschman (847/491-2458; e-mail s-roschman)
Publicity Manager: Laura Leichum (847/491-5315; e-mail: lleichum)
  Sales Coordinator: Parneshia Jones (847/491-7420; e-mail: p-jones3)
  Sales Representatives: Blake Delodder (301/322-4509; e-mail:
  bdelodder@press.uchicago.edu); Gary Hart (323/663-3529; e-mail:
  ghart@press.uchicago.edu); Bailey Walsh (608/218-1669; e-mail:
  bwalsh@press.uchicago.edu); Luis Borella (206/932-3013; e-mail: luis@redsides.com);
  Henry Hubert (303/422-8640; e-mail: hjhubert@earthlink.net); Don Morrison (800/446-
  4095; 615/269-8977; e-mail: msgbooks@aol.com); Bill Verner (919/286-4839; e-mail:
  vermin@mindspring.com); Arthur Viders (813/886-4868; e-mail:
  aviders@tampabay.rr.com)
Art Director: Marianne Jankowski (847/467-5368)
Production Manager: Michael Brooks (847/491-8113; e-mail: m-brooks2)
TriQuarterly Associate Editor: Ian Morris (847/467-7351; e-mail: i-morris)
Assistant Business Manager: Kirstie Felland (847/491-8310; e-mail: kfelland)

Full Member

Established: 1959
Title output 2002: 52
Titles currently in print: 900

Admitted to AAUP: 1988
Title output 2003: 45
Journals published: 2

Editorial Program

The Press publishes in drama/performance studies; Chicago region; fiction; poetry; Latino
fiction and biography; literary criticism; literature in translation; law; philosophy; Slavic
studies; and the following journals: *TriQuarterly* and *Renaissance Drama*.

  Special Series: Avant-Garde and Modernism Studies; European Classics; European Drama
Classics; European Poetry Classics; Jewish Lives; Law-in-Context; Marlboro Travel; The

Northwestern-Newberry Edition of the Writings of Herman Melville; Rethinking Theory; Studies in Phenomenology and Existential Philosophy; Studies in Russian Literature and Theory; Topics in Historical Philosophy; Writings from an Unbound Europe.
Imprints: Hydra Books; TriQuarterly Books; The Marlboro Press; Latino Voices.
Distributed Presses: FC2; Glas; Jannes Art Press; Paper Mirror Press; Tia Chucha Press.

University of Notre Dame Press

310 Flanner Hall
Notre Dame, IN 46556

Phone: (574) 631-6346
Fax: (574) 631-8148
E-mail: nd.undpress.1@nd.edu
Indiv: (user I.D.)@nd.edu
Web site: www.undpress.nd.edu

Orders:
University of Notre Dame Press
Chicago Distribution Center
11030 South Langley Avenue
Chicago, IL 60628
Phone: (800) 621-2736
Fax: (800) 621-8476

UK and European Representative:
Eurospan

Staff
Director: Barbara Hanrahan (574/631-3265; e-mail: hanrahan.4)
Acquisitions Editor: TBA
　Editorial Assistant: Lowell Francis (574/631-4913; e-mail: francis.24)
　Secretary: Gina Bixler (574/631-6346; e-mail: bixler.1)
Manuscript Editorial: Rebecca DeBoer, Managing Editor (574/631-4908; e-mail: deboer.8)
　Assistant Editor: Katie Lehman (574/631-4911; e-mail: mlehman.2)
Marketing: Julie Beckwith, Manager (574/631-3267; e-mail: beckwith.7)
　Assistant Manager: Ann Bromley (574/631-4910; e-mail: bromley.1)
　Exhibits Coordinator: Beth VerVerlde (574/631-4905; e-mail: vervelde.1)
Design and Production: Wendy McMillen, Manager (574/631-4907; e-mail: mcmillen.3)
　Assistant Production Manager: Emily McKnight (574/631-3266; e-mail: mcknight.3)
　Art Director and Web Administrator: Margaret Gloster (574/631-4906; e-mail: gloster.1)
Business: Diane Schaut, Manager (574/631-4904; e-mail: schaut.1)
　Assistant: Deborah Campbell (574/631-8680; e-mail: campbell.87)

Full Member
Established: 1949
Title output 2002: 53
Titles currently in print: 840

Admitted to AAUP: 1959
Title output 2003: 52
Journals published: 1

Editorial Program
Religion; theology; philosophy; ethics; political science; medieval studies; classics; Catholic studies; business ethics; American history; European history; Latin American studies; religion and literature; Irish studies; history and philosophy of science; international relations; peace studies; patristics; political theory; and the journal *US Catholic Historian*. Submissions are not invited in the hard sciences, mathematics, psychology, or novel-length fiction.

Special series, joint imprints, and/or copublishing programs: Andrés Montoya Poetry Prize; Christianity and Judaism in Antiquity; The Collected Works of Jacques Maritain; Contemporary European Politics and Society; Erasmus Institute Publications; Ernest Sandeen Prize in Poetry; Faith and Reason; The Irish in America; Kellogg Institute for International Studies; The Medieval Book; Publications in Medieval Studies; Notre Dame Texts in Medieval Culture; Poetics of Orality and Literacy; Richard Sullivan Prize in Short Fiction; Studies in American Catholicism; Studies in Spirituality and Theology; Thomistic Studies; Ward-Phillips Lectures in English Language and Literature; William and Katherine Devers Series in Dante Studies; The Works of Cardinal Newman Collected.

Ohio University Press

Scott Quadrangle
Athens, OH 45701-2979

Phone: (740) 593-1155
Fax: (740) 593-4536
E-mail: (user I.D.)@ohio.edu
Web site: www.ohiou.edu/oupress/

UK and European Representative:
Eurospan

Orders:
Ohio University Press
Chicago Distribution Center
11030 South Langley Avenue
Chicago, IL 60628
Phone: (800) 621-2736
Fax: (800) 621-8476

Canadian Representative:
Cariad, Ltd.

Staff
Director: David Sanders (740/593-1157; e-mail: dsanders1)
Senior Editor: Gillian Berchowitz (740/593-1159; e-mail: berchowi)
Managing Editor: Nancy Basmajian (740/593-1161; e-mail: basmajia)
   Project Editors: Sharon Rose (740/597-1592; e-mail: roses); Rick Huard (740/597-1941; e-mail: huard)
Marketing and Sales: Richard Gilbert, Marketing Manager (740/593-1160; e-mail: gilbert)
   Publicity Manager: Jeff Kallet (740/593-1158; e-mail: kallet)
   Marketing Associate: Carolyn King (740/597-2998; e-mail: kingc3)
Production Manager: Beth Pratt (740/593-1162; e-mail: prattb)
Business: Bonnie Rand, Chief Financial Officer (740/593-1156; e-mail: rand)
   Customer Service Manager: Judy Wilson (740/593-1154; e-mail: wilson1)

Full Member
Established: 1964
Title output 2002: 47
Titles currently in print: 780

Admitted to AAUP: 1966
Title output 2003: 50

Editorial Program

Special series, joint imprints, and/or copublishing programs: African Series; The Complete Works of Robert Browning; The Complete Works of William Howard Taft; The Collected Letters of George Gissing; Eastern African Series; Gender and Ethnicity in Appalachia; Global and Comparative Studies; Latin America Series; Law, Society, and Politics in the Midwest; Ohio Bicentennial; Perspectives on the History of Congress and Perspectives on the Art and Architecture of the United States Capitol (for the US Capitol Historical Society); Polish and Polish-American Studies Series; Research in International Studies; Series in Continental Thought; Series in Ecology and History; Southeast Asia Series; Western African Series; White Coat Pocket Guide.

The Ohio State University Press

180 Pressey Hall
1070 Carmack Road
Columbus, Ohio 43210-1002

Phone: (614) 292-6930
Fax: (614) 292-2065
E-mail: ohiostatepress@osu.edu
Indiv: (user I.D.)@osu.edu
Web site: www.ohiostatepress.org

Orders:
The Ohio State University Press
Chicago Distribution Center
11030 South Langley Avenue
Chicago, IL 60628
Phone: (800) 621-2736
Fax: (800) 624-8476

Staff

Director: Malcolm Litchfield (614/292-7818; e-mail: litchfield.6)
 Permissions Coordinator and Assistant to the Director: Patt McLaughlin (614/292-6930; e-mail: mclaughlin.111)
Acquisitions Editorial:
 Editors: Heather Miller (history, literature, women's studies, women and health, urban studies) (614/292-3668; e-mail: miller.1438); Malcolm Litchfield (political science, business history) (614/292-7818; e-mail: litchfield.6); Eugene O'Connor (classics) (614/ 292-3667; e-mail: oconnor.136)
Manuscript Editorial: Eugene O'Connor, Managing Editor (614/292-3667; e-mail: oconnor.136)
 Copyediting Coordinator: Maggie Diehl (614/247-6996; e-mail: diehl.48)
Marketing: Laurie Avery, Manager (614/292-1462; e-mail: avery.21)
 Marketing Assistant: Linda Aselton Patterson (614/292-6824; e-mail: patterson.52)
Design and Production:
 Production Coordinators: Jason Stauter (614/292-3686; e-mail: stauter.1); Jennifer Forsythe (614/292-3550; e-mail: forsythe.36)
Journals: Eavon Lee Mobley, Manager (614/292-3666; e-mail: mobley.2)
 Journals Subscription Manager: Jodie Moffett (614/292-1407; e-mail: moffett.8)
 Editorial Assistant: Marie Bontempo (614/292-3664; e-mail: bontempo.1)
Business: Kathleen Edwards, Assistant Director (614/292-3692; e-mail: edwards.206)

Full Member

Established: 1957
Title output 2002: 26
Titles currently in print: 290

Admitted to AAUP: 1961
Title output 2003: 25
Journals published: 5

Editorial Program

Scholarly studies with special interests in American history; business and economic history; history of crime; classics, literary criticism; political science; regional studies; urban studies; Victorian studies; women's health; and gender and sexuality studies.

Journals: *Geographical Analysis; Journal of Higher Education; Journal of Money, Credit and Banking; Narrative; American Periodicals.*

Special Series: The Centenary Edition of the Works of Nathanial Hawthorne; The Complete Works of Aphra Behn; The History of Crime and Criminal Justice; Historical Perspectives on Business Enterprise; The Ohio State University/ The Journal Award in Poetry; The Ohio State University Prize in Short Fiction; Parliaments and Legislatures; The Theory and Interpretation of Narrative; Urban Life and Urban Landscape; Victorian Critical Interventions; Women and Health; Vascular Flora of Ohio.

The Press distributes the publications of The Accounting Hall of Fame at The Ohio State University.

University of Oklahoma Press

2800 Venture Drive
Norman, OK 73069

Phone: (405) 325-2000
Faxes: (405) 325-4000 (director/rights/acquisitions/marketing);
(405) 307-9048 (manuscript editing/production/finance)
E-mail: (user I.D.)@ou.edu
Web site: www.oupress.com

Orders:
Phone: (800) 627-7377)
Fax: (405) 364-5798; (800) 735-0476

UK Representative:
Aldington Books

Canadian Representative:
Hargreaves, Fuller & Co.

Staff

Director: John Drayton (405/325-3189; e-mail: jdrayton)
  Secretary to the Director: Minna Fielding (405/325-3189; e-mail: mfielding)
  Rights and Permissions: Angelika Tietz (405/325-5326; e-mail: atietz)
Editorial: Charles E. (Chuck) Rankin, Associate Director and Editor-in-Chief (405/325-5609; e-mail: cerankin)
  Acquisitions: TBA (regional studies and textbooks); John Drayton (classical studies) (405/325-3189; e-mail: jdrayton); Alessandra Jacobi (Native American and Latin American studies) (405/325-2365; e-mail: jacobi); Charles E. (Chuck) Rankin (American West, military history) (405/325-5609; e-mail: cerankin); Karen Wieder (literature) (405/325-2916; e-mail: kwieder)

Manuscript Editing: Alice K. Stanton, Managing Editor (405/325-4922; e-mail: astanton)
Associate Editors: Julie Shilling (405/325-3268; e-mail jshilling); Marian Stewart (405/325-7991; e-mail: mstewart)
Marketing and Sales: Dale Bennie, Assistant Director and Sales/Marketing Manager (405/325-3207; e-mail: dbennie)
Publicity: Caroline Dwyer Gilley (802/656-9105, fax 802/656-9106; e-mail: cdwyer)
Assistant Sales Manager (Exhibits): Jo Ann Reece (405/325-2734; e-mail: jreece)
Advertising Manager (Direct Mail): Joy Warren (405/325-3202; e-mail: joywarren)
Designer: Tony Roberts (405/325-4283; e-mail: tonyroberts)
Production: Patsy Willcox, Assistant Director and Production Manager (405/325-3186; e-mail: pwillcox)
Assistant Production Manager: Connie Arnold (405/325-3185; e-mail: carnold)
Production Editor: Susan Garrett (405/325-2408; e-mail: sgarrett)
Business: Diane Cotts, Assistant Director and Chief Financial Officer (405/325-3276; e-mail: dcotts)
Distribution and Operations Manager: Rick Stinchcomb (405/325-2013; e-mail: rstinchcomb)
Office Manager: Charolette Hackney (405/325-2326; e-mail: chackney)
Customer Service: Kathy Benson (405/325-2287; e-mail: kbenson)
Accounts Receivable: Martha Eaton (405/325-2443; e-mail: meaton)

Full Member
Established: 1928

Admitted to AAUP: 1937

Title output 2002: 90

Title output 2003: 79

Titles currently in print: 1,045

Editorial Program
Scholarly books, general nonfiction, and fiction with special interests in the American West, Native America, Latin America, area studies, Classics, language and literature, art, archaeology, political science, and natural history.

Special Series: American Exploration and Travel; American Indian Literature and Critical Studies; Animal Natural History; Campaigns and Commanders; Chicana and Chicano Visions of the Americas; Civilization of the American Indian; Congressional Studies; Gilcrease-Oklahoma Series on Western Art and Artists; Julian J. Rothbaum Distinguished Lecture Series; Literature of the American West; Sam Noble Oklahoma Museum of Natural History Publications; Oklahoma Series in Classical Culture; Oklahoma Western Biographies; Series for Science and Culture; Variorum Chaucer; and Western Frontier Library.

Oregon State University Press

102 Adams Hall
Corvallis, OR 97331-2005

Phone: (541) 737-3166
Fax: (541) 737-3170
E-mail: osu.press@oregonstate.edu
Indiv: (user I.D.) @oregonstate.edu
Web site: oregonstate.edu/dept/press/

Order Fulfillment & Distribution:
The University of Arizona Press
330 S. Toole, Suite 200
Tucson, AZ 85701
Phone: (800) 426-3797;
(520) 626-4218 (in Arizona & outside
continental US)

Canadian Distributor:
University of British Columbia Press

Staff

Director: Karen Orchard (541/737-3864; e-mail: karen.orchard)
Acquisitions Editor: Mary Elizabeth Braun (541/737-3873; e-mail: mary.braun)
Managing Editor & Production Manager: Jo Alexander (541/737-3866; e-mail: jo.alexander)
Marketing Manager: Tom Booth (503/796-0547; Fax: 503/796-0549; e-mail:
  tbooth@teleport.com)
Business Manager: Pennie Coe (541/737-3872; e-mail: pennie.coe)

Affiliate Member

Established: 1961
Title output 2002: 14
Titles currently in print: 167

Admitted to AAUP: 1991
Title output 2003: 12

Editorial Program

The Oregon State University Press primarily publishes books dealing with the history, natural history, cultures, and literature of the Pacific Northwest, as well as natural resources and natural resource issues.

Oxford University Press

Editorial Offices:
198 Madison Avenue
New York, NY 10016
Phone: (212) 726-6000
Fax: (212) 726-6440
E-mail: (firstname.lastname)@oup.com
Web site: www.oup.com

Customer Service:
Orders/Prices: (800) 451-7556
Inquiries: (800) 445-9714
ELT: (800) 441-5445
Journals: (800) 852-7323
Music Retail: (800) 292-0639
Fax: (919) 677-1303

UK Office:
Walton Street
Oxford OX2 6DP
United Kingdom
Phone: +44 1865 353767
Fax: +44 1865 353646

Canadian Office:
70 Wynford Drive
Don Mills, ON M3C 1J9
Canada
Phone: (416) 441-2941
Fax: (416) 444-0427

Distribution Center &
Journals Office:
2001 Evans Road
Cary, NC 27513
Phone: (919) 677-0977
Dist. Fax: (919) 677-8877
Journals Fax: (919) 677-1714

English Language Teaching:
Phone: (212) 726-6300
Fax: (212) 726-6389

Staff

President: Laura N. Brown
   Assistant to the President: Arlene Jacks
Executive Vice President and Chief Operating Officer: Barbara Wasserman
   Assistant to the Chief Operating Officer: Mai Plummer
Senior Vice President and Chief Financial Officer: Ellen Taus
   Assistant to the Chief Financial Officer: Elizabeth Himmelsbach
Senior Vice President: Brinton Strode (distribution/MIS)
Vice Presidents: Joan Bossert (associate publisher, academic science); Ellen Chodosh (trade publisher); Casper Grathwohl (publisher, professional/scholarly reference and on-line); Karen Day (associate publisher, professional/scholarly reference); Niko Pfund (publisher, academic and professional); Christopher Rogers (higher education publisher); Nancy Toff (young adult reference); Evan Schnittman (business development)
Academic and Professional
   Publisher: Niko Pfund
   Editorial: Joan Bossert (science and professional books); Catharine Carlin (psychology); Terry Vaughn (finance and economics); Dedi Felman (law, politics, and sociology); Susan Ferber (world history); Bill Lamsback & Marion Osman (medicine); Peter Prescott (life sciences); Elissa Morris (literature and classics); Peter Ohlin (philosophy and linguistics); Fiona Stevens (medicine); Cynthia Read (religion); Kim Robinson (music); Carrie Pedersen (epidemiology)

Marketing: Greg Bussy (medicine); Michael Groseth (academic, humanities, and social sciences); Michael Sieden (science and professional books)

Editing/Design/Production: Nancy Hoagland

Higher Education

Publisher: Chris Rogers

Editorial: Janet Beatty (English); Peter Coveney (history); Danielle Christensen (engineering); Peter Labella (media studies and popular culture, politics and sociology); Robert Miller (philosophy, religion, and classics)

Marketing and Sales: Scott Burns

Editing/Design/Production: Elyse Dubin (higher education and medicine)

Trade

Publisher: Ellen Chodosh

Editorial: Peter Ginna (trade); Donald Kraus (Bibles); Linda Robbins (trade paperbacks); Elda Rotor (trade); Timothy Bartlett (trade)

Marketing: Dino Battista (trade); Kurt Hettler (trade paperbacks)

Publicity: Sara Leopold (trade)

Sales: Hargis Thomas (Bibles)

Editing/Design/Production: Ruth Manes

Design and Production: Brice Hammack

Reference & Online

Publisher: Casper Grathwohl

Associate Publisher: Karen Day

Director Marketing & Sales: Rebecca Seger

Associate Director Marketing & Sales: Lisa Nachtigall

Editorial: Timothy DeWerff (dev. and production); Stephen Wagley (humanities and social sciences); Erin McKean (US dictionaries); Nancy Toff (young adult reference); Stephen Wagley (humanities and social sciences)

Marketing and Sales: John Perata (schools reference); Doug Doremus (library sales); Rebecca Seger (scholarly reference); Christine Kuan (Grove Art)

Business Development

Vice President-Director: Evan Schnittman

Director of Technology & Producer Online EDP & Technology: Corey Podolsky

Director Subsidiary Rights: Margie Mueller

Manager—Foreign Rights: Ashley Mabbitt

Sales

Director of Sales: TBA

Director—Trade Sales: Thomas Willshire

Associate Sales Director: William Johnson

Manager—Special Sales: Vera Plummer

Mary Jarrad (trade sales)

Operations

Executive Vice President and Chief Operating Officer: Barbara Wasserman

Brinton Strode (distribution—Cary); Helene Klappert (human resources); Dennis Teston (manufacturing and design); Judith Lanham (publishing database); Terese Dickerson (office services)

Finance

Senior Vice President and Chief Financial Officer: Ellen Taus

Director of Financial Analysis: William Weinberg

Music
  Director, US Music: Christopher Johnson
  Frances Levy (rights and rental library); Louis Fifer (sales and marketing); Sean Finnegan (production); Brian Hill (copyrights and promotions)
English Language Teaching Division
  Deputy Managing Director: Neil Butterfield
  Executive Publishers: Nancy Leonhardt and Janet Aitchison
  Managing Editor: Judith Cunninghan
  Marketing and Sales: TBA
  Production: Shanta Persaud (United States)
  Design: Lynn Luchetti
Journals (North Carolina)
  Erich Staib (manager); Carolyn Wilson (US subscriber services); Patricia Hudson (marketing manager)
Distribution Center:
  Kenneth Guerin (inventory planning/control); Banks Honeycutt (credit and collection); Donna Jones (customer service); Cameron Shaw (warehouse operations); Dottie Warlick (accounting services); Daniel Wingard (Cary facilities); Marilyn Okrent (human resources); Lee West (information services)

Full Member

Established: 1895	Admitted to AAUP: 1950
Title output 2002: 1,917	Title output 2003: 2,138
Titles currently in print: 19,848	Journals published (US only): 36

Editorial Program
Scholarly monographs; general nonfiction; Bibles; college textbooks; medical books; music; reference books; journals; children's books; English language teaching. Submissions are not invited in the area of fiction.

The following Oxford journals are published in the US: *American Journal of Epidemiology*; *American Law and Economics Review*; *American Literary History*; *Behavioral Ecology*; *Brief Treatment and Crisis Intervention*; *Clinical Psychology: Science and Practice*; *Communication Theory*; *Contemporary Economic Policy*; *Economic Inquiry*; *Enterprise & Society: The International Journal of Business History*; *Environmental Practice*; *Glycobiology*; *Holocaust and Genocide Studies*; *Human Communication Research*; *Journal of Communication*; *Journal of Deaf Studies and Deaf Education*; *Journal of Econometrics*; *Journal of Heredity*; *Journal of Law, Economics, & Organization*; *Journal of Pediatric Psychology*; *Journal of Public Administration Research and Theory*; *Journal of the American Academy of Religion*; *Journal of the History of Medicine and Allied Sciences*; *Journal of the National Cancer Institute*; *Journal of Urban Health*; *Modern Judaism*; *Molecular Biology and Evolution*; *The Musical Quarterly*; *The Opera Quarterly*; *Political Analysis*; *Psychotherapy Research*; *Public Health Reports*; *Public Opinion Quarterly*; *The Review of Financial Studies*; *Social Politics*; *Toxicological Sciences*; *The World Bank Economic Review*; and *The World Bank Research Observer*.

University of Pennsylvania Press

4200 Pine Street
Philadelphia, PA 19104-4011

Phone: (215) 898-6261
Fax: (215) 898-0404
E-mail: (user I.D.)@pobox.upenn.edu
Web site: www.upenn.edu/pennpress

Warehouse & Returns:
Maple Press Company
Lebanon Distribution Center
704 Legionnaire Drive
Fredericksburg, PA 17026

UK Representative:
University Presses Marketing

Order Department:
P.O. Box 50370
Baltimore, MD 21211-4370
Phone: (800) 537-5487
Fax: (410) 516-6998
E-mail (inquiries only):
custerv@pobox.upenn.edu

Canadian Representative:
Scholarly Book Services

Staff

Director: Eric Halpern (215/898-1672; e-mail: ehalpern)
  Assistant to the Director: Christopher Jack (215/898-6263; e-mail: cjack)
Acquisitions: Peter Agree, Social Sciences Editor (anthropology, human rights, political
  science) (215/573-3816; e-mail: agree); Jerome E. Singerman, Humanities Editor (humanities, Jewish studies) (215/898-1681; e-mail: singerma); Jo Joslyn (art & architecture) (215/
  898-5754; e-mail: joslyn); Eric Halpern (classics, ancient history) (215/898-6263; e-mail:
  ehalpern); Robert Lockhart (American history, regional books) (215/898-1677; e-mail:
  rlockhar)
  Acquisitions Assistants: Theodore Mann (215/898-3252; e-mail: tcmann); Eleanor
  Goldberg (215/898-6262; e-mail: ejg)
Manuscript Editing and Production: George Lang, Editing & Production Manager (215/
  898-1675; e-mail: gwlang)
  Managing Editor: Alison Anderson (215/898-1678; e-mail: anderaa)
  Associate Managing Editor: Erica Ginsburg (215/898-1679; e-mail: eginsbur)
  Design Coordinator: John Hubbard (215/573-6118; e-mail: wmj)
  Editing & Production Coordinator: Renee Ricker (215/898-7588; e-mail: ricker)
  Editorial/Production Assistant: Susan Staggs (215/898-1676; e-mail: sstaggs)
Marketing: Laura Waldron, Marketing Director (215/898-1673; e-mail: lwaldron)
  Rights & Publicity Manager: Jessica Pigza (215/898-1674; e-mail: jpigza)
  Direct Mail & Advertising Manager: Laura Lindquist (215/898-9184; e-mail: laurajl)
  Rights & Reprints Administrator: Francisco Aguirre (215/898-8678; e-mail: faguirre)
  Marketing Assistant: Laura Giuliani (215/898-6264; e-mail: laa)
Business: Julie Schilling, Business Manager (215/898-1670; e-mail: juliesch)
  Financial Coordinator: Kathy Ranalli (215/898-1682; e-mail: ranalli)
  Customer Service Representative: Marlene DeBella (215/898-1671; e-mail: custserv)

Full Member

Established: 1890   Admitted to AAUP: 1967

Title output 2002: 76   Title output 2003: 78

Titles currently in print: 975

Editorial Program

Scholarly and semipopular nonfiction, with special interests in American history and culture; ancient, medieval, and Renaissance studies; anthropology; landscape architecture; studio arts; human rights; Jewish studies; Pennsylvania regional studies; and the following journals. *Early American Studies, Hispanic Review, Journal of the Early Republic, Jewish Quarterly Review,* and *PaleoAnthropology.*

Special series, joint imprints, and/or copublishing programs: The Arts and Intellectual Life in Modern America; Contemporary Ethnography; Critical Authors & Issues; Divinations: Rereading Late Ancient Religion; Early American Studies; Encounters with Asia; Ethnography of Political Violence; Jewish Culture and Contexts; Material Texts; Metropolitan Portraits; Middle Ages Series; Penn Studies in Landscape Architecture; Pennsylvania Studies in Human Rights; Personal Takes; Politics and Culture in Modern America; Rethinking the Americas.

The Press copublishes selected titles in the series The Complete Potter and Ceramics Handbooks. Pine Street Books is a trade imprint.

The Pennsylvania State University Press

820 North University Drive
University Park, PA 16802-1003

Phone: (814) 865-1327
Fax: (814) 863-1408
E-mail: (user I.D.)@psu.edu
Web site: www.psupress.org

Orders:
Phone: (800) 326-9180
Fax: (877) 778-2665

UK Representative:
Eurospan

Canadian Distributor:
University of Toronto Press

Staff
Director: Sanford G. Thatcher (e-mail: sgt3)
Acquisitions Editorial: Peter J. Potter, Editor-in-Chief (e-mail: pjp8)
  Art History and Humanities Editor: Gloria Kury (e-mail: gxk17)
  Editorial Assistants: Stephanie Grace (e-mail: sjg166); Sarah Wheeler (e-mail: sbw132)
Manuscript Editorial: Cherene Holland, Managing Editor (e-mail: cah8)
  Manuscript Editors: Patricia Mitchell (e-mail: pam18); Laura Reed-Morrison
  (e-mail: lxr168)
Marketing: Tony Sanfilippo, Marketing and Sales Manager (814/863-5994; e-mail: ajs23)
  Publicity Manager: Anne Davis (814/863-0524; e-mail: akd115)
  Exhibits Manager: Heather Smith (e-mail: hms7)
  Advertising Manager: Brian Beer (e-mail: bxb110)
Design and Production: Jennifer Norton, Manager (814/863-8061; e-mail: jsn4)
  Chief Designer: Steven Kress (e-mail: srk5)
Journals: Mary Lou McMurtrie, Manager (814/863-5992; e-mail: mlm2)
Business: Clifford Way Jr., Manager (814/863-5993; e-mail: cgw3)
  Inventory Control Specialist: Kevin Trostle (e-mail: kjt2)
  Accounting Assistant: Kathy Vaughn (e-mail: kmv1)
  Warehouse Staff: Jon Bierly (e-mail: jwb9); Kristin Harrington (e-mail: kah32)
Information Systems Manager: Ed Spicer (e-mail: res122)

Full Member
Established 1956
Title output 2002: 54
Distributed titles 2002: 6
Titles currently in print: 1,200

Admitted to AAUP: 1960
Title output 2003: 40
Distributed titles 2003: 4
Journals published: 11

Editorial Program
Scholarly books in the humanities and social sciences, with current emphasis on art, architecture, art history; philosophy; Latin American studies; Russian and East European studies; international relations, political theory, comparative politics, US politics; American and European history; medieval studies; women's studies; rural studies; and the following journals (* available online): *Book History**; *Chaucer Review**; *Comparative Literature Studies**; *The Good Society**; *Journal of General Education**; *Journal of Nietzsche Studies**; *Journal of Policy History**; *Journal of Speculative Philosophy**; *Pennsylvania History*; *Philosophy and Rhetoric**;

and *SHAW: The Annual of Bernard Shaw Studies**. Submissions are not invited in fiction, poetry, or drama.

Special imprints: Keystone Books

Special series: American and European Philosophy; Buildings, Landscapes, and Societies; Edinburgh Edition of Thomas Reid; Essays on Human Rights; Issues in Policy History; Literature and Philosophy; Magic in History; New Modernisms; Penn State Library of Jewish Literature; Penn State Series in the History of the Book; Pennsylvania German History and Culture; Re-Reading the Canon (feminist interpretations of major philosophers); Rural Studies; Studies of the Greater Philadelphia Philosophy Consortium.

University of Pittsburgh Press

Eureka Building, 5th Floor
3400 Forbes Avenue
Pittsburgh, PA 15260

Phone: (412) 383-2456
Fax: (412) 383-2466
E-mail: (user I.D.)@pitt.edu
Web site: www.pitt.edu/~press

Orders:
University of Pittsburgh Press
Chicago Distribution Center
11030 South Langley Avenue
Chicago, IL 60628
Phone: (773) 568-1550
Fax: (773) 660-2235

UK Representative:
Eurospan

Canadian Representative:
Scholarly Book Services

Staff

Director: Cynthia Miller (e-mail: cymiller)
  Assistant to the Director: Sue Hasychak (e-mail: susief)
  Subsidiary Rights Manager: Margie Bachman (e-mail: mkbachma)
Acquisitions Editors: Nathan MacBrien (international studies, Latin American studies, Russian and East European studies) (e-mail: macbrien); Kendra Boileau Stokes (US history, US political science, composition and literacy, philosophy of science) (e-mail: kbstokes)
Editorial/Production and Design: F. Ann Walston, Production Director (e-mail: awalston)
  Senior Editor: Deborah Meade (e-mail: dmeade)
  Editor: Sara Lickey (e-mail: sal41)
  Production Coordinator: Amy Sykes (e-mail: abs22)
Marketing: Lowell Britson, Marketing Director
  Direct Mail/Advertising Manager: Lydia Wiseman (e-mail: law31)
  Publicist: Maria Sticco (e-mail: mes5)
Business: Cindy Wessels, Business Manager (e-mail: caw1)

Full Member

Established: 1936

Title output 2002: 46

Titles currently in print: 412

Admitted to AAUP: 1937

Title output 2003: 42

Editorial Program

History; political science; international studies; composition and literacy studies; poetry; philosophy of science; Pittsburgh and western Pennsylvania. The Press does not invite submissions in the hard sciences, original fiction (except DHLP), festschriften, memoirs, symposia, or unrevised doctoral dissertations.

Special series, joint imprints, and/or copublishing programs: the Agnes Lynch Starrett Poetry Prize; Cuban Studies; the Drue Heinz Literature Prize; Illuminations: Cultural Formations of the Americas; Golden Triangle Books; Milton Studies; Pitt Latin American Series; Pitt Poetry Series; Pitt Series in Russian and East European Studies; Pittsburgh Series in Composition, Literacy, and Culture; Pittsburgh/Konstanz Series in Philosophy and History of Science.

The Press distributes and copublishes selected titles with the Carnegie Museum of Art, the Carnegie Museum of Natural History, the Historical Society of Western Pennsylvania, the Mattress Factory, and the Westmoreland Museum of American Art.

Princeton University Press

Executive Offices:

41 William Street

Princeton, NJ 08540-5237

Phone: (609) 258-4900

Fax: (609) 258-6305

E-mail:

(firstname_lastname)@ pupress.princeton.edu

Web site: www.pup.princeton.edu

Order Fulfillment (US and Canada):

California/Princeton Fulfillment Services

1445 Lower Ferry Road

Ewing, NJ 08618

Phone: (800) 777-4726; (609) 883-1759

Fax: (800) 999-1958; (609) 883-7413

European Editorial Office:

3 Market Place

Woodstock, Oxfordshire

OX20 1SY United Kingdom

Phone: +44 1993 81 4500

Fax: +44 1993 81 504

E-mail: (firstinitial)(lastname)@pupress.co.uk

UK Distributor:

John Wiley & Sons

Staff

Director: Walter H. Lippincott (609/258-4903)

Assistant to the Director: Martha Camp (609/258-4953)

Associate Director and Controller: Patrick Carroll (609/258-2486)

Acquisitions Editorial: Sam Elworthy, Editor-in-Chief (609/258-5716)

Publisher: Peter Dougherty, Group Publisher, Social Sciences (economics) (609/258-6778); Executive Editors: Robert Kirk (ornithology, natural history) (609/258-4884); Brigitta van Rheinberg (history) (609/258-4935)

Senior Editors: Vickie Kearn (mathematics) (609/258-2321); Anne Savarese (reference) (609/258-4937)
Acquisitions Editors: Fred Appel (music, religion) (609/258-2484); Ingrid Gnerlich (physical sciences) (609/258-5775); Ian Malcolm (philosophy, political theory, sociology) (609/258-4569); Charles Myers (political science) (609/258-4922); Tim Sullivan (economics, sociology, organizational behavior) (609/258-4908); Hanne Winarsky (art, literature) (609/258-4469)
Manuscript Editorial: Neil Litt, Director of Editing, Design and Production (609/258-5066)
Managing Editor: Elizabeth Byrd (609/258-2589)
Assistant Managing Editor: Linny Schenck (609/258-0183)
Electronic Manuscripts Manager: Eileen Reilly (609/258-2719)
Production Manager: Anju Makhijani (609/258-4929)
Marketing: Adam Fortgang, Assistant Press Director and Marketing Director (609/258-4896)
Advertising Manager: Ray Potter (609/258-4924)
Assistant Marketing Director: Leslie Nangle (609/258-5881)
Exhibits Manager: Melissa Burton (609/258-4915)
Text Promotion Manager: Julie Haenisch (609/258-6856)
Sales Director: Eric Rohmann (609/258-4898)
Subsidiary Rights Manager: Ben Tate (609/258-5121)
Publicity Manager: Kathryn Rosko (609/258-7879)
Business: Patrick Carroll, Controller (609/258-2486)
Assistant to the Controller: Persa Ducko (609/258-2485)
Associate Controller: Debbie Greco (609/882-0550)
Intellectual Property Manager: Daphne Ireland (609/258-5228)
Information Systems: Patrick Carroll, Acting Director of Information Technology (609/258-2846)
Director of Computing and Publishing Technology: Chuck Creesy (609/258-5745)
Webmaster: Ann Ambrose (609/258-7749)
European Office:
Publishing Director, Europe: Richard Baggaley (economics, finance) (+44 1993 81 4501)
Editor: Ian Malcolm (classics, philosophy, political theory) (+44 1993 81 4502)
Publicity and Marketing Manager: Louise Corless (+44 1993 81 4503)

Full Member

Established: 1905	Admitted to AAUP: 1937
Title output 2002: 301	Title output 2003: 282
Titles currently in print: 5,244	Journals published: 1

Editorial Program

Humanities: American, Asian, and European history; classics; fine arts (art history, music, painting and sculpture); philosophy; political theory; literature; religion.

Reference Books: humanities; social science and science.

Science: astrophysics; biology; earth science; mathematics; natural history; ornithology; physics.

Social science: anthropology; economics; law (constitutional and international); political science; sociology. The Press does not publish drama or fiction.

Journal: *Annals of Mathematics*

Special imprints: The Bollingen Series, established in 1941 by the Bollingen Foundation, has been published by Princeton University Press since 1967. The Press is not accepting further contributions to the series.

Special monograph series: Annals of Mathematics Studies; A.W. Mellon Lectures in the Fine Arts; The Bard Music Festival; British Artists; Buddhism; Charles Beebe Martin Classical Lectures; The Cultural Lives of Law; Encountering Jung; Eliot Janeway Lectures on Historical Economics; Ethikon Series in Comparative Ethics; Frontiers of Economic Research; Historical, International, and Comparative Perspectives; In-formation; Index of Christian Art Resources; Jews, Christians and Muslims from the Ancient to the Modern World; Literature in History Series; Mathematical Notes; Monographs in Behavior and Ecology; Monographs in Population Biology; New Forum Books; Philosophy Now; Physical Chemistry; Politics and Society in Twentieth Century America; Porter Lectures; Princeton Computer Science Notes; Princeton Economic History of the Western World; Princeton Field Guides; Princeton Illustrated Checklists; Princeton Library of Asian Translations; Princeton Mathematical Series; Princeton Modern Greek Studies; Princeton Monographs in Philosophy; Princeton Opera Series; Princeton Pocket Guides; Princeton Readings in Religion; Princeton Series in Applied Mathematics; Princeton Series in Astrophysics; Princeton Series in Computer Science; Princeton Series in Finance; Princeton Series in Geochemistry; Princeton Series in International Economics; Princeton Series in Physics; Princeton Series in Theoretical and Computational Biology; Princeton Studies in American Politics; Princeton Studies in Complexity; Princeton Studies in Cultural Sociology; Princeton Studies in International History and Politics; Princeton Studies in Legal Theory; Princeton Studies in Muslim Politics; Princeton Studies on the Near East; The Roundtable Series in Behavioral Economics; Science and Engineering; Translation/Transnation; Where to Watch Birds.

Poetry series: Facing Pages; The Lockert Library of Poetry in Translation.

Original source series: The Collected Papers of Albert Einstein; Collected Works of Spinoza; Complete Works of W.H. Auden; Kierkegaard's Writings; The Papers of Thomas Jefferson; The Papers of Woodrow Wilson; The Philosophical, Political and Literary Works of David Hume; Selected Writings of Wilhelm Dilthey; The Writings of Henry D. Thoreau.

University of Puerto Rico Press

Street Address:
Edificio Editorial/ Diálogo
Jardín Botánico Área Norte
Carretera No. 1, KM 12.0
Río Piedras, San Juan, PR 00931

Mailing Address:
PO Box 23322
U.P.R. Station
San Juan, PR 00931-3322

Phone: (787) 250-0000, 0435
Fax: (787) 753-9116, 751-8785

Staff
President, Editorial Board: Angel Collado Schwarz
Executive Director: Manuel G. Sandoval
Editorial: Marta Aponte, Director of Acquisitions and Editorial
    Editors: Jesús Tomé; Rosa V. Otero, Salvador O. Rosorio
Sales Director: José A. Burgos
    Promotions Manager: Ruth Morales
    Exhibits Manager: Moraima Clavell
Chief Financial Officer and Administrator: Carlos González
    Accountant: Clara Ortiz
    Accounts Receivable: TBA
Warehouse Manager: Miguel Rodríguez
    Inventory Manager: Amoury de Jesús
Journals: *Revista La Torre*, Director, Juan Nieves
    Journals Marketing: Judith de Ferdinandy

Full Member
Established: 1932
Title output 2002: 13
Titles currently in print: 900

Admitted to AAUP: 1977
Title output 2003: 30
Journals published: 1

Editorial Program
Scholarly studies on Puerto Rico, the Caribbean and Latin America; philosophy; history; architecture; law; social sciences; health; women's studies; economics; literary theory and criticism; creative poetry and prose; literary anthologies; nature studies; flora; fauna; ecosystems; children' s books; reference; other general interest publications.

Special series: literary anthologies; philosophy; creative literature; scholarly nonfiction; nature.

Special imprints: Aquí y Ahora (current literature); Colección Puertorriqueña (literary classics); Colección Eugenio María de Hostos (complete works); San Pedrito (children's books); Mujeres de Palabra (women's literature); Colección Sinsonate (poetry).

Journal: *Revista La Torre* (the humanities). In distribution: *Revista de Estudios Hispánicos* (Spanish language studies); and *Historia y Sociedad* (Puerto Rican and Caribbean history); *Diálogos* (philosophy).

Purdue University Press

South Campus Courts, Building E
509 Harrison Street
West Lafayette, IN 47907-2025

Orders:
Phone: (800) 247-6553

Phone: (765) 494-2038
Fax: (765) 496-2442
E-mail: pupress@purdue.edu
Indiv: (user I.D.)@purdue.edu
Web site: www.thepress.purdue.edu

European Distributor:
Eurospan

Canadian Distributor:
Scholarly Book Service

Staff
Director: Thomas Bacher (765/494-2038; e-mail: bacher)
Acquisitions Editorial: Thomas Bacher
Manuscript Editorial: Margaret Hunt (765/494-6259; e-mail: mchunt)
Marketing & Sales: Thomas Bacher
Design & Production: Bryan Shaffer (765/494-8428; e-mail: bshaffer)
Journals: Thomas Bacher
Business & Warehouse: Thomas Bacher

Full Member
Established: 1960
Title output 2002: 31
Titles currently in print: 300

Admitted to AAUP: 1993
Title output 2003: 25
Journals published: 3

Editorial Program
General scholarly titles, innovative nonfiction, and interdisciplinary studies across a broad range of fields with special interest in agriculture, business, engineering, health, military history, philosophy, technology, and veterinary medicine.

Series include: Central European Studies; Comparative Cultural Studies; History of Philosophy; Philosophy and Communications; and Purdue Studies in Romance Literature.

Imprints include NotaBell Books—an eclectic reprint collection of non-traditional classics; Ichor Business Books—practical, high-level, how-to titles for today's business and professional challenges; Litera Scripta Manet—a non-traditional reprint series that re-publishes out-of-print scholarly information.

RAND Corporation

Street Address:
1700 Main Street
Santa Monica, CA 90401

Mailing Address:
PO Box 2138
Santa Monica, CA 90407-2138

Phone: (310) 393-0411
Fax: (310) 451-7026
E-mail: (user I.D.)@rand.org
Web site: www.rand.org/publications

Customer Service:
Phone: (877) 584-8642
Fax: (412) 802-4981
E-mail: order@rand.org

US Distributor:
National Book Network
Phone: (800) 462-6420 or (717) 794-3800
Fax: (800) 338-4550

UK and European Distributor:
Eurospan

Staff
Director, Publications: Jane Ryan (ext. 7260; e-mail: ryan)
Associate Director, Publications: Paul Murphy (ext. 7806; e-mail: murphy)
Managing Editor: Peter Hoffman (ext. 7556; e-mail: peterh)
Marketing Director: John Warren (ext. 6293; e-mail: jwarren)
Art Director: Ron Miller (ext. 6384; e-mail: ronkm)
Editor, RAND Journal of Economics: Paula Larich (ext. 6617; e-mail: larich)
Business Manager: Erin Miller (ext. 7251; e-mail: erin_miller)
Computing Manager: Edward Finkelstein (ext. 7417; e-mail: edwardf)

Associate Member
Established: 1948
Title output 2002: 158
Titles currently in print: 10,000

Admitted to AAUP: 2000
Title output 2003: 140
Journals published: 1

Editorial Program
For more than 50 years, decision-makers in the public and private sectors have turned to the RAND Corporation for objective analysis and effective solutions that address the challenges facing the nation and the world. Publication topics include policy issues such as education; environment and energy; health care; immigration, labor, and population; international affairs; national security; public safety and justice; science and technology; and terrorism and homeland security. Unsolicited manuscripts are not accepted.

Resources for the Future/RFF Press

1616 P Street, N.W.
Washington, DC 20036-1400

Phone: (202) 328-5000
Fax: (202) 328-5002
E-mail: rffpress@rff.org
Indiv: (user I.D)@rff.org
Web site: www.rffpress.org

Book Orders and Customer Service:
c/o Hopkins Fulfillment Services
PO Box 50370
Baltimore, MD 21211-4370
Phone: (410) 516-6965
Fax: (410) 516-6998; (800) 537-5487

Staff
Publisher: Don Reisman (202/328-5064; e-mail: reisman)
Acquisitions: Don Reisman
Production: John Deever (202/328-5067; e-mail: deever)
Marketing, Exhibits, Business: Meg Keller (202/328-5086; e-mail: keller)

Associate Member
Established: 1952
Title output 2002: 11
Titles currently in print: 85

Admitted to AAUP: 1988
Title output 2003: 12

Editorial Program
Scholarly, text, and general interest books in environmental and resource economics; environmental politics, policy, and regulation; risk analysis and management; climate change; land, forest, water, and mineral use; conservation; biodiversity; environmental history; sustainable development at local, national, and global levels; outer space as a natural resource; and the use of science in formulating public policy.

The Rockefeller University Press

1114 First Avenue, 4th Floor
New York, NY 10021-8325

Phone: (212) 327-7938
Fax: (212) 327-8587
E-mail: (user I.D.)@rockvax.rockefeller.edu
Web site: www.rockefeller.edu/rupress

Staff

Executive Director: Michael J. Held (212/327-8571; e-mail: held)
  Assistant to the Director: JoAnn Greene (212/327-8025; e-mail: greenej)
Manuscript Editorial: Michael T. Rossner, Executive Editor, *The Journal of Cell Biology* (212/ 327-8881; e-mail: rossner); Jennifer Bell, Executive Editor, *The Journal of Experimental Medicine* (212/327-8361; e-mail: bellj); David Greene, Managing Editor, *The Journal of General Physiology* (212/327-8615; e-mail: jgp)
Marketing: Bruce Lyons, Director (212/327-8663; e-mail: lyonsb)
  Advertising: Lorna Petersen, Advertising Sales Director (212/327-8880; e-mail: petersl)
Journals: Robert O'Donnell, Electronic Publishing and Production Director (212/327-8545; e-mail: odonner)
Business: Raymond T. Fastiggi, Finance Director (212/327-8567; e-mail: fastigg)
  Circulation Manager: Joyce Buffa (212/327-8572; e-mail: buffaj)
  Circulation Director: Gregory Malar (212/327-7948; e-mail: malarg)

Affiliate Member

Established: 1958
Title output 2002: 0
Titles currently in print: 39

Admitted to AAUP: 1982
Title output 2003: 0
Journals published: 3

Editorial Program

Scholarly works on scientific subjects, primarily in the biomedical sciences. The Press is interested in related subjects, such as historical, philosophical, or biographical studies that illuminate the goals of our scientific frontiers, along with problems and opportunities that this research poses. Manuscripts from nonscientific fields are unlikely to be considered.

The Press publishes the following journals: *The Journal of Cell Biology*; *The Journal of Experimental Medicine*; and *The Journal of General Physiology*. Occasionally a book is published under a joint imprint and/or copublishing arrangement.

Russell Sage Foundation

112 East 64th Street
New York, NY 10021-7383

Phone: (212) 750-6000
Fax: (212) 371-4761
E-mail: pubs@rsage.org
Indiv: (firstname)@rsage.org
Web site: www.russellsage.org

Orders:
Russell Sage Foundation
CUP Services
750 Cascadilla St.
P.O. Box 6525
Ithaca, NY 14851
Phone: (800) 666-2211; (607) 277-2211
Fax: (800) 688-2877; (607) 277-6292

UK and European Representative:
University Presses Marketing

Staff
Director of Publications: Suzanne Nichols (212/750-6026)
Publications Assistant: Lianne Stachnick (212/750-6038)
Director of Public Relations: David A. Haproff (212/750-6037)
Public Relations Assistant: Angela Gloria (212/750-6021)
Production Editor: Genna Patacsil (212/750-6034)
Exhibits/Permissions: Lianne Stachnick (212/750-6038)
Foundation President: Eric Wanner

Associate Member
Established: 1907
Title output 2002: 22
Titles currently in print: 400

Admitted to AAUP: 1989
Title output 2003: 22

Editorial Program
Scholarly books on current research and policy issues in the social sciences. Recent research programs sponsored by the Russell Sage Foundation include the future of work, sustainable employment, current US immigration, the analysis of the 1990 and 2000 US Census, the social psychology of cultural contact, the role of trust in shaping social relations, the social dimensions of inequality, and behavioral economics.

Copublishing programs: Joint publications with Harvard University Press, The MIT Press, and Princeton University Press.

Rutgers University Press

Livingston Campus
100 Joyce Kilmer Avenue
Piscataway, NJ 08854-8099

Phone: (732) 445-7762
Fax: (732) 445-7039
E-mail: (user I.D.)@rci.rutgers.edu
Web site: rutgerspress.rutgers.edu

Warehouse, Fulfillment, and Customer Service:
Phone: (732) 445-7762, ext. 613
Fax: (800) 446-9323

UK and European Representative:
Eurospan

Canadian Representative:
Scholarly Book Services

Staff

Director: Marlie Wasserman (ext. 624; e-mail: marlie)
  Assistant to the Director/Subsidiary Rights Manager/E-book Coordinator: Michele Gisbert (ext. 623; e-mail: gisbert)
  Unit Computing Specialist: Thomas Markowski (ext. 650; e-mail: tmmark)
Acquisitions Editorial: Leslie Mitchner, Associate Director and Editor-in-Chief (humanities, literature, art, film) (ext. 601; e-mail: lmitch)
  Editors: Kristi Long (sociology, anthropology, religion, Latin American studies) (ext. 604; e-mail: kristil); Audra Wolfe (sciences, health, psychology, environment, history of science, regional) (ext. 603; e-mail: audraw); Melanie Halkias (history, Asian-American studies) (ext. 602; e-mail: halkias)
  Editorial Assistants: Molly Babb (ext. 630; e-mail: mbabb); Adi Hovav (ext. 603; e-mail: adih)
Manuscript Editorial and Production: Marilyn Campbell, Managing Editor (ext. 606; e-mail: marilync)
  Senior Production Coordinator: Anne Hegeman (ext. 608; e-mail: hegeman)
  Production Editors: Nicole Lokach (ext. 607; e-mail: nlokach); Alison Hack (ext. 605; e-mail: ahack)
Marketing: Gary Fitzgerald, Marketing and Sales Director (ext. 627; e-mail: garyfitz)
  Publicity Director: Jonathan Reilly (ext. 626; e-mail: joreilly)
  Promotions Manager: Donna Liese (ext. 628; e-mail: dliese)
  Marketing Assistant/Exhibits: Arlene Bacher (ext. 622; e-mail: bacher)
  Marketing and Web Coordinator: Jessica Pellien (ext. 625; e-mail: pellien)
Business: Molly Venezia, Chief Operations Officer (ext. 610; e-mail: mvenezia)
  Accountant: Winnie Westcott (ext. 614; e-mail: wwestcot)
  Accounting: Eileen Kornberg (ext. 612; e-mail: kornberg)
  Fulfillment: Penny Borden (ext. 613; e-mail: pborden)
  Credit and Collection Manager: Linda Bond (ext. 644; e-mail: lbond)
  Order Entry: Debra Sinowell (ext. 633; e-mail: debbies)

Full Member

Established: 1936
Title output 2002: 88
Titles currently in print: 1,795

Admitted to AAUP: 1937
Title output 2003: 88

Editorial Program

American studies; anthropology; art history and criticism; Asian studies; Asian-American studies; Black studies and literature; environmental studies; film and media; history; history of science/technology; Jewish studies; life and health sciences; literary studies; public policy; regional studies; religion; sociology; women's studies.

Special Series: Art & Public Policy; Childhood Studies; Critical Issues in Health Care; Depth of Field; Screen Decades; Subterranean Lives: Chronicles of Alternative America; Studies in Medical Anthropology.

Joint Imprint: The Jane Voorhees Zimmerli Art Museum. The Press distributes publications of the New Jersey Historical Society, the Harriet Beecher Stowe Center, the Montclair Art Museum, and the Newark Museum.

The University of Scranton Press

445 Madison Avenue
Scranton, PA 18510-4660

Phone: (570) 941-4228
Fax: (570) 941-6256
E-mail: salesoffice@scranton.edu
Web site: www.scrantonpress.com

Orders:
Phone: (800) 941-3081; (800) 941-8804
(Print On Demand orders handled directly)

Staff

Director: Richard W. Rousseau, S.J. (570/941-7449; e-mail: richard.rousseau@scranton.edu)
Production Manager: Patricia Mecadon (570/941-4228; e-mail: mecadonpl@scranton.edu)
Cover Designer: Trinka Ravaioli Pettinato (570/558-0203; e-mail:
  grapevine_design@yahoo.com)

Affiliate Member

Established: 1988
Title output 2002: 10
Titles currently in print: 90

Admitted to AAUP: 1997
Title output 2003: 5

Editorial Program

Theology and religious studies, including the relation between culture, literature, art, and religion; philosophy, including philosophy of religion; regional trade titles in the history and traditions of Northeastern Pennsylvania.

Smithsonian Books

Street Address:
750 Ninth Street, N.W.
Suite 4300
Washington, DC 20560-0001

Mailing Address:
PO Box 37012
Victor Building MRC 950
Washington, DC 20013-8012

Phone: (202) 275-2300
Fax: (202) 275-2274; (202) 275-2245
E-mail: inquiries@sipress.si.edu
Indiv: (first initial)(last name)@sipress.si.edu

New York Office:
Smithsonian Books
245 5th Avenue
New York, NY 10016

Order Fulfillment:
Distributed by W.W. Norton
Phone: (800) 233-4830

Staff
Director: Don Fehr (202/275-2183) and (212/679-4515)
Subrights/Permissions: Janey Tannenbaum (212/679-4298)
Acquisitions Editor: Caroline Newman (202/275-2214)
Editors: Robert Poarch (202/275-2215), Joanne Reams (202/275-2238)
Marketing and Sales: Janey Tannenbaum; Marketing Director (212/679-4298)
   Publicity Manager: Matt Litts (202/275-2206)
   Sales Manager: TBA
   Advertising Manager: Chris Orcutt (212/679-4109)
Design and Production: Carolyn Gleason, Production Director (202/275-2223)
Contributions and Studies Series Program: Diane Tyler, Managing Editor (202/275-2233)
Business Manager: Prospero Hernandez (202/275-2198)

Full Member
Established: 1846
Title output 2002: 67
Titles currently in print: 800

Admitted to AAUP: 1966
Title output 2003: 64

Editorial Program
Adult trade and scholarly non-fiction.

Society of Biblical Literature

The Luce Center
825 Houston Mill Road, Suite 350
Atlanta, GA 30329

Orders:
Phone: (877) 725-3334

Phone: (404) 727-3100
Fax: (404) 727-3101
E-mail: sblexec@sbl-site.org
Indiv: (firstname.lastname)@sbl-site.org
Web site: www.sbl-site.org

Staff
Executive Director: Kent Richards (404/727-3038)
Director of Development and Board Relations: Susan Madara (404/727-3103)
Director of Administrative and Technology Services: Missy Colee (404/727-3124)
Bookkeeper: Lorian Warrilow (404/727-9095)
Editorial Director: Bob Buller (970/669-9900)
Managing Editor: Leigh Andersen (404/727-2327)
Marketing Manager: Kathie Klein (404/727-2325)
Director of Research and Development: Patrick Durusau (404/727-2337)
Technology Manager: Lauren Hightower (404/727-3114)
Web Site Manager: Sharon Johnson (404/727-3102)

Associate Member
Established: 1880
Title output 2002: 19
Titles currently in print: 369

Admitted to AAUP: 2003
Title output 2003: 33
Journals published: 3

Editorial Program
The SBL publishes works in biblical and religious studies. Monographic publications include major reference works; commentaries; text editions and translations; collections of essays; doctoral dissertations; and tools for teaching and research fields; archaeological, sociological, and historical studies; volumes that use archaeological and historical data to illuminate Israelite religion or the culture of biblical peoples; scholarly works on the history, culture, and literature of early Judaism; scholarly works on various aspects of the Masorah; scholarly congress proceedings; critical texts of the Greek Fathers including evaluations of data; philological tools; studies employing the methods and perspectives of linguistics, folklore studies, literary criticism, structuralism, social anthropology, and postmodern studies; studies of the Septuagint including textual criticism, manuscript witnesses and other versions, as well as its literature, historical milieu, and thought; studies related to the Jewish apocrypha and pseudepigrapha of the Hellenistic period, and the subsequent development of this literature in Judaism and early Christianity; studies in biblical literature and/or its cultural environment; text-critical works related to Hebrew Bible/Old Testament and New Testament including investigations of methodology, studies of individual manuscripts, critical texts of a selected book or passage, or examination of more general textual themes; translations of ancient Near Eastern texts; translations of ancient texts from the Greco-Roman world.

Special Series: Academia Biblica; Archaeology and Biblical Studies; Brown Judaic Studies; Early Judaism and Its Literature; Global Perspectives on Biblical Scholarship; Masoretic Studies; Resources for Biblical Study; Semeia Studies; Septuagint and Cognate Studies; Studies in Biblical Literature; Symposium Series; Text-Critical Studies; The New Testament in the Greek Fathers; Writings from the Ancient World; Writings from the Greco-Roman World.

Journals: *Journal of Biblical Literature*, *Review of Biblical Literature*, and *Studia Philonica*.

Joint imprints and co-publishing programs: SBL Handbook of Style for Ancient Near Eastern, Biblical, and Early Christian Studies with Hendrickson Publishers; HarperCollins Study Bible (NRSV), HarperCollins Bible Dictionary, Revised Edition, HarperCollins Bible Commentary, Revised Edition, and Harper's Bible Pronunciation Guide with HarperCollins; Hardback editions with Brill Academic Publishers of Leiden, The Netherlands.

University of South Carolina Press

1600 Hampton Street
5th Floor
Columbia, SC 29208

Phone: (803) 777-5243
Fax: (803) 777-0160
E-mail: (user I.D.)@sc.edu
Web site: www.sc.edu/uscpress

Business Office and Warehouse:
718 Devine Street
Columbia, SC 29208
Phone: (800) 768-2500
Fax: (800) 868-0740
E-mail: (user I.D.)@sc.edu

UK and European Distributor:
Eurospan

Canadian Distributor:
Scholarly Book Services

Staff

Director: Curtis L. Clark (803/777-5245; e-mail: cclark)
  Assistant Director for Operations: Linda Fogle (803/777-4848; e-mail: lfogle)
  Assistant to the Director: Karen Riddle (803/777-5245; e-mail: riddlek)
Acquisitions Editors: Linda Fogle (regional, trade) (803/777-4848; e-mail: lfogle); Alexander Moore (African-American studies, history, Southern studies) (803/777-8070; e-mail: alexm); Barry Blose (literature, religious studies, rhetoric/communication, social work) (803/777-4859; e-mail: barryb)
Manuscript Editorial: Bill Adams, Managing Editor (803/777-5075; e-mail: adamswb)
  Editor: Scott Burgess (803/777-5877; e-mail: sburgess)
  Editorial Assistant: Karen Beidel (803/777-9055; e-mail: kcbeidel)
Marketing: TBA, Manager
  Sales Assistant: Carolyn Dibble (803/777-5029; e-mail: cdibble)
  Advertising and Design Manager: Lynne Parker (803/777-5231; e-mail: parkerll)
Design and Production: Pat Callahan, Design and Production Manager (803/777-2449; e-mail: mpcallah)
  Book Designer: Brandi Lariscy-Avant (803/777-9056; e-mail: lariscyb)
  Design and Production Assistant: Ashley Mathias (803/777-2238; e-mail: samathi)

Business/Warehouse: Dianne Smith, Business Manager and Permissions (803/777-1773; e-mail: dismith)
Assistant Business Manager: Vicki Sewell (803/777-7754; e-mail: sewellv)
Customer Service Representative: Libby Mack (803/777-1774; e-mail: lmack)
Warehouse Assistant: Eddie Hill (803/777-0184; e-mail: jehill)

Full Member

Established: 1944

Admitted to AAUP: 1948

Title output 2002: 42

Title output 2003: 50

Titles currently in print: 700

Editorial Program

Scholarly works, mainly in the humanities and social sciences, and general interest titles, particularly those of importance to the state and region. Subjects include African-American studies; history, especially American history, military history, maritime history, and Southern history; literature and literary studies; religious studies, including comparative religion; Southern studies; rhetoric/communication; and social work.

Special series, joint imprints, and/or copublishing programs: The Belle W. Baruch Library in Marine Science; Chief Justiceships of the United States Supreme Court; The Papers of Henry Laurens; The Papers of John C. Calhoun; Social Problems and Social Issues; Southern Classics; Studies in Comparative Religion; Studies in Maritime History; Studies in Rhetoric/Communication; Studies on Personalities of the New Testament; Studies on Personalities of the Old Testament; Understanding Contemporary American Literature; Understanding Contemporary British Literature; Understanding Modern European and Latin American Literature; and Women's Diaries and Letters of the South.

Southern Illinois University Press

Street/Warehouse Address:
1915 University Press Drive
Carbondale IL 62901

Mailing Address:
P.O. Box 3697
Carbondale IL 62902-3697

Phone: (618) 453-2281
Fax: (618) 453-1221
E-mail: (user I.D.)@siu.edu
Web site: www.siu.edu/~siupress

Orders:
Phone: (618) 453-6619; (800) 346-2680
Fax: (618) 453-3787; (800) 346-2681

UK and European Distributor:
Eurospan

Canadian Representative:
Scholarly Book Services

Staff

Director: John F. Stetter (618/453-6615; e-mail: jstetter)
Rights and Permissions Manager: Mona E. Ross (618/453-6616; e-mail: monasiu)
Acquisitions Editorial: Karl Kageff, Editor-in-Chief: (communication, film, theater) (618/453-6629; e-mail: kageff)
Editor: John F. Stetter (618/453-6615; e-mail: jstetter)
Sponsoring Editor: Kristine Priddy (618/453-6631; e-mail: mkpriddy)

Editorial Assistant: Bridget Brown (618/453-2178; e-mail: bcbrown)
Manuscript Editorial: Carol A. Burns, Managing Editor (618/453-6627; e-mail: cburns)
  Associate Editor: Wayne Larsen (618/453-6628; e-mail: wlarsen)
  Project Editor: Kathleen Kageff (618/453-6613; e-mail: kbkageff)
Marketing and Sales: Larry Townsend, Director of Sales and Marketing (618/453-6623; e-mail: townsend)
  Assistant Marketing Manager: Jonathan Haupt (618/453-6624; e-mail: jnathan)
  Publicity Manager: Jane Carlson (618/453-6633; e-mail: jcarlson)
Design and Production: Barbara Martin, Design and Production Manager (618/453-6614; e-mail: bbmartin)
  Production Editor: Teresa White (618/453-6620; e-mail: twhite)
  Book Designer: Mary Rohrer (618/453-6612; e-mail: mrohrer)
  Compositor: Kyle Lake (618/453-6635; e-mail: kylelake)
Business: Lisa Falaster, Business Manager: (618/453-6610; e-mail: lisafala)
  Order Entry: Angela Moore-Swafford (618/453-6619; e-mail: angmoore); Dawn Vagner (618/453-2281; e-mail: dvagner)
  Computer Tech: Eric Crawford (618/453-2281; e-mail: drofwarc)
  Warehouse/Shipping Manager: David A. Robinson, Warehouse Manager (618/453-4439; e-mail: shipper1)
  Internet Sales Manager: J.D. Tremblay (618/453-6634; e-mail: shipper2)

Full Member

Established: 1956   Admitted to AAUP: 1980
Title output 2002: 55   Title output 2003: 51
Titles currently in print: 1,250

Editorial Program

Scholarly books, primarily in the humanities and social sciences. Particular strengths are film studies; theatre and stagecraft; regional, Civil War, and military history; speech, rhetoric, and composition studies; American literature; civil rights; criminology; philosophy; aviation; contemporary poetry; and baseball literature and history. Submissions in fiction and festschriften are not invited

Special Series: American Civil Liberties Union Handbooks; Aviation Management; Contemporary Studies in Crime and Justice; The Crab Orchard Review Award Series; The Crab Orchard Review First Book Series; The Holmes-Johnson Series in Criminology; The Illustrated Flora of Illinois; Landmarks in Rhetoric and Public Address; The Papers of Ulysses S. Grant; Shawnee Classics; Shawnee Books; Studies in Rhetorics and Feminisms; Studies in Writing and Rhetoric; Theater in the Americas; The Works of John Dewey; Writing Baseball.

Southern Methodist University Press

Street Address:
314 Fondren Library West
6404 Hilltop Lane
Dallas, TX 75275

Mailing Address:
P.O. Box 750415
Dallas, TX 75275-0415

Phone: (214) 768-1432
Fax: (214) 768-1428
E-mail: (user I.D.)@mail.smu.edu

Orders:
Phone: (800) 826-8911

Staff
Director: Keith Gregory (214/768-1432; e-mail: keithg)
Acquisitions Editor: Kathryn M. Lang (214/768-1433; e-mail: klang)
Marketing and Production Manager: George Ann Ratchford (214/768-1434; e-mail: ggoodwin)

Full Member
Established: 1937
Title output 2002: 11
Titles currently in print: 198

Admitted to AAUP: 1946
Title output 2003: 6

Editorial Program
Ethics and human values; fiction; medical humanities; performing arts; Southwestern studies; and sports.

Stanford University Press

1450 Page Mill Road
Palo Alto, CA 94304-1124

Phone: (650) 723-9434
Fax: (650) 725-3457
E-mail: (user I.D.)@stanford.edu
Web site: www.sup.org

Orders:
Stanford University Press
Chicago Distribution Center
11030 South Langley Avenue
Chicago, IL 60628
Phone: (800) 621-2736; (773) 568-1550
Fax: (800) 621-8471

European Representative:
Eurospan

Canadian Representative:
Lexa Publishers' Representatives

Staff
Director: Geoffrey Burn (650/736-1942; e-mail: grhburn)
Rights, Permissions, and Contracts: Ariane de Pree-Kajfez, Rights Manager (650/725-0815; e-mail: arianep)
Acquisitions Editorial: Alan Harvey, Publishing Director (650/723-6375; e-mail: aharvey)
  Program Director Scholarly Publishing (and Humanities Editor): Norris Pope (650/725-0827; e-mail: npope)
  Acquiring Editors: Muriel Bell (Asian studies, Asian American studies, and US foreign

policy) (650/725-0824; e-mail: muriel); Kate Wahl (sociology, anthropology) (650/723-9598; e-mail: kwahl); Amanda Moran (law, politics, and policy) (650/725-0845; e-mail: amoran); Martha Cooley (economics, business, and finance) (650/724-7079; e-mail: mcooley)

Associate Editor: Carmen Borbon-Wu (650/724-7080; e-mail: carmenb)

Assistant Editor: Mariah Isely (650/736-0924; e-mail: isely)

Editorial Assistant: Angie Michaelis (650/723-9598; e-mail: angiem)

Editorial, Design, and Production: Patricia Myers, EDP Director (650/724-5365; e-mail: pmyers)

Senior Production Editor: Judith Hibbard (650/736-0719; e-mail: jhibbard)

Production Editors: Tim Roberts (650/724-9990; e-mail: tim.roberts); Mariana Raykov (650/725-0835; e-mail: mraykov); John Feneron (650/725-0828; e-mail: johnf)

Art & Design Manager: Rob Ehle (650/723-1132; e-mail: ehle)

Production Manager: Harold Moorehead (650/725-0836; e-mail: hmoorehead)

Marketing: David Jackson, Marketing Director (650/736-1782; e-mail: david.jackson)

Marketing and Publicity Manager: Puja Sangar (650/724-4211; e-mail: psangar)

Advertising and Direct Mail Coordinator: Jana Unkel (650/736-1781; e-mail: jana.unkel)

Exhibits Manager: Christie Cochrell (650/725-0820; e-mail: cochrell)

Business: John Zotz, Chief Operating Officer (650/723-3230; e-mail: jnzotz)

Business Manager: Jean Kim (650/725-0838; e-mail: plcmnkim)

Systems Administrator: Chris Cosner (650/724-7276; e-mail: ccosner)

Full Member

Established: 1925	Admitted to AAUP: 1937
Title output 2002: 146	Title output 2003: 135
Titles currently in print: 1,600	

Editorial Program

Scholarly titles and textbooks in philosophy, history, literature, religion, sociology, anthropology, and political science; and on Asia, Latin America, and the Western United States. Scholarly titles, textbooks, and professional titles in business, economics, law, and policy. Special Series: Asian America; Asian Religions and Cultures; Asian Security; Atopia: Philosophy, Political Theory, Aesthetics; Cold War International History Project; Comparative Studies in History, Institutions, and Public Policy; The Complete Works of Friedrich Nietzsche; Contemporary Issues in Asia and the Pacific; Contraversions: Jews and Other Differences; Cultural Memory in the Present; Cultural Sitings; Divinations: Rereading Late Ancient Religion; Figurae: Reading Medieval Culture; Innovation and Technology in the World Economy; Jurists: Profiles in Legal Theory; Latin American Development Forum; Law, Society, and Culture in China; The Making of Modern Freedom; Meridian: Crossing Aesthetics; Social Science History; Stanford Business Classics; Stanford Nuclear Age Series; Stanford Studies in International Economics and Development; Stanford Studies in Jewish History and Culture; Studies in Kant and German Idealism; Studies in Social Inequality; Studies of the East Asian Institute; Writing Science.

Special Imprints: Stanford Business Books; Stanford Law and Politics; Stanford Social Sciences

Co-publishing arrangements: The Press co-publishes with the World Bank and the Woodrow Wilson Center

State University of New York Press

90 State Street, Suite 700
Albany, NY 12207-1707

Phone: (518) 472-5000
Fax: (518) 472-5038
E-mail: info@sunypress.edu
Indiv: (user I.D.)@sunypress.edu
Web site: www.sunypress.edu

UK Representative:
Andrew Gilman
University Presses Marketing

Canadian Representative:
Lexa Publishers' Representatives

Customer Service:
c/o CUP Services
PO Box 6525
Ithaca, NY 14851
Phone: (607) 277-2211;
(800) 666-2211 (US only)
Fax: (607) 277-6292;
(800) 688-2877 (US only)
E-mail: orderbook@cupserv.org

UK and European Distributor:
NBN International

Staff

Director: Priscilla Ross (518/472-5026; e-mail: rosspr)
  Assistant to the Director: Janice Vunk (518/472-5025; e-mail: vunkja)
  Rights & Permissions: Jennie Doling (518/472-5024; e-mail: dolingje)
  Receptionist: Darlene Knight (518/472-5000; e-mail: knightda)
Acquisitions Editorial: James Peltz, Associate Director and Editor-in-Chief (518/472-5031;
  e-mail: peltzja)
  Assistant to the Editor-in-Chief: Katy Leonard (518/472-5035; e-mail: leonarka)
  Senior Acquisitions Editors: Jane Bunker (518/472-5003; e-mail: bunkerja); Nancy
  Ellegate (518/472-5004; e-mail: ellegana)
  Acquisitions Editors: Michael Rinella (518/472-5030; e-mail: rinellmi); Lisa Chesnel (518/
  472-5020; e-mail: chesneli)
  Editorial Assistant: Allison Lee (518/472-5018; e-mail: leeal)
Marketing: Fran Keneston, Director of Marketing and Publicity (518/472-5023; e-mail:
  kenestfr)
  Senior Marketing Manager: Anne Valentine (518/472-5032; e-mail: valentan)
  Marketing Manager: Michael Campochiaro (518/472-5043; e-mail: campocmi)
  Promotions Manager: Susan Petrie (518/472-5008; e-mail: petriesu)
  Exhibits Coordinator: Michelle Alamillo (518/472-5039; email: alamilmi)
  Review Clerk: Trisha Smith (518/472-5006; e-mail: smithtr)
Sales: Dan Flynn, Sales Manager (518/472-5036; e-mail: flynnda)
  Sales Assistant: Judy Trenchard (518/472-5010; e-mail: trenchju)
Production: Marilyn Semerad, Production Manager (518/472-5019; e-mail: semerama)
  Senior Production Editors: Judith Block (518/472-5015; e-mail: blockju); Diane Ganeles
  (518/472-5014; e-mail: ganeledi); Michael Haggett (518/472-5042; e-mail: haggetmi);
  Laurie Searl (518/472-5033; e-mail: searlla)
  Production Editor: Kelli Williams (518/472-5041; e-mail: williake)
  Production Assistant: Stephanie Wilsey (518/472-5002; e-mail: wilseyst)

Business: Frank Mahar, Business Manager (518/472-5022; e-mail: maharfr)
  Accountants: Fortunata Migliore (518/472-5027; e-mail: migliofo); Tania Micale (518/472-5016; e-mail: micaleta)
Information Systems: Bob Sajeski, LAN Administrator (518/472-5021; e-mail: sajeskro)
  Director of Electronic Sales, Marketing, and Product Development: Dana Yanulavich (518/472-5028; e-mail: yanulada)

Full Member

Established: 1966	Admitted to AAUP: 1970
Title output 2002: 192	Title output 2003: 180
Titles currently in print: 3,509	

Editorial Program

Scholarly titles and serious works of general interest in most areas of the humanities and the social sciences, with special interest in African-American studies; anthropology; Asian studies; communication; cultural studies; education; environmental studies; film studies; Holocaust studies; Jewish studies; literature and literary theory and criticism; Middle Eastern studies; philosophy; political science; psychology; religious studies; rhetoric and composition; sociology; sports studies; and women's studies.

Syracuse University Press

Street Address:
621 Skytop Road, Suite 110
Syracuse, NY 13244-5290

Warehouse Address:
1600 Jamesville Avenue
Syracuse, NY 13244-5160

Phone: (315) 443-5534
Fax: (315) 443-5545
E-mail: (user I.D.)@syr.edu
Web site: syracuseuniversitypress.syr.edu

Orders:
Phone: (315) 443-2597; (800) 365-8929
Fax: (866) 536-4771

Canadian Sales Representative:
Cariad, Ltd.

UK Distributor:
Eurospan

Staff
Director: Peter B. Webber (315/443-5535; e-mail: pbwebber)
  Assistant to the Director: Ellen S. Goodman (315/443-5541; e-mail: esgoodma)
  Development Director: Anne Carlson (315/443-1364; e-mail: akcarlso)
Acquisitions Editorial: Mary Selden Evans, Executive Editor (315/443-5543; e-mail: msevans)
  Acquisitions Editor: Glenn Wright (315/443-5647; e-mail: glwright)
Manuscript Editorial: John Fruehwirth, Managing Editor (315/443-5544; e-mail: jjfruehw)
  Copy Editor: Marian Buda (315/443-5542; e-mail: mebuda)
Marketing: Theresa A. Litz, Marketing Manager (315/443-5546; e-mail: talitz)
  Publicity and Advertising Manager: Therese Walsh (315/443-5546; e-mail: twalsh01)
  Design Specialist: Lynn Hoppel (315/443-5547; e-mail: lphoppel)
Design and Production: Mary Peterson Moore, Manager (315/443-5540; e-mail: mpmoore)
  Senior Designers: Victoria Lane (315/443-5540; e-mail: vmlane); Fred Wellner (315/443-5540; e-mail: fawellne)
  Electronic Manuscripts Manager: Mike Rankin (315/443-5540; e-mail: mwrankin)
Business: Alice Randel Pfeiffer, Comptroller (315/443-5536; e-mail: arpfeiff)
  Assistant Comptroller: Karen Boland (315/443-5539; e-mail: kcboland)
  Warehouse Manager: Jeff McManus (315/443-5537)
  Warehouse Assistant: Anthony Carbone (315/443-5537)
  Order Supervisor: Lori Lazipone (315/443-5538; e-mail: ljlazipo)
The Encyclopedia of New York State:
  Copy Editor: Kay Steinmetz (315/443-9155; e-mail: kasteinm)

Full Member
Established: 1943
Title output 2002: 75
Titles currently in print: 1,450

Admitted to AAUP: 1946
Title output 2003: 55

Editorial Program
Scholarly books and works of general interest in the areas of Jewish, Middle East, Irish, New

York State, women's, Native American, and Medieval studies; Arab-American writing; religion; television; sports history; journalism; biography; human and urban geography; politics; and conflict resolution. Selected fiction and memoirs.

Special series, joint imprints, and/or copublishing programs: The Adirondack Museum/ Syracuse University Press; The Albert Schweitzer Library; Arab-American Writing; Contemporary Issues in the Middle East; Gender, Culture, and Politics in the Middle East; Gender and Globalization; Irish Studies; Iroquois and Their Neighbors; Judaic Traditions in Literature, Music, and Art; Library of Modern Jewish Literature; The Martin Buber Library; Medieval Studies; Middle East Literature in Translation; Modern Intellectual and Political History of the Middle East; Modern Jewish History; Mohamad El-Hindi Books on Arab Culture and Islamic Civilization; New York State Studies; Religion and Politics; Religion, Theology and the Holocaust; Space, Place, and Society; Sports and Entertainment; Syracuse Studies in Peace and Conflict Resolution; The Television Series; and Women in Religion.

The Press distributes books bearing the imprints of Adirondack Museum; American University of Beirut; Moshe Dayan Center for Middle Eastern and African Studies (Tel-Aviv University); American University in Cairo Press; New Netherlands Project; Jusoor; National Library of Ireland; Munson-Williams-Proctor Institute; and Corning Museum of Glass.

In 2005 the Press will produce the print edition of the *Encyclopedia of New York State*.

Teachers College Press

1234 Amsterdam Avenue
New York, NY 10027-6696

Phone: (212) 678-3929
Fax: (212) 678-4149
E-mail: (user I.D.)@columbia.edu
Web site: www.tcpress.com

Warehouse:
Teachers College Press
PO Box 20
Williston, VT 05495-0020
Phone: (800) 864-7626

Returns:
12 Winter Sport Lane
Williston, VT 05495

European Representative:
Eurospan

Canadian Representative:
Guidance Centre

Staff

Director: Carole Pogrebin Saltz (212/678-3927; e-mail: cps8)
    Assistant to Director: Catherine Chandler (212/678-3965; e-mail: coc2101)
    Rights and Permissions Manager/Special Sales Coordinator: Amy Kline (212/678-3827; e-mail: ard14)
Acquisitions Editorial: Brian Ellerbeck, Executive Acquisitions Editor (administration, school change, leadership, policy, special and gifted education, curriculum studies, cultural studies) (212/678-3908; e-mail: bhe3)
    Acquisitions Editors: Susan Liddicoat (early childhood education, sociology, educational research, teacher education/foundations, higher education, women's studies) (212/678-3928; e-mail: sal17); Carol Collins (language and literacy, teacher research, counseling/psychology, infancy/child development) (212/678-3909; e-mail: ccc27)
    Assistant Acquisitions Editor: Adee Braun (212/678-3905; e-mail: braun@tc.columbia.edu)
Marketing: Leyli Shayegan, Director, Sales and Marketing and Assistant Director (212/678-3475; e-mail: ls175)
    Marketing Manager: Nancy Power (212/678-3915; e-mail: nep5)
    Graphic Arts Manager: David Strauss (212/678-3982; e-mail: dms38)
    Publicity Coordinator: Jessica Balun (212/678-3963; e-mail: jab2126)
    Outreach Coordinator: Michael McGann (212/678-3919; e-mail: mim11)
Production: Peter Sieger, Production Manager (212/678-3926; e-mail: prs7)
    Senior Production Editor: Karl Nyberg (212/678-3806; e-mail: kan10)
    Production Editors: Lyn Grossman (212/678-3902; e-mail: lg124); Aureliano Vazquez (212/678-3945; e-mail: av314); Lori Tate (212/678-3907; e-mail: lat18)
    Production Assistants: Debra Jackson-Whyte (212/678-3926; e-mail: daj61); Shannon Waite (212/678-3914; e-mail: stw2005)
Business: Mary Lynch, Senior Financial Manager (212/678-3913; e-mail: mal48)
    Business Assistant: Lisa Forsythe (212/678-3917; e-mail: laf2002)
    Secretary/Receptionist: Marcia Ruiz (212/678-3929; e-mail: myr3)

Full Member

Established: 1904   Admitted to AAUP: 1971
Title output 2002: 61   Title output 2003: 60
Titles currently in print: 517

Editorial Program

Scholarly, professional, text, and trade books on education, education-related areas, and feminist studies. Multimedia instructional materials, tests, and evaluation materials for classroom use at all levels of education.

Specific areas of interest in education are: curriculum; early childhood; school administration and educational policy; counseling and guidance; mathematics; philosophy; psychology; language and literacy; science; sociology; special education; social studies; teacher education; cultural studies; women and higher education.

Special series: Advances in Contemporary Educational Thought; Athene Series in Women's Studies; Between Teacher & Text; Counseling and Development; Critical Issues in Curriculum; Critical Issues in Educational Leadership; Early Childhood Education; Education and Psychology of the Gifted; John Dewey Lecture; Language and Literacy; Multicultural Education; Politics of Identity and Education; Practitioner Inquiry; Professional Ethics in Education; Reflective History; The Series on School Reform; Sociology of Education; Teaching for Social Justice; Ways of Knowing in Science and Mathematics.

Temple University Press

1601 N. Broad Street, USB Room 306
Philadelphia, PA 19122-6099

Phone: (215) 204-8787; (800) 447-1656
Fax: (215) 204-4719
E-mail: (firstname.lastname)@temple.edu
Web site: www.temple.edu/tempress

UK Distributor:
Eurospan

Orders:
Temple University Press
Chicago Distribution Center
11030 South Langley Avenue
Chicago, IL 60628
Phone: (800) 621-2736
Fax: (800) 621-8471

Canadian Distributor:
Lexa Publishers' Representatives

Staff

Director: Alex Holzman (215/204-3436)
  Rights and Permissions Administrator and Assistant to the Director: Matthew Kull (215/204-5707)
Acquisitions: Janet M. Francendese, Assistant Director and Editor-in-Chief (215/204-3437)
  Senior Editors: Micah Kleit (215/204-3439); Peter Wissoker (202/986-7379)
  Assistant Editor: William Hammell (215/204-3782)
Marketing: Ann-Marie Anderson, Assistant Director and Director of Marketing (215/204-1108)
  Advertising and Promotion Manager: Irene Imperio (215/204-1099)
  Publicity Manager: Gary Kramer (215/9204-3440)
  Webmaster and Site Designer: Dawn Danish
Production: Charles H. E. Ault, Assistant Director and Director of Production and Electronic Publishing (215/204-3389)
  Senior Production Editor: Jennifer French (215/204-3388)
  Production Coordinator: David Wilson (215/204-7296)
Business: Barry Adams, Assistant Director and Financial Manager (215/204-3444)
  Customer Service/Operations Manager: Karen Baker (215/204-8606)

Full Member

Established: 1969
Title output 2002: 58
Titles currently in print: 1,055

Admitted to AAUP: 1972
Title output 2003: 47

Editorial Program

African-American Studies; American studies; anthropology; Asian studies; Asian American studies; cinema and media studies; communication; criminology; disability studies; education; ethnicity and race; gay and lesbian studies; gender studies; geography; health; labor studies; Latin American studies; law and society; Philadelphia regional studies; political science and public policy; religion; sociology; sports; urban studies; US and European history; women's studies.

Special series: America in Transition: Radical Perspectives; American Subjects; Animals, Culture, and Society; Asian American History and Culture; Critical Perspectives on the Past; Emerging Media; Gender, Family, and the Law; Labor in Crisis; Mapping Racisms; The New

Academy; Place, Culture, and Politics; Politics, History, and Social Change; Queer Politics, Queer Theories; Rhetoric, Culture, and Public Address; Sound Matters; Studies in Latin American and Caribbean Music; Teaching/Learning Social Justice; Voices of Latin American Life; Wide Angle Books.

Temple University Press distributes books for the Asian American Writers' Workshop.

University of Tennessee Press

600 Henley Street
Suite 110 Conference Center
Knoxville, TN 37902

Phone: (865) 974-3321
Fax: (865) 974-3724
E-mail: custserv@utpress.org
Indiv: (user I.D.)@utk.edu
(unless otherwise indicated)
Web site: utpress.org

Orders:
Univ. of Tennessee Press
Chicago Distribution Center
11030 South Langley Avenue
Chicago, IL 60628
Phone: (800) 621-2736
Fax: (773) 660-2235

Staff
Director: Jennifer M. Siler (e-mail: jsiler)
Acquisitions Editorial: Scot Danforth, Acquisitions Editor (e-mail: danforth)
Manuscript Editorial: Stanley Ivester, Managing Editor (e-mail: ivester)
  Manuscript Editor: Gene Adair (e-mail: adair@utpress.org)
  Editorial Assistant: Thomas Wells (e-mail: twells)
Marketing: Cheryl Carson, Manager (e-mail: ccarson3)
  Exhibits/Publicity Manager: Tom Post (e-mail: tpost)
Design and Production: Barbara Karwhite, Manager (e-mail:karwhite@utpress.org)
  Book Designer: Cheryl Carrington (e-mail: carringt)
Business: Tammy Berry, Manager (e-mail: tberry)
  Receptionist/Bookkeeper: Bethany McMillan (e-mail: mcmillan@utpress.org)
Electronic Projects Manager: Jennifer M. Siler (e-mail: jsiler)

Full Member
Established: 1940
Title output 2002: 38
Titles currently in print: 643

Admitted to AAUP: 1964
Title output 2003: 41

Editorial Program
American studies; Appalachian studies; African-American studies; history; religion; folklore; vernacular architecture; historical archaeology; material culture; literature; and literary fiction. Submissions in poetry, textbooks, and translations are not invited.

Special series, joint imprints, and/or copublishing programs: Appalachian Echoes; Correspondence of James K. Polk; Outdoor Tennessee; The Papers of Andrew Jackson; Perspectives in Vernacular Architecture; Sport and Popular Culture; Tennesseana Editions; Tennessee Studies in Literature; Vernacular Architecture Studies; and Voices of the Civil War.

University of Texas Press

Street Address:
2100 Comal Street
Austin, TX 78722

Mailing Address:
P.O. Box 7819
Austin, TX 78713-7819

Phone: (512) 471-7233
Fax: (512) 232-7178
E-mail: utpress@uts.cc.utexas.edu
Indiv: (user I.D.)@utpress.ppb.utexas.edu
Web site: www.utexaspress.com

Orders:
Phone: (800) 252-3206
Fax: (800) 687-6046

Staff

Director: Joanna Hitchcock (512/232-7604; e-mail: joanna)
   Assistant to the Director: Dreya Johannsen (512/232-7603; e-mail: dreya)
   Development Officer: Tim Staley (512/232-7605; e-mail: tim)
Rights and Permissions Manager: Laura Young Bost (512/232-7625; e-mail: laura)
   Rights and Permissions Assistant: Peggy Gough (512/232-7624; e-mail: peggy)
Assistant Director and Editor-in-Chief: Theresa May (social sciences) (512/232 7612;
   e-mail: theresa)
   Acquisitions Editors: William Bishel (natural sciences, Texas and the Southwest) (512/232-
   7609; e-mail: wbishel); Jim Burr (humanities) (512/232-7610; e-mail: jim)
   Associate Editor: Allison Faust (512/232-7615; e-mail: allison)
   Assistant Editor: Wendy Moore (512/232-7608; e-mail: wendy)
Managing Editor: Carolyn Cates Wylie (512/232-7613; e-mail: carolyn)
   Assistant Managing Editor: Leslie Tingle (512/232-7614; e-mail: leslie)
   Manuscript Editors: Jan McInroy (512/232-7616; e-mail: jan); Lynne Chapman (512/232-
   7607; e-mail: lynne)
Sales and Marketing Manager: David Hamrick (512/232-7627; e-mail: dave)
   Texas Sales Manager: Darrell Windham (512/471-4032; e-mail: darrell)
   Assistant Marketing Manager: Nancy Bryan (512/232-7628; e-mail: nancy)
   Direct Mail and Website Manager: Sharon Casteel (512/232-7631; e-mail: sharon)
   Publicist: Heather Crist (512/232-7634; e-mail: heather)
   Exhibits and Events Manager: Lauren Zachry-Reynolds (512/232-7630; e-mail: lauren)
   Marketing Fellow: Casey Kittrell (512/232-7633; e-mail: casey)
Assistant Director and Design/Production Manager: David Cavazos (512/232-7638; e-mail:
   david)
   Art Director: Ellen McKie (512/232-7640; e-mail: ellen)
   Designers: Teresa W. Wingfield (512/232-7641; e-mail: teresa); Heidi Haeuser (512/232-
   7642; e-mail: heidi)
   Production Editor: Regina Fuentes (512/232-7639; e-mail: regina)
   Production Assistant: Frank Minogue (512/232-7637; e-mail: frank)
   Production Fellow: Michael Williams (512/232-7643; e-mail: michael)
Journals Manager: Sue Hausmann (512/232-7620; e-mail: sue)
   Journals Production Manager: Karen Crowther (512/232-7619; e-mail: karen)

Journals Production Assistant: Karen Broyles (512/232-7622; e-mail: kbroyles)
Journals Promotion Manager: Leah Dixon (512/232-7618; e-mail: leah)
Journals Circulation and Rights and Permissions Manager: Stacey Salling (512/232-7617; e-mail: stacey)
Journals Circulation Assistant: Christina Rivera (512/232-7621; e-mail: christina)
Assistant Director and Financial Officer: Joyce Lewandowski (512/232-7646; e-mail: joyce)
   Accounts Receivable: Margaret Cano (512/232-7648; e-mail: margaret)
   Accounts Payable: Linda Ramirez (512/232-7649; e-mail: linda)
   Business Assistant: Nancy Monroe (512/232-7647; e-mail: nmonroe)
   Fulfillment Manager: Shirley Stewart (512/232-7652; e-mail: shirley)
   Customer Service: Brenda Jo Hoggatt (512/232-7650; e-mail: brenda_jo)
Warehouse (512/471-3634)
   Warehouse Manager: Donald Martinez (512/232-7654; e-mail: donald)
   Warehouse Supervisor: George Mill (512/232-7656; e-mail: george)
   Warehouse Staff: Michael Murillo (512/232-7655); Rogelio Rocha Jr. (512/232-7657); Andrew Murillo (512/232-7658; e-mail: andy)
Senior LAN Administrator: William Braddock (512/232-7644; e-mail: william)

Full Member

Established: 1950	Admitted to AAUP: 1954
Title output 2002: 91	Title output 2003: 84
Distributed titles 2002: 6	Distributed titles 2003: 6
Titles currently in print: 964	Journals published: 11

Editorial Program

Scholarly books in the humanities, natural sciences, and social sciences; regional books; and serious nonfiction of general interest; humanities (art of the ancient world, classics and the ancient world, Egyptology, film and media studies, literary modernism, Middle Eastern studies and translations of Middle Eastern literature, Old World archaeology, Texas architecture); natural sciences (botany, conservation, cookbooks and gardening, environmental studies, geography, marine science, natural history, ornithology); social sciences (American studies, anthropology, applied language, Chicano/a studies, Latin American and pre-Columbian studies, translations of Latin American literature, Mexican American studies, Native American studies, New World archaeology, Texas and the Southwest, women's studies); and the following journals (* indicates journals available electronically): *Archaeoastronomy*; *Asian Music*, *Cinema Journal**; *The Journal of Individual Psychology*; *The Journal of the History of Sexuality**; *Latin American Music Review**; *Latin American Research Review**; *Libraries and Culture**; *Texas Studies in Literature and Language**; *The Velvet Light Trap*; and the *Journal of Latin American Geography for the Conference of Latin Americanist Geographers*. Original fiction, poetry, and children's books are not invited.

Special series, joint imprints, and/or copublishing programs: Center for Mexican American Studies, History, Culture, and Society Series; Chicana Matters Series; Constructs Series; Focus on American History Series; Harry Ransom Humanities Research Imprint Series; Handbook of Latin American Studies; Inter-America Series; Legendary Past Series; Literary Modernism Series; Middle East Monograph Series; Modern Middle East Literature in Translation Series; Modern Middle East Series; New Interpretations of Latin America Series; Oratory of Classical Greece Series; Southwest Writers Series; Surrealist Revolution Series;

Texas Archaeology and Ethnohistory Series; Texas Film and Media Studies Series; Texas Field Guides; Texas Pan American and Literature in Translation Series; Wittliff Gallery Series of Southwestern and Mexican Photography.

The Press distributes publications for the Austin Museum of Art; Bat Conservation International; Center for Middle Eastern Studies; Center for Mexican American Studies; Institute of Mesoamerican Studies (SUNY/Albany); McNay Art Museum; Museum of Fine Arts Houston; and Teresa Lozano Long Institute of Latin American Studies.

Endowed Book Series: Clifton and Shirley Caldwell Texas Heritage Series; Peter T. Flawn Series in Natural Resource Management and Conservation; Joe R. and Teresa Lozano Long Series in Latin American and Latino Art and Culture; Linda Schele Series in Maya and Pre-Columbian Studies; Jack and Doris Smothers Series in Texas History, Life, and Culture; Louann Atkins Temple Women and Culture Series; Bill and Alice Wright Photography Series.

Texas A&M University Press

Street Address:
John H. Lindsey Building, Lewis Street
College Station, TX 77843

Mailing Address:
4354 TAMU
College Station, TX 77843-4354

Phone: (979) 845-1436
Fax: (979) 847-8752
E-mail: upress@tampress.tamu.edu
Indiv: (user I.D.)@tampress.tamu.edu
Web site: www.tamu.edu/upress/

Orders:
Phone: (800) 826-8911
Fax: (888) 617-2421

Staff
Director: Charles Backus (979/458-3980; e-mail: backus)
　Assistant to the Director/Rights & Permissions: Linda Lou Salitros (979/845-1438; e-mail: lls)
Acquisitions Editorial: Mary Lenn Dixon, Editor-in-Chief (Texas and Western history, borderland studies, presidential studies, anthropology) (979/845-0759; e-mail: mld)
　Louise Lindsey Merrick Editor for the Natural Environment: Shannon Davies (512/327-3183; e-mail: smdavies@aol.com)
　Acquisitions Editor: TBA (military history, Eastern European studies, business history, nautical archaeology) (979/458-3977)
　Associate Editor (copyedit): Stephanie Attia George (979/845-0758; e-mail: seg)
　Assistant Editor (copyedit): Jennifer Ann Hobson (979/458-3979; e-mail: jah)
　Acquisitions Assistant: Diana Vance (979/458-3975; e-mail: dlv)
　Editorial Assistant: Janet Mathewson (979/458-3978; e-mail: jmm)
Marketing: Gayla Christiansen, Marketing Manager (979/845-0148; e-mail: gec)
　Publicity and Advertising Manager: Jennifer McDonald (979/458-3982; e-mail: jam)
　Graphics/Web Manager: Kyle Littlefield (979/458-3983; e-mail: k-littlefield)
　Exhibits Manager: TBA (979/458-3984)
　Sales Manager: Steve Griffis (979/458-3981; e-mail: srg)
Production: Susan Pettey, Production Manager (979/845-0760; e-mail: sap)
Design: Mary Ann Jacob, Design Manager (979/845-3694; e-mail: maj)
　Design and Production Assistant: Kevin Grossman (979/458-3995; e-mail: klg)

Financial: Dianna Sells, Financial Manager (979/845-0146; e-mail: dsh)
  Finance Assistant: Johnny Ruiz (979/458-3974; e-mail: jar)
Business Operations Manager: Sharon Pavlas-Mills (979/458-3994; e-mail: sym)
  Accounts Receivable Manager: Ellen Compton (979/458-3989; e-mail: esc)
  Order Fulfillment Supervisor: Vicky Ramos (979/458-3990; e-mail: vrr)
  Orders Clerk: Brandy Petereit (979/458-3991; e-mail: bjp)
Warehouse Manager: Mike Martin (979/458-3986; e-mail: mam)
  Assistant Warehouse Manager: Dennis McDowell (979/458-3987; e-mail: drm)

Full Member

Established: 1974
Title output 2002: 57
Titles currently in print: 875

Admitted to AAUP: 1977
Title output 2003: 61

Editorial Program

Texas and the Southwest; American and Western history; natural history; the environment; women's studies; military history; economics; business; architecture; art; veterinary medicine; presidential studies; borderland studies. Submissions are not invited in poetry.

Special series: C. A. Brannen Series in Military Memoirs; Canseco-Keck History; Carolyn and Ernest Fay Series in Analytical Psychology; Centennial of Flight Series; Centennial Series of the Association of Former Students; Charles and Elizabeth Prothro Texas Photography; Clayton Wheat Williams Texas Life; Eastern European Series; Ed Rachal Foundation Series in Nautical Archaeology; Elma Dill Russell Spencer Foundation; Environmental History Series; Fronteras Series; Gulf Coast Studies Series; Joe and Betty Moore Texas Art; Kenneth E. Montague Business and Oil History; Landmark Speeches on American Politics; Louise Lindsey Merrick Texas Environment; Presidential Rhetoric; The Presidency and Leadership Studies; Rio Grande/Rio Bravo; Sam Rayburn Rural Life; Sara and John H. Lindsey Series in the Arts and Humanities; Studies in Architecture and Culture; Tarleton State University Southwestern Studies in the Humanities; Texas A&M Economics; Texas A&M Foreign Relations and the Presidency; Texas A&M Military History; Texas A&M Southwestern Studies; Texas A&M University Anthropology; University of Houston Mexican American Studies; W. L. Moody Jr. Natural History; Wardlaw Books; West Texas A&M University.

TCU Press

Box 298300
Fort Worth, TX 76129

Phone: (817) 257-7822
Fax: (817) 257-5075
Web site: www.prs.tcu.edu

Staff
Director: Judy Alter (e-mail: j.alter@tcu.edu)
Editor: Susan Petty (e-mail: s.petty@tcu.edu)
Acquisitions Editor: James W. Lee (e-mail: j.lee@tcu.edu)

Affiliate Member
Established: 1966   Admitted to AAUP: 1982
Title output 2002: 12   Title output 2003: 10
Titles in print: 216

Editorial Program
Humanities and social sciences, with special emphasis on Texas and Southwestern history and literature; American studies; fiction; and women's studies.
    Special series: The Chisholm Trail Series; The Texas Tradition Series.

Texas Tech University Press

Street Address:
Administrative Support Center
2903 Fourth Street, Suite 201
Lubbock, TX 79409-1037

Mailing Address:
Box 41037
Lubbock, TX 79409-1037

Phone: (806) 742-2982
Fax: (806) 742-2979
E-mail: (firstname.lastname)@ttu.edu
Web site: www.ttup.ttu.edu

Orders:
Phone: (806) 742-2982; (800) 832-4042

Staff
Director: Noel R. Parsons
Acquisitions: Judith Keeling, Editor-in-Chief (humanities)
   Editor: Noel R. Parsons (sciences)
Managing Editor: Katherine Dennis
Marketing Manager: Courtney Burkholder
   Marketing Assistant: John Brock
Design and Production Manager: Barbara Werden
Journals Editor: Virginia Downs
Business Manager: Joel Nichols
   Customer Service: Sandra Fielding; LaTisha Roberts; Isabel Williams
Warehouse & Shipping Manager: Ramon Luna

Full Member
Established: 1971
Title output 2002: 24
Titles currently in print: 300

Admitted to AAUP: 1987
Title output 2003: 21
Journals published: 5

Editorial Program
Natural sciences and natural history; environmental studies and literature of place; regional
history and culture; Western Americana; Vietnam War and Southeast Asian studies; eigh-
teenth-century studies; Joseph Conrad studies; costume and textile history and conservation;
poetry (by invitation only); regional fiction.
   Journals: *Conradiana*; *The Eighteenth Century*; *Helios*; *Intertexts*; and *The William Carlos
Williams Review*.
   Special series: Costume Society of America; Discourses in Native America; Double
Mountain Books: Classic Reissues of the American West; Fashioning the Eighteenth Cen-
tury; Grover E. Murray Studies in the American Southwest; Modern Southeast Asia; Plains
Histories; and Walt McDonald First-Book Series in Poetry.

Texas Western Press

University of Texas at El Paso
500 West University Avenue
El Paso, TX 79968-0633

Phone: (915) 747-5688
Fax: (915) 747-7515
E-mail: twpress@utep.edu
Indiv: (user I.D.)@utep.edu
Web site: www.utep.edu/~twp

Orders:
Phone: (800) 488-3789; (915) 747-5688

Staff
Acting Director: Jon Amastae (915/747-5688; e-mail: amastae)
Marketing: Jon Amastae
Production: Jon Amastae
Business: Jon Amastae
   Accounts Supervisor: Carmen Tavarez (915/747-5688; e-mail: ctavarez)
Secretary: Carmen Tavarez

Full Member
Established: 1952
Title output 2002: 2
Titles currently in print: 54

Admitted to AAUP: 1986
Title output 2003: 2

Editorial Program
Scholarly books and serious nonfiction with special interests in the history and cultures of the Southwest; selected art and photography; US-Mexico border studies; environmental studies; and the following series: Southwestern Studies and The Borderlands/La Frontera.

University of Tokyo Press

7-3-1 Hongo, Bunkyo-ku
Tokyo 113-8654, Japan

Phone: +81-3-3811-8814
Fax: +81-3-3814-9458, +81-03-3812-6958
E-mail: info@utp.or.jp

US Representative:
Columbia University Press

Staff
President: Takeshi Sasaki
Chairman of the Board: Fumihiko Gomi
Managing Director: Isao Watanabe
Associate Director and CFO: Masami Yamaguchi
Chief Operating Officer: Jiichiro Oe
Editor-in-Chief: Hidetoshi Takenaka
Marketing Director: Tomohiko Takahashi
Production Director: Masayuki Nagasaka
Executive Assistant, International Publications: Mitsuo Takayanagi

International Member
Established: 1951
Title output 2002: 140 (2 in English)
Titles currently in print: 3,740

Admitted to AAUP: 1970
Title output 2003: 125

Editorial Program
Titles published in Japanese reflect the research carried out at the university in the humanities, social sciences, and natural sciences.

Continuing series are published in biology, earth sciences, sociology, economics, philosophy, and Japanese art and historical studies. Special projects include publication of textbooks and reprinting of historical source materials.

English-language publishing began in 1960; special strengths include Japanese and Asian studies (including history, economics, law, and sociology). English-language publications also include translations of historical and important literary works and diaries.

University of Toronto Press, Inc.

Scholarly Publishing Division:
10 St. Mary Street, Suite 700
Toronto, ON M4Y 2W8
Canada

Phone: (416) 978-2239
Fax: (416) 978-4738
E-mail: publishing@utpress.utoronto.ca
Indiv: (user I.D.)@utpress.utoronto.ca
Web site: www.utpress.utoronto.ca

European Representative:
Premier Book Marketing

Journals Division/Orders/Customer Service:
5201 Dufferin Street
Downsview, ON M3H 5T8
Canada
Phone: (800) 565-9523; (416) 667-7791
Fax: (416) 667-7832; (800) 221-9985

US Warehouse:
2250 Military Road
Tonawanda, NY 14150
Phone: (716) 693-2768

UK Representative:
Yale University Press

Staff

President, Publisher and CEO: John Yates (416/978-2239, ext. 222; e-mail: jyates)

Senior Vice President, Administration: Kathryn Bennett (416/978-2239, ext. 224; e-mail: kbennett)

Senior Vice President, Scholarly Publishing: Bill Harnum (416/978-2239, ext. 243; e-mail: bharnum)

Vice President, Order Fulfillment and Management Information Services: Hamish Cameron (416/978-2239, ext. 252; e-mail: hcameron)

Vice President, Finance: Curt Auwaerter (416/667-7765)

Vice President, Journals: Anne Marie Corrigan (416/667-7838; e-mail: acorrigan)

Editorial (416/978-2239): Virgil Duff, Executive Editor (social sciences) (ext. 240; e-mail: vduff)

Editors: Len Husband (Canadian history) (ext. 238; e-mail: lhusband); Siobhan McMenemy (Canadian film and literature history) (ext. 231; e-mail: smcmenemy); Ron Schoeffel (ext. 241; e-mail: rschoeffel); Jill McConkey (humanities) (ext. 233; e-mail: jmcconkey)

Humanities Editor and Foreign Rights: Suzanne Rancourt (medieval and Renaissance studies, English language and literature) (ext. 239; e-mail: rancourt)

Permissions: Walter Brooker (ext. 226; e-mail: wbrooker)

Reference Division Manager: Elizabeth Lumley (ext. 245; e-mail: elumley)

Managing Editor: Anne Laughlin (ext. 236; e-mail: alaughlin)

Marketing and Sales (416/978-2239): Melissa Pitts, Sales and Marketing Manager (ext. 254; e-mail: mpitts)

Publicist: Ruta Liormanis (ext. 248; e-mail rliormanis)

Advertising/Web Coordinator: Don Bassingthwaite (ext. 249; e-mail: dbassing)

Catalogue Coordinator: Douglas Hildebrand (ext. 260; e-mail: dhildebrand)

Production: Ani Deyirmenjian, Manager (ext. 227; e-mail: adeyirmenjian)

Journals: (5201 Dufferin St.)

Vice-President, Journals: Anne Marie Corrigan (416/667-7838; e-mail: acorrigan)

Manager, Circulation and Distribution: Joanne Raines (416/667-7766; e-mail: jraines)

Journals Marketing and Online Manager: Tamara Hawkins (416/667-7849; e-mail: thawkins)
Journals Advertising and Marketing Coordinator: Audrey Greenwood (416/667-7766; e-mail: agreenwood)
Printing Division: Trevor Williamson, Operations Manager (416/667-7778)
  Sales Manager: Reg Hunt
  Bindery Manager: Mike Cummins (416/667-7754); Creative Services: (416/978-2261)

Full Member

Established: 1901	Admitted to AAUP: 1937
Title output 2002: 145	Title output 2003: 142
Titles currently in print: 1,600	Journals published: 32

Editorial Program

Classical studies; medieval studies; Renaissance studies; Slavic studies; environmental studies; Erasmian studies; Victorian studies; English literature; Canadian studies; Canadian literature; literary theory and criticism; modern languages and literatures; philosophy; political science; law and criminology; religion and theology; education; music; art history; geography; Canadian and international history; sociology; anthropology; Native studies; social work; and women's studies.

The Press also publishes the following journals: *Bookbird*; *Canadian Historical Review*; *Canadian Journal on Aging*; *Canadian Journal of Information and Library Sciences*; *Canadian Journal of Linguistics*; *Canadian Journal of Mathematics*; *Canadian Journal of Science, Mathematics, and Technology*; *Canadian Journal of Sociology*; *Canadian Journal of Women and the Law*; *Canadian Mathematics Bulletin*; *Canadian Modern Language Review*; *Canadian Public Policy*; *Canadian Review of American Studies*; *Canadian Theatre Review*; *Cartographica*; *Diaspora: A Journal of Transnational Studies*; *Eighteenth Century Fiction*; *Eye on Science*; *Francophonies d'Amérique*; *Histoire Sociale*; *INFOR*; *Journal of Canadian Studies*; *Journal of Scholarly Publishing*; *Journal of Veterinary Medical Education*; *Modern Drama*; *Seminar*; *Simile: Studies in Media and Information Literacy Education*; *The Tocqueville Review*; *Ultimate Reality and Meaning*; *University of Toronto Law Journal*; *University of Toronto Quarterly*; and *Victorian Periodicals Review*. Submissions are not invited in poetry or fiction.

Special series, joint imprints and/or copublishing programs: Anthropological Horizons; Benjamin Disraeli Letters; Chaucer Bibliographies; Collected Works of A.M. Klein; Collected Works of Bernard Lonergan; Collected Works of E.J. Pratt; Collected Works of Erasmus; Collected Works of George Grant; Collected Works of Northrop Frye; Collected Works of John Stuart Mill; Dictionary of Canadian Biography; Erasmus Studies; Historical Atlas of Canada; Hong Kong Bank of Canada Papers on Asia; Italian Linguistics and Language Pedagogy; Lonergan Studies; McMaster Old English Studies and Texts; Medieval Academy Reprints for Teaching; Mental and Cultural World of Tudor and Stuart England; Ontario Historical Studies Series; Phoenix Supplementary Volumes; Publications of the Osgoode Society; Records of Early English Drama; Reprints in Canadian History; Renaissance Society of America Reprint Texts; Robson Classical Lectures; Royal Inscriptions of Mesopotamia; State and Economic Life Series; Studies in Gender and History; Studies in Social History; Themes in Canadian Social History; Theory/Culture; Toronto Italian Studies; Toronto Medieval Bibliographies; Toronto Medieval Texts and Translations; Toronto Old English Series; Toronto Studies in Philosophy; Studies in Early English Drama; Toronto Studies in Semiotics; University of Toronto Romance Series; University of Toronto Ukrainian Studies.

United Nations University Press

53-70, Jingumae 5-chome
Shibuya-ku, Tokyo 150-8925
Japan

Orders:
Fax: +81-3-3406-7345
E-mail (orders): sales@hq.unu.edu

Phone: +81-3-3499-2811
Fax: +81-3-3406-7345
E-mail: press@hq.unu.edu
Indiv: (user I.D.)@hq.unu.edu
Web site: www.unu.edu

US Distributor:
Brookings Institution Press

UK Distributor:
UPM (through Brookings)

Staff
Head of Publications: Scott McQuade (5467-1319; e-mail: mcquade)
Administrative Assistant: Atsuko Sato (5467-1291; e-mail: atsuko)
Assistant Editor: Gareth Johnston (5467-1315; e-mail: johnston)
Marketing and Sales: Marc Benger, Manager (5467-1310; e-mail: benger)
  Sales Assistant: Mikako Torii (5467-1313; e-mail: torii)
Design and Production: Yoko Kojima, Manager (5467-1316; e-mail: kojima)

International Member
Established: 1990
Title output 2002: 8
Titles currently in print: 170

Admitted to AAUP: 1997
Title output 2003: 17

Editorial Program
The United Nations University Press is the publishing division of the United Nations University, a UN organ established by the General Assembly in 1972. The UNU Press publishes scholarly books and periodicals in the social sciences, humanities, and pure and applied natural sciences, with concentrations in peace and conflict resolution, development, environment and sustainability, and science and technology.

United States Institute of Peace Press

1200 17th Street, N.W., Suite 200
Washington, DC 20036-3011
Phone: (202) 429-3814
Fax: (202) 429-6063
E-mail: (user I.D)@usip.org
Web site and online catalog: www.usip.org

Customer Service:
P.O. Box 605
Herndon, VA 20172
Phone: (800) 868-8064 ;(703) 661-1590
Fax: (703) 661-1501

UK and European Representative:
University Presses Marketing

Canadian Representative:
Renouf Books

Staff
Director: TBA
Editor: Peter Pavilionis (202/429-3812; e-mail: peter_pavilionis)
Sales and Marketing Manager: Kay Hechler (202/429-3816; e-mail: kay_hechler)
Production Manager: Marie Marr (202/429-3815; e-mail: marie_marr)

Associate Member
Established: 1991
Title output 2002: 7
Title currently in print: 80

Admitted to AAUP: 1993
Title output 2003: 6

Editorial Program
The Press publishes books that are based on work supported by the Institute. The Institute is an independent, nonpartisan federal institution mandated by Congress to promote research, education, and training on the peaceful resolution of international conflicts. The Institute's publications range across the entire spectrum of international relations, including: conflict management and resolution, diplomacy and negotiation, human rights, mediation and facilitation, foreign policy, ethnopolitics, political science, and religion and ethics. The Institute also publishes reports and a newsletter, *Peace Watch*.

W. E. Upjohn Institute for Employment Research

300 Westnedge Avenue
Kalamazoo, MI 49007-4686

Phone: (269) 343-4330
Fax: (269) 343-7310
E-mail: publications@upjohninstitute.org
Indiv: (last name)@upjohninstitute.org
Web site: www.upjohninstitute.org

Staff
Director of Publications: Kevin Hollenbeck (269/343-5541)
  Assistant to the Director: Claire Black (269/343-5541)
Manager of Publications and Marketing: Richard Wyrwa (269/343-5541)

Associate Member
Established: 1945   Admitted to AAUP: 1997
Title output 2002: 10   Title output 2003: 12
Titles currently in print: 190   Journals published: 1

Editorial Program
Scholarly works on employment-related issues; labor economics; current issues in the social sciences, with an emphasis on public policy. Books are authored mainly by researchers awarded grants through the Institute's annual Competitive Grant Program; also by resident research staff and other scholars in the academic and professional communities. The Institute also publishes working papers and technical reports authored by the resident research staff; a quarterly journal on the West Michigan economy, *Business Outlook for West Michigan*, and a quarterly newsletter, *Employment Research*.

University of Utah Press

1795 E. South Campus Drive, #101
Salt Lake City, UT 84112-9402

Phone: (801) 581-6771
Fax: (801) 581-3365
E-mail: info@upress.utah.edu
Indiv: (user I.D.)@upress.utah.edu
Web site: www.uofupress.com

Orders:
Phone: (800) 773-6672

Canadian Representative:
Scholarly Book Services

Staff
Director: Jeffrey L. Grathwohl (e-mail: jgrathwohl)
Acquisitions Editor: Peter DeLafosse (e-mail: pdelafosse)
Managing Editor: Glenda Cotter (e-mail: gcotter)
Marketing Manager: Marcelyn Ritchie (801/585-9786; e-mail: mritchie)
   Assistant Marketing Manager: Rachael Coonradt (e-mail: rcoonradt)
Production Manager: Virginia Fontana (e-mail: jfontana)
Business Manager: Sharon Day (e-mail: sday)
Customer Service: Sydney Grubb (e-mail: sgrubb)

Full Member
Established: 1949
Title output 2002: 26
Titles currently in print: 319

Admitted to AAUP: 1979
Title output 2003: 26

Editorial Program
Anthropology and archaeology; linguistics; Mesoamerica; Native America; Western American history; Utah; regional studies; geography; natural history.
   Special series: Agha Shahid Ali Prize in Poetry; Anthropology of Pacific North America; Foundations of Archaeological Inquiry; Publications in the American West; Tanner Lectures on Human Values; University of Utah Anthropological Papers.

Utah State University Press

Utah State University
7800 Old Main Hill
Logan, UT 84322-7800

Orders:
Phone: (800) 239-9974

Phone: (435) 797-1362
Fax: (435) 797-0313
E-mail: (firstname.lastname)@usu.edu
Web site: www.usu.edu/usupress

Staff

Director: Michael Spooner
Executive Editor: John R. Alley Jr.
Marketing Manager: Brooke Bigelow
Business Manager: Cathy Tarbet
Office Assistant: Sandra Reed

Affiliate Member

Established: 1972
Title output 2002: 15
Titles currently in print: 164

Admitted to AAUP: 1984
Title output 2003: 16

Editorial Program

Scholarly books with special emphasis on Western American history; regional (Mountain West) studies; composition studies; folklore studies; regional natural history; Native American studies; Western women's history; and Mormon history. Submission by invitation only in fiction and poetry.

Special series: Kingdom in the West; Life Writings of Frontier Women; May Swenson Poetry Award; Western Experience.

Vanderbilt University Press

Street Address:
112 21st Avenue South
University Plaza Suite 201
Nashville, TN 37203

Mailing Address:
VU Station B 351813
Nashville, TN 37235

Phone: (615) 322-3583
Fax: (615) 343-8823
Email: vupress@vanderbilt.edu
Indiv: (user I.D.)@vanderbilt.edu
Online catalog and Web site: www.vanderbilt.edu/vupress

Customer Service/Order Fulfillment:
OU Press Book Distribution Center
4100 28th Avenue NW
Norman, OK 73069
Phone: (800) 627-7377
Fax: (800) 735-0476

UK Distributor:
Eurospan

Staff

Director: Michael Ames (e-mail: michael.ames)
Editorial Coordinator: Betsy Phillips (e-mail: betsy.t.phillips)
Editing and Production Manager: Dariel Mayer (e-mail: dariel.mayer)
Marketing Manager: Sue Havlish (e-mail: sue.havlish)
Business Manager: Donna Gruverman (e-mail: donna.gruverman)

Affiliate Member

Established: 1940
Title output 2002: 18
Titles currently in print: 180

Admitted to AAUP: 1993
Title output 2003: 10

Editorial Program

Scholarly books and serious nonfiction in most areas of the humanities, the social sciences, health care, and higher education. Special interests include Hispanic and Latin American studies, health care and social issues, English and American literature, gender studies, human rights, and regional books.

Copublishing program: Country Music Foundation.

The University of Virginia Press

Street Address:
Bemiss House
210 Sprigg Lane
Charlottesville, VA 22903-0608

Mailing Address:
P.O. Box 400318
Charlottesville, VA 22904-4318

Phone: (434) 924-3468
Fax: (434) 982-2655
E-mail: upressva@virginia.edu
Indiv: (user I.D.)@virginia.edu
Web site: www.upress.virginia.edu

Warehouse Address:
500 Edgemont Road
Charlottesville, VA 22903-0608
Phone: (434) 924-6305
Fax: (434) 982-2655

UK/European Representative:
Eurospan

Canadian Representative:
Scholarly Book Services

Staff

Director: Penelope Kaiserlian (434/924-3131; e-mail: pkaiserlian)
  Assistant to the Director and Rights & Permissions: Mary E. MacNeil (434/924-3361; e-mail: mmm5w)
Acquisitions Editorial: Cathie Brettschneider (humanities) (434/982-3033; e-mail: cib8b); Richard K. Holway (history and social sciences) (434/924-7301; e-mail: rkh2a); Boyd Zenner (architecture, environmental studies, ecocriticism, and regional) (434/924-1373; e-mail: bz2v)
  Editorial Assistant: Angie Hogan (434/924-4725; e-mail: arh2h)
Manuscript Editorial: Ellen Satrom, Managing Editor (434/924-6065; e-mail: egs6s)
  Senior Editor: Susan Lee Foard (434/924-6067; e-mail: slf9d)
  Project Editor: Mark Mones (434/924-6066; e-mail: emm4t)
Marketing: Mark Saunders, Marketing Director (434/924-6065; e-mail: mhs5u)
  Marketing Manager: Nancy Mills (434/924-6070; e-mail njm8j)
  Publicist: Emily Grandstaff (434/982-2932; e-mail: ekg4a)
  Electronic Marketing and Exhibits Manager: Jason Coleman (434/924-4150; e-mail: jgc3h)
Design and Production: Martha Farlow, Production Manager (434/924-3585; e-mail: mfarlow)
  Design/Production Assistant: Brooke Kelley (434/982-2704; e-mail: bwk4u)
Business: David E. Garrett, Chief Financial Officer and Operations Manager (434/982-2666; e-mail: deg4x)
  Accountant: F. Duncan Pickett (434/924-6068; e-mail: fdp7e)
  Customer Service Manager: Brenda Fitzgerald (434/924-3469; e-mail bwf)
  Business Assistant: V. Juanita Cranor (434/924-3468; e-mail: vjc7y)
  Warehouse Manager: Johnny Tyler (434/924-6305; e-mail: jrt3u)
Electronic Imprint: Mark H. Saunders, Manager (434/924-6065; e-mail: mhs5u)
  Administrative and Editorial Assistant: Mary Ann Lugo (434/982-2310; e-mail: ml2z)
  Systems Engineer/Programmer: Oludotun Akinola (434/924-4423; e-mail: oa2m)
  Managing Editor: David Sewell (434/924-9973; e-mail: drs2n)
  Programmer/Analyst and XML Designer: Shannon Shiflett (434/924-4544; e-mail shiflett)

Full Member

Established: 1963

Title output 2002: 54

Titles currently in print: 916

Admitted to AAUP: 1964

Title output 2003: 53

Editorial Program

American history; African-American studies; Southern studies; political science; literary and cultural studies, with particular strengths in African and Caribbean studies; Victorian studies; religious studies; architecture and landscape studies; regional trade; Virginiana.

Special series: The American South; CARAF BOOKS (Caribbean and African Literature translated from French); The Carter G. Woodson Institute Series in Black Studies; Cultural Frames, Framing Cultures; History of Early Modern Germany; Jeffersonian America; A Nation Divided: New Studies in Civil War History; Race and Ethnicity in Urban Politics; Reconsiderations in Southern African History; Studies in Religion; Under the Sign of Nature; Victorian Literature and Culture; The Virginia Bookshelf.

Multi-volume series: The Correspondence of William James; The Letters of Christina Rossetti; The Letters of Matthew Arnold (completed); The Papers of George Washington; The Papers of James Madison.

The Press distributes the Washington Bookshelf series, published by the Mount Vernon Ladies Association.

University of Washington Press

Street Address:

1326 Fifth Avenue, Suite 555

Seattle, WA 98101-2604

Phone: (206) 543-4050 (General)

(206) 543-8870 (Business Office)

Fax: (206) 543-3932 (General)

(206) 685-3460 (Business Office)

E-mail: (user I.D.)@u.washington.edu

Web site: www.washington.edu/uwpress/

UK Representative:

Combined Academic Publishing

Mailing Address:

P.O. Box 50096

Seattle, WA 98145-5096

Orders:

Phone: (800) 441-4115

Fax: (800) 669-7993

Canadian Sales Group:

University of British Columbia Press

Staff

Director: Pat Soden (206/543-8271; e-mail: patsoden)

Assistant to Director and Subsidiary Rights Manager: Denise Clark (206/543-4057; e-mail: ddclark)

Associate Director and General Manager: Mary Anderson (206/221-5892; e-mail: maryande)

Associate Director and CFO: Dorothy Anthony (206/543-2857; e-mail: djabooks)

Development Director: Nina McGuinness (206/543-4053; e-mail: ninamg)

Development Assistant: Hady De Jong (206/221-4991; e-mail: hadydej)

Acquisitions Editorial: Michael Duckworth, Executive Editor (206/221-4940; e-mail: michaeld)

Acquisitions Editors: Lorri Hagman (206/221-4989; e-mail: lhagman); Jacqueline Ettinger

(206/221-4984; e-mail: jetting)
  Acquisitions Assistant: Beth Fuget (206/616-0818; e-mail: bfuget)
Manuscript Editorial: Marilyn Trueblood, Managing Editor (206/221-4987; e-mail: marilynt)
  Assistant Managing Editor: Mary Ribesky (206/685-9165; e-mail: ribesky)
  Copyeditor: Kerrie Maynes (206/221-5889; e-mail maynesk)
  Assistant Editor and Electronic Marketing Specialist: Kathleen Pike Jones (206/221-4986; e-mail: kpike)
Marketing Manager: Alice Herbig (206/221-4994; e-mail: aherbig)
  Sales Manager: Marcelle Garrard (206/221-4995; e-mail: mgarrard)
  Publicist: Gigi Lamm (206/221-4996; e-mail: glamm)
  Exhibits and Text Promotion: Beth DeWeese (206/221-5890; e-mail: edeweese)
  Advertising and Direct Mail: Alice Schroeter (206/685-9874; e-mail: aschroet)
  Distribution and Fulfillment Coordinator: Kyle Hansen (206/543-8870; e-mail: khansen)
Design and Production: John Stevenson, Production Manager (206/221-5893; e-mail: jasbooks)
  Art Director: Audrey Meyer (206/685-9877; e-mail: asmeyer)
  Designer and Assistant Production Manager: Pamela Canell (206/221-4993; e-mail: pcanell)
  Production Coordinator: Diane Murphy (206/221-4992; e-mail: kdm)
  Design/Production Assistant: Ashley Saleeba (206/221-7004; e-mail: asaleeba)
Assistant Business Manager: Patricia Kain (206/685-3286; e-mail: pkain)
  Credit and Accounts Receivable Manager: Linda Tom (206/543-8658; e-mail: lindatom)
  Orders/MIS Support: Gayle Morriss (206/543-2862; e-mail: gmorriss)
  Warehouse Manager: Eric Ramhorst (206/543-4342; e-mail: amhort)

Full Member

Established: 1909   Admitted to AAUP: 1937
Title output 2002: 64   Title output 2003: 63
Titles currently in print: 1,400

Editorial Program

African studies; anthropology; Asian-American studies; Asian studies; art; aviation history; environmental studies; forest history; regional history and culture of the Northwest; Native American studies; Slavic studies; Middle Eastern studies; international studies; Western American history; Jewish studies.

Special series, joint imprints, and/or copublishing programs: American Ethnic and Cultural Studies; Asian Art and Culture; Asian Law Series; Classics in Tlingit Oral Literature; Columbia Northwest Classics; Emil and Kathleen Sick Series in Western History and Biography; Fabric Folios; Gandharan Buddhist Texts; Global Diasporas; Henry M. Jackson Lectures on Modern Chinese Studies and Publications in Korean Studies; History of East Central Europe Series; The Jackson School Publications in International Studies; Jacob Lawrence Series on American Artists; Jessie and John Danz Lecture Series; McLellan Books; Pacific Northwest Poetry Series; Publications on Near Eastern Studies; The Samuel and Althea Stroum Lectures in Jewish History; Samuel and Althea Stroum Books; The Scott and Laurie Oki Series in Asian-American Studies; Studies in Modernity and National Identity; Studies on Ethnic Groups in China; Thomas Burke Memorial Washington State Museum Monographs; Weyerhaeuser Environmental Books.

Washington State University Press

Cooper Publications Building
P.O. Box 645910
Pullman, WA 99164-5910

Phone: (509) 335-3518
Fax: (509) 335-8568
E-mail: wsupress@wsu.edu
Indiv: (user I.D.)@wsu.edu
Web site: wsupress.wsu.edu

Orders:
Phone: (800) 354-7360; (509) 335-7880

Canadian Representative:
University of British Columbia Press

Staff
Director: Mary Read (509/335-3518; e-mail: read)
Editor-in-Chief: Glen Lindeman (509/335-3518; e-mail: lindeman)
Production Coordinator: Jean Taylor (509/335-3518; e-mail: taylorj)
Production Editor: Nancy Grunewald (509/335-3518; e-mail: grunewan)
Marketing Coordinator: Caryn Lawton (509/335-3518; e-mail: lawton)
Order Fulfillment Coordinator: Jenni Lynn (509/335-7880; e-mail: jslynn)

Affiliate Member
Established: 1927
Title output 2002: 9
Distributed titles 2003: 3
Titles currently in print: 150

Admitted to AAUP: 1987
Title output 2003: 8

Journals published: 1

Editorial Program
Pacific Northwest; natural history; history, politics, and culture relating to the region; Western American history; ethnic studies; Native American studies; women's studies; environmental issues; essays; and memoirs. The Press distributes publications for the Washington State University Museum of Art, Oregon Writers Colony, and the Pacific Institute.

Journal: *Northwest Science*

Wayne State University Press

4809 Woodward Avenue
Detroit, MI 48201-1309

Phone: (313) 577-4600
Fax: (313) 577-6131
E-mail: (user I.D.)@wayne.edu
Web site: wsupress.wayne.edu

Orders:
Phone: (800) WSU-READ (978-7323)

Canadian Distributor:
Scholarly Book Services

UK/European Distributor:
Eurospan

Staff
Director: Jane Hoehner (313/577-4606; e-mail: jane.hoehner)
  Acquisitions/Permissions Assistant: Mollika Basu (313/577-4607; e-mail: ar9413)
Acquisitions Editorial: Kathryn Wildfong, Acquisitions Manager (313/577-6070; e-mail:
  k.wildfong) (Great Lakes, Africana, Judaica, German literary criticism, Armenian studies)
  Editors: Annie Martin (313/577-8335; e-mail: annie.martin) (film and television, fairy tale
  studies, childhood studies); Jane Hoehner (speech and language pathology)
Manuscript Editorial: Kristin Harpster Lawrence, Managing Editor (313/577-4604; e-mail:
  khlawrence)
  Manuscript Editor: Adela Garcia (313/577-6128; e-mail: adela.garcia)
  Editorial Assistant: Carrie Downes (313/577-6123; e-mail: carrie.downes)
Marketing: Renee Tambeau, Marketing Director (313/577-4603; e-mail: renee.tambeau)
  Promotions Assistant: Brandon Kelly (313/577-6077; e-mail: b.kelley)
Design and Production: Maya Rhodes, Production Coordinator (313/577-4600; e-mail:
  m.rhodes)
Business: Theresa Mahoney, Business Manager (313/577-3671; e-mail: ab7620)
  Fulfillment Manager: Theresa Martinelli (313/577-6126; e-mail: theresa.martinelli)
  Customer Service: Colleen Stone (313/577-6120; e-mail: colleen.stone)
  Warehouse Manager: Todd Richards (313/577-4619; e-mail: aa5624)
  Shipping: John Twomey (313/577-4609; e-mail: ai7331)
Electronic Publishing Coordinator: John Stephenson (313/577-2109; e-mail: j.stephenson)

Full Member
Established: 1941
Title output 2002: 62
Distributed titles 2003: 4
Titles currently in print: 817

Admitted to AAUP: 1956
Title output 2003: 34

Journals published: 6

Editorial Program
Scholarly books and serious nonfiction, with special interests in regional and local history;
Africana; Judaica; Armenian studies; film and television studies; childhood studies; fairy tales
and folklore; literary criticism; speech and language pathology; labor studies; urban studies;
and gender and ethnic studies. The Press publishes the following journals: *Criticism; Discourse; Framework; Human Biology; Marvels and Tales; Merrill-Palmer Quarterly.*

Special series: African American Life; American Jewish Civilizations; American Studies; Classical Studies Pedagogy; Contemporary Approaches to Film and Television; Fairy Tale Studies; Great Lakes Books; Kritik: German Literary Theory and Culture; Landscapes of Childhood; Painted Turtle Press; Raphael Patai Series in Jewish Folklore and Anthropology; TV Milestones; William Beaumont Hospital Series in Speech and Language Pathology.

Joint imprints and copublishing programs: Hebrew Union College Press, Cranbrook Institute of Science, Detroit Institute of Arts.

Wesleyan University Press

Editorial Offices:
215 Long Lane
Middletown, CT 06459-0433

Phone: (860) 685-7711
Fax: (860) 685-7712
E-mail: (user I.D.)@wesleyan.edu
Web site: www.wesleyan/edu/wespress/

UK and European Representative:
Eurospan

Book Distribution Center:
Wesleyan University Press
c/o University Press of New England
37 Lafayette Street
Lebanon, NH 03766-1466
Phone: (800) 421-1561
Fax: (603) 643-1540

Staff
Acting Director/Editor-in-Chief: Suzanna Tamminen (860/685-7727; e-mail: stamminen)
  Acquisitions Editor: TBA
Marketing: Leslie Starr, Marketing Manager (860/685-7725; e-mail: Lstarr)
  Marketing Associate: Kim Radowiecki (860/685-7716; e-mail: kradowiecki)
  Publicist: Stephanie Elliot (860/685-7723; e-mail: selliot)

Full Member
Established: 1959

Title output 2002: 38
Titles currently in print: 413

Admitted to AAUP: 2001
(Former membership: 1966-1991)
Title output 2003: 41

Editorial Program
The current editorial program focuses on poetry, music, dance, science fiction studies, film/TV/media studies, regional studies, and American studies.
  Special series: Early Classics of Science Fiction; Music/Culture; Wesleyan Poetry.

The West Virginia University Press

Street Address:
G3 White Hall
Morgantown, WV 26506

Mailing Address:
PO Box 6295
Morgantown, WV 26506

Phone: (304) 293-8400
Fax: (304) 293-6585
Web site: www.wvupress.com

Staff

Director/Editor: Patrick Conner (ext. 4505; e-mail: pconner@wvu.edu)
   Rights and Permissions: Stephanie Grove (ext. 4501; e-mail: press03@mail.wvu.edu)
   Office Manager: Floann Downey (ext. 4500; e-mail: fdowney2@wvu.edu)
   Public Relations: Bonnie Anderson (304/293-3107 ext. 33404; e-mail: banders@wvu.edu)
Marketing Director: Geoff George (ext. 4504; e-mail: press02@wvu.edu)
Production Manager/Designer: Than Saffel (ext. 4503; e-mail: than.saffel@mail.wvu.edu)
Journals Manager: Hilary Attfield (ext. 4502; e-mail: hattfiel@wvu.edu)
Business Manager: Michelle Marshall (304/293-3107 ext. 33407; e-mail:
   michele.marshall@mail.wvu.edu)
   Accounting: Sherry McGraw (ext. 4501; e-mail: press09@mail.wvu.edu)

Affiliate Member

Established: 1963

Admitted to AAUP: 2003

Title output 2002: 7

Title output 2003: 8

Titles currently in print: 43

Journals published: 4

Editorial Program

Serious works of nonfiction in American history, with an emphasis on West Virginia and
Appalachia; art history, economic history; ethnic studies; West Virginia and Appalachian
fiction and poetry; medieval studies; regional studies in Appalachia; American studies;
natural history. A second imprint, Vandalia Press, publishes fiction and non-fiction of
interest to the general reader concerning Appalachia and, more specifically, West Virginia.

The Press also publishes the following journals: *Essays in Medieval Studies; Labor Studies
Journal; Tolkien Studies;* and *Victorian Poetry.*

Special Series: Medieval European Studies; West Virginia and Appalachia.

Wilfrid Laurier University Press

75 University Avenue West
Waterloo, ON N2L 3C5
Canada

Phone: (519) 884-0710 ext. 6124
Fax: (519) 725-1399
E-mail: press@wlu.ca
Indiv: (user I.D.)@press.wlu.ca
Web site: www.wlupress.wlu.ca

US Distributor:
Wilfrid Laurier University Press

UK Representative:
Gazelle Book Services, Ltd.

Staff
Director: Brian Henderson (ext. 6123; e-mail: brian)
Acquisitions Editorial: Jacqueline Larson, Acquisitions Editor (ext. 2843; e-mail: jlarson)
Manuscript Editorial: Carroll Klein, Managing Editor (ext. 6119; e-mail: carroll)
Marketing: Penny Grows, Marketing Manager (ext. 6605; e-mail: pgrows)
  Web Page and Marketing Coordinator: Leslie Macredie (ext. 6281; e-mail: leslie)
  Publicist: Clare Ferguson (ext. 2665; e-mail: clare)
Design and Production: Heather Blain-Yanke, Production and Editorial Projects Manager
  (ext. 6122; e-mail: heather)
Journals: Cheryl Beaupré, Customer Service Coordinator (ext. 6124; e-mail: cheryl)
Business: Greg Clark, Financial Supervisor (ext. 6121; e-mail: greg)
Information Systems: Steve Izma, Computing Systems Administrator (ext. 6125;
  e-mail: steve)

Full Member
Established: 1974
Title output 2002: 17
Titles currently in print: 254

Admitted to AAUP: 1986
Title output 2003: 23
Journals published: 8

Editorial Program
Canadian literature; cultural studies; history; literary criticism; literature in translation;
philosophy; life writing; sociology / anthropology; native studies; film studies; art and art
history; religious studies; social work; women's studies.
  Journals (* indicates journals available electronically): *Anthropologica*; *Canadian Bulletin of
Medical History*; *Canadian Social Work Review*; *Dialogue: Canadian Philosophical Review*;
Leisure/Loisir; *Studies in Religion* *; *Topia: A Canadian Journal of Cultural Studies*; *Toronto
Journal of Theology*.
  Special series and joint imprints: Aboriginal Studies; Canadian Corporation for Studies in
Religion Series: Editions SR; Collected Works of Florence Nightingale; Comparative Ethics;
Cultural Studies; Family in Canada; Film Studies; The Future of Canada; Life Writing;
Studies in Childhood; Studies in Christianity and Judaism; Studies in Women and Religion.
  Copublications with Calgary Institute for the Humanities.

The University of Wisconsin Press

1930 Monroe Street, 3rd Floor
Madison, WI 53711-2059

Phone: (608) 263-1110
Fax: (608) 263-1132
E-mail: uwiscpress@uwpress.wisc.edu
Indiv: (user I.D)@wisc.edu
Web site: www.wisc.edu/wisconsinpress

Orders:
The University of Wisconsin Press
Chicago Distribution Center
11030 South Langley Avenue
Chicago, IL 60628-3892
Phone: (800) 621-2736; (773) 702-7000
Fax: (800) 621-8476; (773) 702-7212

UK Distributor:
Eurospan

Staff

Director: Robert Mandel (608/263-1101; e-mail: ramandel)
  Associate Director: Steve Salemson (608/263-0263; e-mail: salemson)
  Outreach Director: Sheila Leary (608/263-0795; e-mail: smleary)
  Popular Press: Gwen Walker (608/263-1123; e-mail: gcwalker)
  Subsidiary Rights & Permissions Manager: Margaret Walsh (608/263-1131; e-mail: mawalsh1)
Acquisitions Editorial: Raphael Kadushin, Senior Acquisitions Editor (608/263-1062; e-mail: kadushin)
  Assistant Editor: Sheila Moermond (608/263-1012; e-mail: samoermond)
Manuscript Editorial: Sue Breckenridge, Managing Editor (608/263-0272; e-mail: subreckenrid)
  Editors: Adam Mehring (608/263-0856; e-mail: amehring); Erin Holman (608/263-1133; e-mail: elholman)
Marketing: Andrea Christofferson, Marketing Manager (608/263-0814; e-mail: aschrist)
  Advertising and Web Manager: Kirt Murray (608/263-0733; e-mail: kdmurray)
  Publicity Manager: Benson Gardner (608/263-0734; e-mail: publicity@uwpress.wisc.edu)
  Exhibits and Direct Mail Coordinator: Kara Zavada (608/263-1136; e-mail: kazavada)
Design and Production: Terry Emmrich, Production Manager (608/263-0731; e-mail: temmrich)
  Assistant Production Manager: Carla Aspelmeier (608/263-0732; e-mail: cjaspelmeier)
  Senior Editor/In-House Compositor: Scott Lenz (608/263-0794; e-mail: sjlenz)
Journals: John Delaine, Manager (608/263-0667; e-mail: jkdelaine)
  Assistant Manager: Susan Kau (608/263-0669; e-mail: szkau)
  Advertising: Adrienne Omen (608/263-0534; e-mail: amomen)
  Journals Marketing Manager: Ken Sullivan (608/263-0753; e-mail: khsullivan)
  Subscription Information/Renewal: Rita Emmert (608/263-0668; e-mail: rmemmert); Judith Choles (608/263-0654; e-mail: jmcholes); Beth Johnson (608/263-1135; e-mail: bajohnso)
Business: Rod Knutson, Business Manager (608/263-0165; e-mail: rpknutso)
  Accounts Payable: Anne Herger (608/263-1137; e-mail: abherger)
  Business office fax: (608/263-1120)
Information Systems: Rob Potter, Network Administrator (608/263-1121; e-mail: rbpotter)

Full Member

Established: 1937

Title output 2002: 90

Distributed titles 2002: 23

Titles currently in print: 2,069

Admitted to AAUP: 1945

Title output 2003: 119

Distributed titles 2003: 32

Journals published: 11

Editorial Program

General scholarly titles, serious fiction and nonfiction, with special interests in: African and African-American studies; classics and humanities; dance and performance studies; gay and lesbian studies; history; Jewish and Holocaust studies; language teaching materials; Latin American studies; regional studies; Slavic studies; and sports history. Brittingham & Felix Pollak Poetry Prize. Poetry contest guidelines available online at *www.wisc.edu/wisconsinpress/ poetryguide.html.*

Journals published: *American Orthoptic Journal; Arctic Anthropology; Contemporary Literature; Ecological Restoration; Journal of Consumer Affairs; Journal of Human Resources; Land Economics; Landscape Journal; Luso-Brazilian Review; Monatshefte;* and *SubStance.*

Special series: Africa and the Diaspora: History, Politics, Culture; African and African Diasporic Religions; The Americas; The Brecht Yearbook; Brittingham Prize in Poetry; Contemporary North American Poetry; Critical Masculinities; The Curti Lectures; The Elvehjem Museum of Art Catalogs; Ethnic Series; Felix Pollak Prize in Poetry; George L. Mosse Series in Modern European Cultural and Intellectual History; Graven Images: Studies in Culture, Law, and the Sacred; History of Anthropology; History of Ireland and the Irish Diaspora; Interpretive Studies in Healthcare and the Human Sciences; Irish Studies in Literature and Culture; Jewish Diasporas; Jewish Voices from Russia and Eastern Europe; Library of American Fiction; Library of Wisconsin Fiction; Library of World Fiction; Living in Latin America; Living Out: Gay and Lesbian Autobiographies; Modern Jewish Philosophy and Religion: Translations and Critical Studies; *Monatshefte* Occasional Volumes; New Badger History; New Studies in Phenomenology and Hermeneutics; Popular Press; Print Culture History in Modern America; Publications of the Wisconsin Center for Pushkin Studies; Ray and Pat Browne Series in Popular Culture; Science and Technology in Society; Shoah Series; Sources in Modern Jewish History; Southeast Asian Studies; Studies in African American Literature, Culture, and History; Studies in American Intellectual and Cultural History; Studies in Dance History; Studies in German Jewish Cultural History and Literature; Studies on Israel; Technical Japanese Series; Terrorism in the 21st Century: Interdisciplinary Perspectives; The University of Wisconsin Press Poetry Series; Voices of the Wisconsin Past; Wisconsin Land and Life; Wisconsin Studies in Autobiography; Wisconsin Studies in Classics; Wisconsin/Warner Bros. Screenplays; Women in Africa and the Diaspora; Writing in Latinidad: Autobiographical Voices of US Latinos/as.

The Woodrow Wilson Center Press

Woodrow Wilson International Center for Scholars
One Woodrow Wilson Plaza
1300 Pennsylvania Avenue, N.W.
Washington, DC 20004-3027

Phone: (202) 691-4041
Fax: (202) 691-4001
E-mail: brinleyj@wwic.si.edu
Indiv: (user I.D.)@wwic.si.edu
Web site: www.wilsoncenter.org/press

Staff
Director: Joseph Brinley (202/691-4042; e-mail: brinleyj)
Editor: Yamile Kahn (202/691-4041; e-mail: kahnym)
Editorial Assistant: Peter Bean (202/691-4000; e-mail: beanpj)
   Administrative Assistant: Pamela J. Moore (202/691-4029; e-mail: moorepam)

Associate Member
Established: 1987   Admitted to AAUP: 1992
Title output 2002: 13   Title output 2003: 18
Titles currently in print: 130

Editorial Program
Woodrow Wilson Center Press publishes work written at or for the Woodrow Wilson International Center for Scholars, the official memorial of the United States to its twenty-eighth president. The Center was created by law in 1968 as a living memorial "symbolizing and strengthening the fruitful relation between the world of learning and the world of public affairs." The Press's books come from both the work of the Center's scholars in residence and from some of the four hundred meetings held at the Center each year.

The Center's interests range widely in areas associated with questions of public policy. The Press has published in American studies; history; international relations; political science; economics and finance; religious studies; urban studies; women's studies; and the study of Africa, Asia, Europe, Latin America, and the Middle East.

All the Press's books are copublished. Partners include Johns Hopkins University Press, Cambridge University Press, Stanford University Press, University of California Press, and Columbia University Press. The Cold War International History Project Series is copublished with Stanford.

Yale University Press

Street Address:
302 Temple Street
New Haven, CT 06511

Mailing Address:
P.O. Box 209040
New Haven, CT 06520-9040

Phone: (203) 432-0960
Faxes: (203) 432-0948 (Main)
(203) 432-1064/2394 (Editorial)
(203) 432-4061 (Production)
(800) 406-9145 (Customer Service)
(203) 432-8485 (Marketing)
(203) 432-5455 (Promotion)
(203) 432-6862 (Computer room)
(203) 432-6862 (Accounting)
E-mail: (firstname.lastname)@yale.edu
Web site and online catalog: www.yale.edu/yup/

London Office:
47 Bedford Square
London WCIB 3DP
United Kingdom
Phone: +44-207-079-4900
Fax: +44-207-079-4901
E-mail: (firstname.lastname)@yaleup.co.uk

Staff

Director: John E. Donatich (203/432-0933)
  Deputy Director for Finance and Operations: John D. Rollins (203/432-0938)
  Publishing Director: Tina C. Weiner (203/432-0962)
  Associate Director and Editorial Director: Jonathan Brent (203/432-0905)
Acquisitions Editorial: Jean E. Thomson Black (science and medicine) (203/432-7534);
  Jonathan Brent (literature, literary studies, theater, Slavic studies) (203/432-0905); Keith
  Condon (political science, psychology) (203/432-0924); Patricia Fidler (art and architec-
  tural history) (203/432-0927); Larisa Heimert (history, intellectual history, American
  studies, biography, and women's studies) (203/432-0935); John Kulka (literature, philoso-
  phy, and political science) (203/432-6807); Mary Jane Peluso (language and reference)
  (203/432-8013); Michael O'Malley (business, economics, law) (203/432-0904)
Manuscript Editorial: Jenya Weinreb, Managing Editor (203/432-0913)
  Assistant Managing Editor: Mary Pasti (203/432-0911)
  Editors: Nancy Brochin (203/432-4823); Laura Jones Dooley (203/432-0915); Dan
  Heaton (203/432-1017); Lawrence Kenney (203/432-0908); Phillip King (203/432-
  1015); Susan Laity (203/432-0922); Margaret Otzel (203/432-0918); Jeffrey Schier (203/
  432-4001)
Marketing: Tina C. Weiner, Publishing Director (203/432-0968)
  Sales Director: Jay Cosgrove (203/432-0967)
  Promotion Director: Sarah F. Clark (203/432-0965)
  Catalogue Manager: Libby Groff (203/432-7933)
  Advertising Manager: Peter Sims (203/432-0974)
  Publicity Manager: Heather D'Auria (203/432-0971)
  Assistant Publicity Manager: Brenda King (203/432-0917)
  Publicists: Brian McKay (203/432-0971); Paige Sampara (203/432-0964)
  Promotion Designers: Amy Andersen (203/432-7086); Thomas Strong (203/432-7993)
  Direct Mail Manager: Debra Bozzi (203/432-0959)
  Electronic Promotions Manager: Timothy Shea (436-1321)

Design and Production: Christina Coffin, Director of Production (203/432-4062)
  Assistant Production Manager: Maureen Noonan (203/432-4064)
  Production Controllers: Mary Mayer (203/432-0925); Genevieve Przygocki (203/432-4060)
  Design Manager: Nancy Ovedovitz (203/432-4067)
  Designers: Rebecca Gibb (203/432-4065); James L. Johnson (203/432-4068); Sonia Scanlon (203/432-4066); Mary Valencia (203/432-8092)
Business: John D. Rollins, Deputy Director for Finance and Operations (203/432-0938)
  Operations Manager: Jim Stritch (203/432-0939)
  Computer Services: Milton Kahl, Manager (203/432-0937)
  Permissions and Ancillary Rights: Donna Anstey, Manager (203/432-0932)
  Intellectual Property and Contracts Manager: Linda B. Klein (203/432-0936)
London Office:
Managing Director and Acquisitions Editor: Robert Baldock
Acquisitions Editors: Gillian Malpass, Heather McCallum, Sally Salvesen
Head of Marketing: Kate Pocock
Foreign Rights Manager: Anne Bihan

Full Member

Established: 1908   Admitted to AAUP: 1937
Title output 2002: 316   Title output 2003: 319
Titles currently in print: 3,800

Editorial Program
Humanities, social and behavioral sciences, natural sciences, medicine. Poetry is not accepted except for submissions to the Yale Series of Younger Poets contest, held annually. Festschriften and collections of previously published articles are not invited and very rarely accepted.

Special series, joint imprints and/or copublishing programs: Annals of Communism; Babylonian Inscriptions in the Collection of James B. Nies; The Bibliography of American Literature; Cassirer Lectures; The Castle Lectures; Children's Literature; Collections in the Yale University Art Gallery; Complete Prose Works of John Milton; Composers of the Twentieth Century; The Culture and Civilization of China; Early Chinese Civilization; The Dialogues of Plato Series; Elizabethan Club; The English Monarchs; The Frederick Douglass Papers; The Freud Lectures at Yale; The Henry L. Stimson Lectures; The Henry McBride Series in Modernism and Modernity; Hermes Books; A History of Modern Criticism, 1750-1950; Music in History; National Gallery London; Oak Spring Garden Foundation; The Papers of Benjamin Franklin; The Papers of Benjamin Henry Latrobe; Planetary Exploration; The Psychoanalytic Study of the Child; Rethinking the Western Tradition; The Selected Papers of Charles Willson Peale and His Family; Selected Works of St. Thomas More; The Silliman Memorial Lectures; Sport and History; The Storrs Lectures; The Terry Lectures; The Works of Jonathan Edwards; Yale Agrarian Studies; The Yale Ben Jonson; Yale College; The Yale Edition of Horace Walpole's Correspondence; The Yale Edition of the Complete Works of St. Thomas More; The Yale Edition of the George Eliot Letters; The Yale Edition of the Swinburne Letters; The Yale Edition of the Works of Samuel Johnson; Yale Fastbacks; Yale French Studies; Yale Historical Publications; Yale Intellectual History of the West; The Yale Institution for Social and Policy Studies; Yale Judaica; Yale Language; The Yale Leibniz; Yale Library of Medieval Philosphy; Yale Music Theory Translation; Yale Musical Instrument; Yale

Near Eastern Researches; Yale Oriental Series: Babylonian Texts; Yale Publications in the History of Art; The Yale Scene: University; Yale Series of Younger Poets; Yale Studies in Hermeneutics; The Yale University Press Pelican History of Art; Yale Western Americana.

Yale University Press also publishes some titles with the Paul Mellon Centre for Studies in British Art.

Airlift Book Company
8 The Arena
Mollison Ave.
Enfield EN3 7NJ
United Kingdom
Phone: +44 020 8804 0400
Fax: +44 020 8804 0044
Web site: www.airlift.co.uk

Aldington Books
Unit 3(b) Frith Business Centre
Frith Road
Aldington, Ashford
Kent TN25 7H5
United Kingdom
Phone: +44 1233 720123
Fax: + 44 1233 721272
E-mail: sales@aldingtonbooks.co.uk
Web site: www.aldingtonbooks.co.uk

Baker & Taylor International
1120 Route 22 East
Bridgewater, NJ 08807
Phone: (800) 775-1500; (908) 541-7000
E-mail: btinfo@btol.com
Web site: www.btol.com

Bill Bailey Publishers' Representatives
16 Devon Square
Newton Abbot
Devon TQ12 2HR
United Kingdom
Phone: +44 1626 331079
Fax: +44 1626 331080
E-mail: billbailey.pubrep@eclipse.co.uk

Book Representation and Distribution Ltd.
Hadleigh Hall
London Road, Hadleigh
Essex SS7 2DE
United Kingdom
Phone: +44 1702 552912
Fax: +44 1702 556095
E-mail: info@bookreps.com
Web site: www.bookreps.com

Broadview Press
280 Perry St., Unit 5
Peterborough, ON K95 7H5
Canada
Phone: (705) 743-8990
Fax: (705) 743-8353
E-mail:
customerservice@broadviewpress.com
Web site: www.broadviewpress.com

Canadian Manda Group
165 Dufferin Street
Toronto, ON M6K 3H6
Canada
Phone: (416) 516-0911
Fax: (416) 516-0917
E-mail: general@mandagroup.com
Web site: www.mandagroup.com

Cariad, Ltd.
180 Bloor St. West
Suite 801
Toronto, ON M5S 2V6
Canada
Phone: (416) 929-2774
Fax: (416) 929-1926

Combined Academic Publishers
15a Lewin's Yard
East Street
Chesham, Buckinghamshire, HP5 1HQ
United Kingdom
Phone: +44 1494 581601
Fax: +44 1494 581602
E-mail:
nickesson@combinedacademic.demon.co.uk
Web site: www.combinedacademic.co.uk

The Crowood Press
The Stable Block
Crowood Lane
Ramsbury, Marlborough
Wiltshire SN8 2HR
United Kingdom
Phone: +44 1672 520320
Fax: +44 1672 520280
E-mail: enquiries@crowood.com
Web site: www.crowoodpress.co.uk

Drake International Services
Market House, Market Place
Deddington
Oxford OX15 OSE
United Kingdom
Phone: +44 1869 338240
Fax: +44 1869 338310
E-mail: info@drakeint.co.uk
Web site: www.drakeint.co.uk

Eurospan University Press Group
3 Henrietta Street, Covent Garden
London WC2E 8LU
United Kingdom
Phone: +44 2072 400856
Fax: +44 2073 790609
E-mail: info@eurospan.co.uk
Web site: www.eurospan.co.uk

Fitzhenry & Whiteside
195 Allstate Parkway
Markham, ON   L3R 4T8
Canada
Phone: (800) 387-9776
Fax: (800)-260-9777
E-mail: godwit@fitzhenry.ca
Web site: www.fitzhenry.ca/

Forest Book Services
The New Building
Ellwood Road
Milkwall Coleford
Glos. GL16 7LE
United Kingdom
Phone: +44 1594 833858
Fax: +441594 833446
Web site: www.forestbooks.com

Gazelle-Drake Book Services, Ltd.
White Cross Mills
High Town
Lancaster LA1 4XS
United Kingdom
Phone: +44 1524-68765
Fax: +44 1524-63232
E-mail: sales@gazellebooks.co.uk
Web site: www.gazellebooks.co.uk

Georgetown Publications, Inc.
579 Richmond Street West, Suite 100
Toronto, ON   L7G 4R9
Canada
Phone: (416) 364-8741
Fax: (416) 367-4242

Gracewing Publishing
2 Southern Avenue
Leominster, Herefordshire HR6 0QF
United Kingdom
Phone: +44 1568 616835
Fax: +44 1568 613289
Web site: www.gracewing.co.uk/

Guidance Centre Suppliers
5201 Dufferin St.
North York, ON M3H 5T8
Canada
Phone: (416) 667-7791
Fax: (416) 667-7832
Web site: http://www.utpress.utoronto.ca/
GCentre/suppliers.html
E-mail: utpbooks@utpress.utoronto.ca

Hargreaves, Fuller & Paton
4335 W. 10th Ave, Suite # 13
Vancouver, BC V6R 2H6
Canada
Phone: (604) 222-2955
Fax: (604) 222-2965
E-mail: harful@telus.net

Jacqueline Gross and Associates Inc.
1 Atlantic Avenue, Suite 105
Toronto, ON M6K 3E7
Canada
Phone: (416) 531- 6737
Fax: (416) 531- 4259
E-mail: gayle@jaquelinegross.com
Web site: www.jacquelinegross.com/

John Wiley & Sons Ltd.
The Atrium
Southern Gate, Chichester
West Sussex, PO 19 8SQ
United Kingdom
Phone: +44 1243 779777
Fax: + 44 1243 775878

Kellington & Associates
338 Riverdale Drive
Toronto, ON M4J 1A2
Canada
Phone: (416) 461-7472
Fax: (416) 461-9173
E-mail: r.kellingtonl@sympatico.ca

Lavis Marketing
73 Lime Walk
Headington, Oxford
Oxfordshire
OX3 7AD
United Kingdom
Phone: +44 1865 767575
Fax: +44 1865 750079
E-mail: lavismarkt@aol.com

Lexa Publishers' Representatives
215 Ashworth Avenue
Toronto, ON M6G 2A6
Canada
Phone: (416) 535-6494
Fax: (416) 535-6599
E-mail: lmcclory@sympatico.ca

Login Brothers Canada
324 Saulteaux Crescent
Winnipeg, MB R3J 3T2
Canada
Phone: (800) 665-1148; (204) 837-2987
Fax: (800) 665-0103; (204) 837-3116
E-mail: sales@lb.ca
Web site: www.lb.ca

Marston Book Services, Ltd.
P.O. Box 269
Abingdon Oxfordshire
OX14 4YN
United Kingdom
Phone: +44 1235 465500
Fax: +44 1235 465555
Web site: www.marston.co.uk/

Premier Book Marketing, Ltd.
Clarendon House
52, Cornmarket St.
Oxford 0X1 3HJ
United Kingdom
Phone: +44 1865-304059
Fax: +44 1865-304035
E-mail: mail@premierbookmarketing.com
Web site: www.premierbookmarketing.com

NBN International.
Estover Road
Plymouth PL6 7PY
United Kingdom
Phone: +44 1752 202301
Fax: +44 1752 202333
E-mail: orders@ nbninternational.com
Web site: www.nbninternational.com

Renouf Books
1-5369 Canotek Road
Ottawa, ON K1J 9J3
Canada
Phone: (888) 551-7470, (613) 745-2665
Fax: (888) 568-8546, (613) 745-7660
Web site: www.renoufbooks.com

Roundhouse Publishing Ltd.
Alan Goodworth
Millstone
Limers Lane
Northam, North Devon EX39 2RG
United Kingdom
Phone: +44 1237 474474
Fax: +44 1237 474774
E-mail: Round.house@ukgateway.net
Web site: www.roundhouse.net

Scholarly Book Services, Inc.
473 Adelaide St. West
4th Floor Rear
Toronto, ON M5V 1T1
Canada
Phone: (800) 847-9736, (416) 504-6545
Fax: (800) 220-9895, (416) 504-0641
Web site: www.sbookscan.com
E-mail: customerservice@sbookscan.com

Taylor and Francis Ltd.
11 New Fetter Lane
London EC4P 4EE
United Kingdom
Phone: + 44 207583 9855
Fax: +44 207842 2298
Web site: www.tandfco.uk

Turnaround Publishers Services
Unit 3 Olympia Trading Estate
Coburg Rd.
Wood Green
London N22 6TZ
United Kingdom
Phone: +44 2088 293000
Fax: +44 2088 815088
Web site: www.turnaround-psl.com
E-mail: sales@turnaround-uk.com

The University Press Group
164 Hillsdale Avenue East
Toronto, ON M4S 1T5
Canada
Phone: (416) 484-8296
Fax: (416) 484-0602
E-mail: dcstimpson@yahoo.com

University Presses Marketing
The Tobacco Factory,
Raleigh Road,
Southville, Bristol BS3 1TF
United Kingdom
Phone: +44 117 9020275
Fax: +44 117 9020294
E-mail: upm01bristol@compuserve.com

Vanwell Publishing Ltd.
1 Northrup Crescent
P.O. Box 2131
St. Catharines, ON L2R 7S2
Canada
Phone: (905) 937-3100 / (800) 661-6136
Fax: (905) 937-1760
E-mail: sales@vanwell.com

William Gills & Associates
7 Yew Lane
Ardargie Forgandenny
Perthshire PH29QX
United Kingdom
Phone: +44-1738-812-619
Fax: +44-1738-812-480
E-mail: bill@booksfromamerica.co.uk
Web site: www.booksfromamerica.co.uk

Windsor Books International
The Boundary
Wheatley Road
Garsington, Oxford OX44 9EJ
United Kingdom
Phone: +44 1865 361122
Fax: +44 1865 361133
E-mail: sales@windsorbooks.co.uk
Web site: www.windsorbooks.co.uk/

THE ASSOCIATION

The Association of American University Presses (AAUP) was established by a small group of university presses in 1937. In the subsequent years, the association has grown steadily. Today AAUP consists of 125 member presses, ranging in size from those publishing a handful of titles each year to those publishing more than a thousand.

AAUP is a nonprofit organization. Its sources of financing are limited to membership dues and to revenues derived from such activities as organizing national conferences and seminars, producing publishing-related books and catalogs, and operating cooperative marketing programs. In addition, grants provided by foundations and government bodies help to finance special projects.

AAUP's member presses provide much of the personnel that guide the association and carry out its work. A thirteen-member board of directors sets policy for the organization. Many individuals serve on committees and task forces. Their activities reflect the diverse concerns of the membership, including keeping up with emerging electronic publishing technologies, production and analysis of industry statistics, maintaining copyright protections, professional development, marketing, and scholarly journals publishing.

The AAUP "Central Office," located in New York City, consists of an executive director and a small professional staff. The office manages member programs and coordinates the work of the board and committees.

AAUP members fall into four categories—full, affiliate, international, and associate. For a complete description of membership requirements, consult the "Guidelines on Admission to Membership and Maintenance of Membership," reproduced on page 209.

2004-2005 AAUP Board of Directors

Douglas Armato, University of Minnesota Press, President (2004-05)

Lynne Withey, University of California Press, President-elect (2004-05)

Seetha Srinivasan, University Press of Mississippi, Past President (2004-05)

Bill Bossier, Louisiana State University Press, Treasurer (2004-05)

Molly Venezia, Rutgers University Press, Treasurer-elect (2004-05)

Holly Carver, University of Iowa Press (2004-07)

Kathyrn Conrad, University of Arizona Press (2002-05)

Alex Holzman, Temple University Press (2004-07)

Daphne Ireland, Princeton University Press (2004-07)

Niko Pfund, Oxford University Press (2002-05)

Janet Rabinowitch, Indiana University Press (2003-06)

John Rollins, Yale University Press, Treasurer (2002-05)

Will Underwood, Kent State University Press (2004-07)

Peter J. Givler, AAUP Central Office, ex officio

2004-2005 AAUP Committees and Chairs

Admissions and Standards Committee
Eric Halpern, Pennsylvania, Chair
Stephen A. Cohn, Duke
Penelope Kaiserlian, Virginia
Additional member TBA

Annual Meeting Program Committee
Janet Francendese, Temple, Chair
Deborah Bruner, Cornell
Holly Carver, Iowa
Barbara Hanrahan, Notre Dame
Elizabeth Hu, British Columbia
Robert Oppedisano, Fordham
Additional members TBA

Business Handbook Committee
Barbara Berg, Northern Illinois, Chair
Caroline Simmons, Getty
Kathy Stein, American Psychiatric

Business Systems Committee
Roger Hubbs, Cornell, Chair
Karen Baker, Temple
Linda Frech, Missouri
Michael Leonard, MIT
William Lindsay, Harvard
Molly Venezia, Rutgers

Copyright Committee
Daphne Ireland, Princeton, Chair
Laura Young Bost, Texas
Melinda Koyanis, Harvard
Tom Robinson, Duke
Sanford G. Thatcher, Penn State
Vicky Wells, North Carolina
Kathryn Wildfong, Wayne State

Design and Production Committee
John Langston, Mississippi, Chair
Adam Grafa, Minnesota
Additional members TBA

Electronic Committee
Paul Murphy, RAND, Chair
Chuck Creesy, Princeton
Steve Izma, Wilfrid Laurier
Michael Jensen, National Academies
Rosemary Tietge, Harvard

Marketing Committee
Glenda Madden, New Mexico, Chair
Jim Denton, Florida
Dave Hamrick, Texas
Michael McCullough, Duke
Additional members TBA

Nominating Committee
Peter Milroy, British Columbia, Chair
Lain Adkins, Chicago
Cynthia Miller, Pittsburgh
Tina Weiner, Yale

Professional Development Committee
Barbara Kline Pope, National Academies, Chair
Richard Brown, Georgetown
Lynne Chapman, Texas
Jennifer Crewe, Columbia
Molly Venezia, Rutgers

Scholarly Journals Committee
Bill Breichner, Johns Hopkins, Chair
Additional members TBA

Central Office Staff

Executive Director: Peter J. Givler
  (e-mail: pgivler@aaupnet.org)

Assistant Director and Controller: Timothy Muench
  (e-mail: tmuench@aaupnet.org)

Administrative Manager: Linda McCall
  (e-mail: lmccall@aaupnet.org)

Marketing Manager: Rachel Weiss
  (e-mail: rweiss@aaupnet.org)

Communications Manager: Brenna McLaughlin
  (e-mail: bmclaughlin@aaupnet.org)

Membership Manager: Susan Patton
  (e-mail: spatton@aaupnet.org)

Marketing/Administrative Assistant: Terriann Pace
  (e-mail: tpace@aaupnet.org)

Program Assistant: Yejide Peters
  (e-mail: ypeters@aaupnet.org)

Mailroom: Chris Williams

Association of American University Presses
71 W. 23rd St., Suite 901
New York, NY 10010

Phone: (212) 989-1010
Fax: (212) 989-0275/0176

E-mail: info@aaupnet.org
Web site: www.aaupnet.org

By-Laws (As revised June 14, 1997)

ARTICLE I: PREAMBLE

This Corporation, existing under the Not-for-Profit Corporation Law of the State of New York, shall be known as the Association of American University Presses, Inc. (hereinafter referred to as the "Association"). The Association expects members to recruit, employ, train, compensate, and promote their employees without regard to race, ethnic background, national origin, status as a veteran or handicapped individual, age, religion, gender, marital status, or sexual preference.

ARTICLE II: PURPOSES

The purposes of the Association shall be:

a) To encourage dissemination of the fruits of research and to support university presses in their endeavor to make widely available the best of scholarly knowledge and the most important results of scholarly research;

b) To provide an organization through which the exchange of ideas relating to university presses and their functions may be facilitated;

c) To afford technical advice and assistance to learned bodies, scholarly associations, and institutions of higher learning; and

d) To do all things incidental to and in furtherance of the foregoing purposes without extending the same.

ARTICLE III: MEMBERSHIP AND AFFILIATION

Section 1: Definition of Membership.

The membership of the Association shall consist of those members who were in good standing at the time of the incorporation of the Association in 1964, except those who have since resigned or whose membership has been otherwise terminated, and all other members who have since been admitted in accordance with the procedures set forth in Section 3 of this Article.

Section 2: Definition of a University Press.

A university press is hereby defined as the scholarly publishing arm of a university or college, or of a group of such institutions within a state or geographic region located within the Americas. A university press as here defined must be an integral part of one or more such colleges and universities, and should be so recognized in the manual of organization, catalogue, or other official publication of at least one such parent institution. The organization and functions of the university press must lie within the prescription of its parent institution or institutions.

Section 3: Eligibility for Membership.

Any university press satisfying the requirements set forth in the "Guidelines on Admission to Membership and Maintenance of Membership" (hereinafter, the "Guidelines") that are in force at the time of application shall be eligible for election to membership in the Association. University presses located in Canada are admitted as Canadian members, which receive all member rights and privileges. A university press shall be elected to membership by a majority vote of the membership on the recommendation of the Board of Directors at the Annual or a Special Meeting of the membership. Such action shall be taken by the Board only on the prior recommendation of the Committee on Admissions and Standards, which shall be responsible for determining that the applying university press satisfies the minimum requirements for membership.

Section 4: Voting and Other Privileges.

Each member of the Association shall be entitled to one vote in such business as may come before the Association. Only members in good standing shall be entitled to vote or otherwise enjoy the privileges of membership in the Association. In these By-Laws the use of the term "member," "member of the Association," or "membership" shall mean university presses which have become members of the Association in accordance with Sections 1 or 3 of this Article III.

Section 5: Cancellation of Membership and Resignation.

A university press, by its very nature, must be devoted to scholarly and educational ends; the failure of a university press to pursue such ends as its fundamental business shall constitute grounds for canceling its membership in the Association. Membership may also be canceled for nonpayment of dues or for continued failure, after admission to membership, to meet the minimum requirements set forth in the Guidelines. Cancellation of membership shall be effected, on recommendation of the Board of Directors, by a two-thirds vote of the members present and voting at the Annual Meeting or a Special Meeting, a quorum being present.

Any member may resign at any time if its current annual dues are paid, provided its resignation is confirmed in a written communication to the President of the Association from a responsible officer or group of officers of the parent institution or institutions. Should a member resign after the due date of the annual dues payment and before the next annual dues payment date, the member is responsible for the payment of such dues at the time of resignation.

Section 6: International Membership.

At the invitation of the Board of Directors, international membership may be applied for by (a) university-affiliated scholarly book publishers in parts of the world not embraced by the Americas and (b) such presses within the Americas that publish primarily in languages other than English. To qualify for international membership in the Association, a publisher in either class must submit a formal application and provide such materials as requested by the Committee on Admissions and Standards, making evident its scholarly publishing program. Admission to international membership shall be by a majority vote of the membership at an Annual or Special Meeting, a quorum being present, on the prior recommendation of the Committee on Admissions and Standards and the Board of Directors.

International membership may be canceled on recommendation of the Board of Directors by a two-thirds vote of the members present and voting at an Annual Meeting or Special Meeting, a quorum being present. International members shall enjoy all rights and privileges of membership except the right to vote in any business being conducted by the Association, the Board of Directors, or the membership. Any reference elsewhere in these By-Laws to a voting right, therefore, shall be read so as to exclude international members. Dues for international members shall be set from time to time by the Board.

Section 7: Affiliate Status.

At the invitation of the Board of Directors, university presses within the Americas may apply for affiliate status provided they satisfy all the requirements set forth in Section C of the Guidelines except for the number of books published and in regard to staffing.

Admission to affiliate status shall be by a majority vote of the membership at an Annual or Special Meeting, a quorum being present, on the prior recommendation of the Committee on Admissions and Standards and the Board of Directors.

Affiliate status may be canceled by a two-thirds majority vote of the membership at an Annual or Special Meeting, a quorum being present. Affiliates shall enjoy such rights and privileges as determined by the Board of Directors, but in no event shall their rights and privileges extend to service on the Board of Directors or on the Standing Committees of the Association or voting on any business conducted by the Association, the Board of Directors, or the membership. Any reference elsewhere in the By-Laws to a voting right shall be read so as to exclude affiliates. Annual fees for the maintenance of affiliate status shall be set from time to time by the Board of Directors.

Section 8: Associate Status.

At the invitation of the Board of Directors, presses of non-degree-granting scholarly institutions and associations may apply for associate status, providing those institutions are incorporated as not-for-profit and that the presses satisfy the requirements for affiliate membership, except that the auspices and structures of the parent organizations of such presses will in all instances be those of non-degree-granting institutions or scholarly associations rather than those of universities. In the absence of an editorial committee or board, an applicant for associate membership shall observe commonly accepted standards of editorial review.

Admission to associate status shall be by a majority vote of the membership at an Annual or Special Meeting, a quorum being present, on the prior recommendation of the Committee on Admissions and Standards and the Board of Directors. Associate members shall enjoy such rights and privileges as determined by the Board of Directors, but in no event shall their rights and privileges extend to serving on the Board of Directors or on the Standing Committees of the Association or to voting on any business conducted by the Association, the Board of Directors, or the membership. Any reference elsewhere in the By-Laws to a voting right, therefore, shall be read so as to exclude associates. Associates shall not be eligible to participate in the Association's statistical programs. Annual fees for associates shall be set from time to time by the Board of Directors. Associates may number no more than thirty percent of the full members of the Association. Associate status may be canceled at any time by a two-thirds vote of the membership at an Annual or Special Meeting, a quorum being present.

ARTICLE IV: MEMBERSHIP MEETINGS

Section 1: The Annual Meeting.

The Annual Meeting of members shall be held at such time and place within or without the State of New York as may be designated by the Board of Directors after giving due weight to preferences expressed by members. Such meetings shall be held for the purpose of electing the Board of Directors, approving the annual budget, and transacting such other business as may be properly brought before the meeting. At each Annual Meeting of members, the Board of Directors shall cause to be presented to the membership a report verified by the President and the Treasurer, or by a majority of the Board, in accordance with the requirements of Section 519 of the New York Not-for-Profit Corporation Law.

Section 2: Special Meetings.

Special Meetings of the members shall be held at such time and place within or without the

State of New York as may be designated by the Board of Directors. Such meetings may be called by (a) the Board of Directors; or (b) the Executive Committee; or (c) the President, the President-elect, or the Executive Director acting on a request received in writing that states the purpose or purposes of the meeting and is signed by 30 percent or more of the members of the Association.

Section 3: Notice of Meetings.
Notice of the purpose or purposes and of the time and place of every meeting of members of the Association shall be in writing and signed by the President, President-elect, or the Executive Director, and a copy thereof shall be delivered personally or by the U.S. Postal Service not less than ten or more than fifty days before the meeting, to each member entitled to vote at such meeting.

Section 4: Representation by Proxy.
A member may authorize a person or persons to act by proxy on all matters in which a member is entitled to participate. No proxy shall be valid after the expiration of eleven months from the date thereof unless otherwise provided in the proxy. Every proxy shall be revocable at the pleasure of the member executing it.

Section 5: Quorum.
Except for a special election of Directors pursuant to Section 604 of the New York Not-for-Profit Corporation Law, the presence at a meeting in person or by proxy of a majority of the members entitled to vote thereat shall constitute a quorum for the transaction of any business, except that the members present may adjourn the meeting even if there is no quorum.

Section 6: Voting.
In the election of members of the Board of Directors and the election of Officers, a plurality of the votes cast at an Annual Meeting shall elect. Any other action requires a majority of votes cast except as otherwise specifically provided in these By-Laws. A vote may be taken without a meeting if a majority of the members in good standing submit written votes in response to a request to this effect from the President, the President-elect, or the Executive Director.

ARTICLE V: DIRECTORS AND OFFICERS

Section 1: The Board of Directors.
The Association shall be managed by its Board of Directors, and, in this connection, the Board of Directors shall establish the policies of the Association while considering the wishes of the membership and the constituency of the Association (which constituency consists of the employees of the member presses), and shall evaluate the performance of the Executive Director. The Board of Directors shall meet at least three times each year, once in the fall and once in the winter and in conjunction with the Annual Meeting of the membership of the Association. The Board of Directors shall consist of not fewer than nine or more than thirteen Directors, all of whom shall be at least nineteen years of age, at least two-thirds of whom shall be citizens of the United States, four of whom shall be the elected Officers of the Association. Directors other than Officers (Directors-at-Large), like Officers, must be on the staff of a member press, except that the Executive Director is an ex officio (nonvoting) member of the Board of Directors and the Executive Committee.

Section 2: Election Procedure and Term of Office.

Directors shall be elected by a plurality vote of the members present at the Annual Meeting. Candidates may be nominated by the Nominating Committee appointed by the Executive Committee, or from the floor. Officers shall be elected for a one-year term, except that the President shall remain on the Board of Directors for an additional year as Past-President; Directors-at-Large shall be elected for a three-year term. Directors shall not succeed themselves except that (a) Directors who are elected Officers shall continue as Directors as long as they remain Officers, and (b) the Treasurer shall remain on the Board for an additional year as a Director-at-large. Each newly elected Director and Officer shall assume office at the close of the Annual Meeting at which the election is held. Any Director or Officer may resign by notifying the President, the President-elect, or the Executive Director. The resignation shall take effect at the time therein specified. Except as provided for in Article IX ("The Executive Director"), Directors shall not receive any compensation for serving as Directors. However, nothing herein shall be construed to prevent a Director from serving the Association in another capacity for which compensation may be received.

Section 3: Officers.

The elected Officers of the Association, each of whom must be on the staff of a member press, shall be a President, a President-elect, a Treasurer, and a Treasurer-elect, each to be elected for a one-year term by a plurality vote of the members present at the Annual Meeting. Between Annual Meetings of members, a Special Meeting of members may elect, by a plurality vote of the members present, an Officer to complete the term of an Officer who has resigned or otherwise ceased to act as an Officer.

Section 4: Duties of Officers.

The President shall serve as presiding officer at all meetings of the membership and all meetings of the Board of Directors and the Executive Committee. The President, with the Executive Director, serves as spokesperson for the Association. At the Annual Meeting of members, the President and the President-elect shall provide a forum for the Association membership and constituency to discuss and assess the Association's program. The President-elect shall discharge the duties of the President in the President's absence, and shall succeed to the office of President in the event of a vacancy in that office, filling out the unexpired term as well as the term to which he or she is elected President.

The Treasurer shall be custodian of the Association's funds, shall be responsible for the preparation of its financial records as the basis for an annual audit, and shall report at the Annual Meeting of members on the Association's financial condition. The Treasurer-elect shall discharge the duties of the Treasurer in the Treasurer's absence, and shall succeed to the office of Treasurer in the event of a vacancy in that office, filling out the unexpired term as well as the term to which he or she is elected Treasurer.

Section 5: Removal from Office and Replacement.

Any Director or elected Officer may be removed from office at any time, for cause or without cause, by a majority vote of the membership or may be removed for cause by a majority vote of the Board acting at a meeting duly assembled, a quorum being present. If one or more vacancies should occur on the Board for any reason, the remaining members of the Board, although less than a quorum, may by majority vote elect a successor or successors for the unexpired term.

Section 6: Board Meetings.

Meetings of the Board of Directors shall be held at such place within or without the State of New York as may from time to time be fixed by resolution of the Board, or as may be specified in the notice of the meeting. Notice of any meeting of the Board need not be given to any Director who submits a signed waiver of such notice. Special Meetings of the Board may be held at any time upon the call of the Executive Committee, the Executive Director, the President, or the President-elect.

Section 7: Board Quorum.

A majority of the members of the Board of Directors then acting, but in no event less than one-half of the entire board of Directors, acting at a meeting duly assembled, shall constitute a quorum for the transaction of business. If at any meeting of the Board there shall be less than a quorum present, a majority of those present may adjourn the meeting without further notice from time to time until a quorum shall have been obtained. The "entire Board of Directors" shall mean the total number of Directors that the Association would have if there were no vacancies.

Section 8: Board Voting.

Except as otherwise specified in these By-Laws, all decisions of the Board shall be by majority vote of the Directors in attendance, a quorum being present. Any Board action may be taken without a meeting if all members of the Board or committee thereof consent in writing to the adoption of a resolution authorizing the action. The resolution and the written consents thereto shall be filed with the minutes of the proceedings of the Board. Any member of the Board or of any committee thereof may participate in a meeting of such Board or committee thereof by means of a telephone or similar communications equipment allowing all persons participating in the meeting to hear each other at the same time. Participation by such means shall constitute presence in person at a meeting.

ARTICLE VI: EXECUTIVE COMMITTEE

The Executive Committee of the Board of Directors shall consist of the Past-President and President of the Association and the President-elect, Treasurer, Treasurer-elect, and the Executive Director (ex officio, nonvoting). The Executive Committee shall advise and confer with the Executive Director, call Special Meetings of the Board of Directors as necessary, appoint committee members not otherwise appointed pursuant to these By-Laws, and serve as the investment committee for the Association. The Executive Committee shall, if necessary, act for the full Board of Directors between meetings of the Board, but only in those matters not establishing policy or not requiring a vote of more than a majority of Directors in attendance.

ARTICLE VII: STANDING COMMITTEES

The Standing Committees of the Association (in addition to the Executive Committee) shall be the Committee on Admissions and Standards, the Committee on the Annual Meeting Program, and the Nominating Committee. The Committee on Admissions and Standards shall be constituted as provided in the Guidelines, and the Nominating Committee shall be appointed by the Executive Committee and confirmed by a vote of the Board of Directors. Appointments to the Committee on the Annual Meeting Program shall be made in accordance with Article VIII of these By-Laws.

ARTICLE VIII: OTHER COMMITTEES

Other committees may be established at the Executive Director's discretion. The Executive Committee shall appoint chairs of said committees (and the Standing Committees) and such of their members as the Executive Committee may care to designate. The Executive Director shall charge the said committees with such duties, including reporting duties, as he or she may deem appropriate. Reports of standing and all other committees shall be made to the Board of Directors, in writing or orally, as requested by the Executive Director.

ARTICLE IX: THE EXECUTIVE DIRECTOR

The Board of Directors may appoint at such times, and for such terms as it may prescribe, an Executive Director of the Association who shall report to the Board of Directors and who is responsible for implementing policy through fiscally sound programs; establishing, charging, and monitoring the work of committees and task forces; and managing the Central Office (such Central Office consisting of salaried employees hired by the Executive Director in order to carry out the business of the Association). The Executive Director shall prepare an operating plan and budget and shall participate in meetings of the Board of Directors and Executive Committee in an ex officio nonvoting capacity as appropriate. Under the authority of the Board of Directors, the Executive Director shall have responsibility for the execution of Association policy, for the furtherance of the Association's interests, and for the day-to-day operation of the Association's business and programs. The Executive Director shall act as secretary at all Board meetings, Executive Committee meetings, and Annual and Special Meetings of the Association, and shall prepare and distribute minutes of the same. The Executive Director shall serve as Corporate Secretary. The Executive Director's salary shall be fixed annually by the Board.

ARTICLE X: REGIONAL ORGANIZATIONS

The Board of Directors may recognize geographical regions within which members of the Association and others may organize themselves for regional meetings to further the aims of the Association.

ARTICLE XI: DUES

The amount of the annual dues payment by members shall be voted each year at the Annual Meeting on recommendation of the Board of Directors. The fiscal year of the Association shall be April 1 to March 31. Dues shall be payable by September 30, at which time any member press that has not paid its dues shall be subject to suspension at the Board's discretion. When a member is suspended for nonpayment of dues, the President of the Association shall so notify the director of the said member and the responsible officer or officers of its parent institution or group of institutions, and shall further advise them that if such member has not paid its dues by the end of the Association's fiscal year its membership shall be subject to cancellation.

ARTICLE XII: BOOKS AND RECORDS

The Association shall keep at its office within the State of New York correct and complete books and records of account; minutes of meetings of the members, of the Board of Directors, and of the Executive Committee; and an up-to-date list of the names and addresses of all members. These books and records may be in written form or in any other form capable of being converted to written form within a reasonable time.

ARTICLE XIII: CHANGES IN BY-LAWS AND GUIDELINES

The members may amend or repeal these By-Laws by two-thirds of the votes cast at any Annual or Special Meeting called for that purpose at which a quorum is present. The members may revise, amend, or repeal the Guidelines by a majority of votes cast at any Annual or Special Meeting of members called for that purpose at which a quorum is present. Whenever there is a conflict between these By-Laws and the Guidelines, any Statement of Governance, or a resolution of the membership, Board of Directors, or Executive Committee, or any other document published by the Association, these By-Laws shall prevail.

Guidelines on Admission to Membership and Maintenence of Membership

As revised January 11, 1995

A. Preamble

The purposes of the Association are to encourage dissemination of the fruits of research and to support university presses in their endeavor to make widely available the best of scholarly know-ledge and the most important results of scholarly research; to provide an organization through which the exchange of ideas relating to university presses and their functions may be facilitated; to afford technical advice and assistance to learned bodies, scholarly associations, and institutions of higher learning; and to do all things incidental to and in furtherance of the foregoing purposes without extending the same.

B. Membership, Associate Membership, and Affiliation

The membership of the Association shall consist of those members who were in good standing at the time of the incorporation of the Association in 1964, except those who have since resigned or whose membership has otherwise been terminated, and all other members who have since been admitted.

A university press is defined as the scholarly publishing arm of a university or college, or a group of such institutions within a state or geographic region located within the Americas. It must be an integral part of one or more such colleges and universities, and should be so recognized in the manual of organization, catalogue, or other official publication of at least one such parent institution. The organization and functions of the university press must lie within the prescription of its parent institution or institutions.

Any press satisfying these requirements shall be eligible in principle for election to membership in the Association. University presses located in Canada are admitted as Canadian members, receiving all membership rights and privileges. A press shall be elected to membership by a majority vote of the full membership on the recommendation of the Board of Directors. Such action shall be taken by the Board only on the prior recommendation of the Committee on Admissions and Standards (see Section E), which shall be responsible for determining that the applying press satisfies the minimum requirements for membership.

A university press, by its very nature, must be devoted to scholarly and educational ends; the failure of a press to pursue such ends as its fundamental business shall constitute grounds for canceling its membership in the Association. Cancellation of membership shall be effected by a two-thirds vote of the membership on the recommendation of the Board of Directors.

At the invitation of the Board of Directors, international membership may be applied for by (a) university-affiliated scholarly book publishers in parts of the world not embraced by the Americas and (b) such presses within the Americas that publish primarily in languages other than English. To qualify for membership in the Association, a publisher in either class must submit a formal application and provide such materials as requested by the Admissions and Standards Committee, making evident its scholarly publishing program.

Admission to international membership shall be by a majority vote of the membership at an Annual or Special Meeting, a quorum being present, on the prior recommendation of the Committee on Admissions and Standards and the Board of Directors. International member-ship may be canceled by a two-thirds vote of the Board of Directors, a quorum being present. International members shall enjoy all rights and privileges of membership except the right to vote in any business conducted by the Association. Any reference elsewhere in the By-Laws to a voting right, therefore, shall be so read as to exclude international members. Uniform dues for international members shall be set from time to time by the Board.

At the invitation of the Board of Directors, university presses within the Americas may apply for affiliate status provided that they satisfy all requirements set forth in Section C of these Guidelines except for the number of books published and in regard to staffing. Admission to affiliate status shall be by a majority vote of the membership, a quorum being present, on the prior recommendation of the Committee on Admissions and Standards which shall be responsible for determining that the applying press satisfies the minimum requirements for affiliation. Affiliate status may be canceled by a two-thirds vote of the membership, a quorum being present. Affiliates shall enjoy such rights and privileges as determined by the Board of Directors, but in no event shall their rights and privileges extend to service on the Board of Directors or on the Standing Committees of the Association or voting in any business conducted by it. Any reference elsewhere in the By-Laws to a voting right, therefore, shall be so read as to exclude affiliates. Uniform annual fees shall be set from time to time by the Board.

At the invitation of the Board of Directors, presses of non-degree-granting scholarly institutions and associations may apply for associate membership, providing those institutions are incorporated as not-for-profit and that the presses satisfy the requirements for affiliate membership, except that the auspices and structures of the parent organizations of such presses will in all instances be those of non-degree-granting institutions or scholarly associations rather than those of universities. In the absence of an editorial committee or board, an applicant for associate membership shall observe commonly accepted standards of editorial review.

Admission to associate status shall be by a majority vote of the membership, a quorum being present, on the prior recommendation of the Committee on Admissions and Standards and the AAUP Board of Directors. Associate members shall enjoy such rights and privileges as determined by the Board of Directors, but in no event shall their rights and privileges extend to service on the Board of Directors or on the Standing Committees of the Association or to voting in any business conducted by it. Any reference elsewhere in the By-Laws to a voting right, therefore, shall be so read as to exclude associate members. Associate members shall not be eligible to participate in the Association's statistical programs. Uniform annual fees for associate members shall be set from time to time by the Board, and associate members may number no more than thirty percent of the full members of the Association. An associate membership may be canceled at any time by a two-thirds vote of the membership, a quorum being present.

C. Desiderata for an Applying Press

In elaboration of the general considerations set forth in the preceding section, the following guidelines have been formally adopted by the Association:

1.   A committee or board of the faculty of the parent institution or institutions shall be charged with certifying the scholarly quality of the books and journals that bear the institutional imprint, and publication of five or more scholarly books each year for a period of not fewer than twenty-four months preceding the date of application shall be required for admission to membership. The word "scholarly" is used here in the sense of original research of a character usually associated with the scholarly interests of a university or college of the first class. (Textbooks, manuals of a synthetic character or intended for class use, and serial publications sponsored by, or under the control of, other departments or divisions of the

university or college are not to be included in the aforementioned minimum scholarly publishing requirement.) A scholarly journals program (one or more journals) may be substituted for one book to satisfy this requirement.

2. An acceptable scholarly publishing program shall have the benefit of the service of not fewer than three full-time employees, of whom one shall have the rank and functions of Director. This official shall report, organizationally, to the President of the university or college, or to an officer at the vice-presidential or decanal level having both academic and fiscal authority, or to the designated representative of a group of such institutions who shall have both kinds of authority.

3. The formal application and supporting data from a press seeking membership in the Association shall be accompanied by a statement from the head of the parent institution, or the designated representative of a group of institutions, outlining the immediate and long-term intentions and financial expectations of the institution or group of institutions for its press, and reflecting a realistic appreciation of the cost of supporting a serious program of scholarly publication.

D. Admission

Admission of a new member to the Association shall take effect immediately following an affirmative vote of a majority of the Association's full membership at the Annual Meeting or a Special Meeting.

E. The Committee on Admissions and Standards

The official agency for the administration of these guidelines shall be the Committee on Admissions and Standards, which shall operate under authority delegated by the Board of Directors, and which shall consist of six members, two of whom shall be appointed for terms of three years each by the incumbent President in each successive year, and three of whom, at least, shall be the director, the editor, and the controller, accountant, or business manager of a member press. In making appointments, the President shall ensure that no member of the committee serves two successive terms. The President shall also appoint a successor to complete the unexpired term of any member of the committee who resigns an appointment or is, for any reason, unable to continue in service; and any person who is appointed as a replacement may, if the President so wishes, be reappointed for a full term following expiration of his or her initial term as a replacement. The President shall also each year appoint a chair of the committee from among its six members. The chairs shall each serve a term of one year, and may not succeed themselves in office.

All inquiries from prospective applicants for membership in the Association are to be directed to the chair of the Committee on Admissions and Standards, who shall advise the candidate of the full substance of these Guidelines on Admission to Membership and Maintenance of Membership, and shall require as evidence of satisfactory compliance with them:

1. Submission to the chair of the committee of one copy of each of 10 or more different scholarly titles published by the applicant and certified by its faculty editorial board or committee, at the rate of five per calendar year in the twenty-four months preceding the date on which the application for membership is filed, and full runs of the issues of any journals for the year or years in which they serve in place of one of the five books.

2. Provision to each member of the committee a complete list, by name and title, of the staff of the applicant press, to be prepared in that form in which such information is given for active members in the most recent edition of the *Directory* of the Association of American University Presses, Inc.

3. Submission to the chair in the original form, and to the other members of the committee as photocopies, of statements from the head of the parent institution, in which are made those affirmations required under Section C, paragraphs 2 and 3, above. The Committee on Admissions and Standards may ask of an applicant press in addition that it furnish, as a supplement to those institutional affirmations required under Section C, paragraph 3, above, copies of its financial operating statements for the two most recently completed fiscal years.

Following the filing of a formal application for membership and notification by the chair to the applicant of its acceptance for consideration, the candidate press shall be regarded as having entered a period of probation, which will last for a period of time no longer than one year, at the end of which, if not sooner, its candidacy will be acted upon as prescribed under the By-Laws, and during which it shall enjoy the following privileges of membership: (a) the right to send delegates to the Annual Meeting, and (b) the right to send representatives to all training sessions, workshops, symposiums, and conferences dealing with professional activities of scholarly publishers and enjoying the support of the Association.

Once a university press satisfying the requirements for membership stated herein has been admitted to active status by action of the membership at the Annual Meeting or a Special Meeting, it shall be required to submit each year to the Central Office of the Association, for publication in the annual *Directory* of members, both a roster of its current staff and an indication of the number of books and journals it has published in each of the two calendar years preceding and that have been certified as to scholarship by its editorial board or committee. And it shall be the responsibility of the Committee on Admissions and Standards to review each listing of an active press in each annual edition of the membership *Directory*, and to undertake action as follows when any member is shown to have fallen below the qualifying criteria for membership: (a) to notify the member of its apparent delinquency under the Guidelines and to offer the full assistance and cooperation of the Association in bringing about satisfactory solutions to its problems; (b) to advise the President and the Board that notification of an apparent delinquency has been sent and an offer of assistance made; (c) to inform the President and the Board of any response received from the member press following its notification; and (d) to recommend to the President and the Board any action that the committee deems appropriate.

With respect to the scholarship of published works, the Association will accept the certification of the press's own faculty board or committee, and will not pass on the scholarship of any individual work. However, the Committee on Admissions and Standards will take into account the observance by the press of commonly accepted standards of editorial review, ordinarily including at least one positive evaluation by a qualified scholar not affiliated with the author's own institution.

When the delinquent press fails to resolve its difficulties within one year of the chair's notice, the Committee on Admissions and Standards shall submit to the Board of Directors a full report of the situation, and recommend, for endorsement by the Board and transmission to the membership for ratification, that the membership of the delinquent press be terminated. Two years from the date of its expulsion, a press shall be entitled to apply for readmission through initiation of the procedures herein prescribed.

PERSONNEL INDEX

Jensen, Michael	106, 198	Kasper, Carol	44
Jerome, Jennifer	49	Kass, Gary	104
Jesionowski, Teresa	52	Kau, Susan	186
Jess, Linda	28	Kaufman, Alex	84
Jestis, Cheryl	73	Kaufman, Debra	55
Johannsen, Dreya	162	Kaur, Manjit	109
Johnson, Beth	186	Kawai, Colins	69
Johnson, Christopher	131	Keane, Kathleen	81
Johnson, Jackie	118	Kearn, Vickie	137
Johnson, James L.	190	Keeling, Judith	167
Johnson, Jennifer	44	Keene, Barbara	95
Johnson, Kim	75	Keeton, Sandi	114
Johnson, Kimberly F.	81	Kehoe, Michael	96
Johnson, Sandra	109	Kelaher, Christopher	33
Johnson, Sharon	148	Keller, Holly	32
Johnson, Thomas	112	Keller, Meg	142
Johnson, William	130	Kelley, Brooke	178
Johnston, Gareth	172	Kelley, Kathryn	109
Jolley, Marc A.	95	Kelley, Pamela	69
Jolluck, Christine	53	Kelly, Brandon	182
Jones, Cheryl	45	Kelly, Fiona	38
Jones, Christopher	45	Kelly, Mark	76
Jones, Donna	131	Kendler, Bernhard	52
Jones, Jackie	58	Keneston, Fran	154
Jones, Kathleen Pike	180	Kenney, Lawrence	189
Jones, Natalie	106	Kepler, Judy	114
Jones, Parneshia	122	Kessler, John	44
Jones, Zina	106	Ketterman, Kathleen	117
Jordan, James D.	48	Keyl, Anne	28
Joslyn, Jo	132	Kidd, Eve	104
Kadushin, Raphael	186	Kieber, Alison	118
Kaemmer, Beverly	100	Kielhorn, Margot	98
Kageff, Karl	151	Kijewski, Kerri	97
Kageff, Kathleen	151	Kilmartin, Kerry	32
Kahl, Milton	190	Kim, Jean	153
Kahn, Yamile	188	Kimball, Katherine B.	112
Kain, Patricia	180	King, Brenda	189
Kaiserlian, Penelope	178, 198	King, Brian	30
Kaldon, Stephen	116	King, Carolyn	124
Kalish, Ilene	115	King, John	34
Kallet, Jeff	124	King, Patrick	37
Kameney, Fred	54	King, Phillip	189
Kane, Sonia	105	King, Susan	104
Kaneshiro, Norman	69	Kingra, Mahinder	52
Kanter, Greg	31	Kingsland, Phyllis	44
Kanyama, Vertelle	44	Kirk, Kara	66
Kaplan, Anne	100	Kirk, Robert	136
Karwhite, Barbara	161	Kirshman, Deborah	36

Maleski, Sheila	53	McCallum, Heather	190
Mallea, Sara Vélez	111	McCarthy, Ellen	96
Malley, Lawrence J.	30	McCarthy, Juliana M.	81
Malpass, Gillian	190	McCaull, June	94
Manaktala, Gita	93	McClure-Parshall, Sally	52
Mandel, Robert	186	McConkey, Jill	170
Maner, Ron	117	McCormick, Mack	87
Manes, Ruth	130	McCoy, Anne	48
Mann, Theodore	132	McCoy, Jim	44
Manning, Kristy	79	McCulloh, Judith M.	73
Manus, Kevin	95	McCullough, Michael	54, 198
Mao, Ling	55	McDermott, Kathleen	67
Markova, Lyudmila	114	McDonald, Amy	118
Markowski, Thomas	145	McDonald, Jennifer	164
Marr, Marie	173	McDowell, Dennis	165
Marsh, Elizabeth	75	McDuffie, John	25
Marshall, Michelle	184	McElroy, Erin	116
Marshall, Stewart	114	McFadden, Patricia	101
Martens, Betsy	52	McGann, Michael	158
Martin, Andy	39	McGilvray, Joan V.	89
Martin, Annie	182	McGonagle, David J.	42
Martin, Barbara	106	McGraw, Sherry	184
Martin, Barbara	151	McGuinness, Nina	179
Martin, Dawn	98	McHugh, Aileen	82
Martin, Larisa	84	McIlraith, Don	37
Martin, Mike	165	McInroy, Jan	162
Martin, Pieter	101	McIntire, Karyn	97
Martin, Roger	90	McIrvin, Michelle	47
Martin, Shari	32	McKay, Brian	189
Martinelli, Theresa	182	McKean, Erin	130
Martinez, Donald	163	McKee, Sarah	64
Martinez, Erica	114	McKie, Ellen	162
Martinez, Tracy	104	McKnight, Emily	123
Maruhn, Elaine	109	McKoy, Marcus	118
Mastromarino, Mark	54	McLaughlin, Brenna	199
Matheson, Laurie C.	73	McLaughlin, Patt	125
Mathewson, Janet	164	McLaughlin, Paul	39
Mathias, Ashley	149	McLeod, Erin Randall	65
Mathis, Steffen	48	McLeod, John	64
Matsumoto, Elyse	69	McLeod, Rebecca	94
Mautner, Stephen M.	106	McManus, Jeff	156
May, Theresa	162	McMenemy, Siobhan	170
Mayer, Dariel	177	McMillan, Amanda	117
Mayer, Loomis	60	McMillan, Bethany	161
Mayer, Mary	190	McMillen, Ronald E.	25
Maynes, Kerrie	180	McMillen, Wendy	123
McAdam, Susanne	90	McMurtrie, Mary Lou	134
McCall, Linda	199	McNaughton, Douglas	58

McQuade, Scott	172	Miyasato, Terri	69
McRory, Susan	84	Mobley, Eavon Lee	125
Meade, Deborah	135	Moen, Jeffery	101
Meade, Mary	97	Moermond, Sheila	186
Mecadon, Patricia	146	Moffett, Jodie	125
Meeker, Dustin	21	Mohney, Chris	60
Meersand, Toby	80	Moir, Robin	101
Mehring, Adam	186	Moise, Loris	88
Mehrjou, Ayda	32	Mones, Mark	178
Meilunas, Mary Kay	108	Monks, Victoria W.	103
Meinders, Anniek	27	Monroe, Nancy	163
Melvin, Terrence	33	Moore, Alexander	149
Merchant, Ann	106	Moore, Anna A.	30
Mesker, Louis W.	74	Moore, Mary Peterson	156
Method, Kathy	85	Moore, Pamela J.	188
Metro, Judy	107	Moore, Wendy	162
Metz, Isabel	102	Moore-Swafford, Angela	151
Meyer, Audrey	180	Moorehead, Harold	153
Meyer, Kathy	57	Morales, Ruth	139
Micale, Tania	155	Moran, Amanda	153
Michaelis, Angie	153	Morgan, Clay	93
Michel, John L.	48	Morgan, Kathi Dailey	64
Migliore, Fortunata	155	Morris, Elissa	129
Mill, George	163	Morris, Ian	122
Millar, Catherine	81	Morris, Michael	52
Miller, Cynthia	135, 198	Morris, Wyn	87
Miller, Erin	141	Morris-Babb, Meredith	59
Miller, Heather	125	Morrison, Don	122
Miller, Robert	130	Morrison, Pamela	54
Miller, Robyn L.	54	Morrison, Richard	101
Miller, Ron	141	Morriss, Gayle	180
Miller, Rose Ann	67	Morrone, Cathy	94
Millholland, Valerie	54	Mortensen, Dee	75
Mills, Eric	108	Morton, Greg	28
Mills, Nancy	178	Mosley, Linda	107
Mills, Ulrike	107	Mostov, Rebecca	96
Milroy, Peter	32, 198	Motherwell, Elizabeth	22
Milstein, Richard	38	Motomura, Akiko	57
Milton, Christina	96	Mueller, Karl	44
Minogue, Frank	162	Mueller, Margie	130
Minovitz, Lise	38	Muench, Timothy	199
Mitchell, Carine	39	Muenning, John	45
Mitchell, David	52	Mullen, Carrie	101
Mitchell, Douglas	43	Mullen, Tess	44
Mitchell, Lauren	103	Mullervy, Deirdre	62
Mitchell, Nicole	64	Mullikin, Melinda G. Smith	65
Mitchell, Patricia	134	Munson, Heather	73
Mitchner, Leslie	145	Munson, Stephanie	52

Salemson, Steve	186	Schuh, Lynda	73
Salisbury, Leila	86	Schultz, Fred L.	108
Salitros, Linda Lou	164	Schultz, Virginia	108
Salling, Stacey	163	Schultz-Nielsen, Axel	50
Saltz, Carole Pogrebin	158	Schwartz, J. Alex	43
Salveson, Sally	190	Schwartz, Marilyn	36
Samaha, Melanie	88	Schwarz, Angel Collado	139
Samen, Anita	44	Schwarz, Helena	48
Sampara, Paige	189	Schwarzchild, Olive	106
Sanders, David	124	Scorziello, Vinnie	93
Sanders-Buell, Sara	107	Scott, Kenneth J.	59
Sandoval, Manuel G.	1396	Seal, Bernard	38
Sanfilippo, Tony	134	Searl, Laurie	154
Sangar, Puja	153	Secondari, Linda	49
Sanmartín, Cristina	93	Secunda, Eve	108
Sarraf, Suzy	107	Sedler, Sandra	69
Sasaki, Takeshi	169	Seger, Rebecca	130
Sato, Atsuko	172	Seiler, Gilbert	82
Satrom, Ellen	178	Sekiya, Yoko	24
Sauers, Sara T.	78	Sell, Laura	54
Saunders, Mark H.	178	Sells, Dianna	165
Savarese, Anne	137	Seltzer, Joyce	67
Savitt, Charles C.	79	Semerad, Marilyn	154
Sayre, Dan	79	Semple, Timothy	112
Scallan, Amanda	88	Severance, Mary	36
Scanlon, Sonia	190	Sewall, Martha	81
Schaffner, Melanie B.	82	Sewell, David	178
Schaut, Diane	123	Sewell, Vicki	150
Scheld, Melissanne	39	Sexsmith, Ann	68
Schenck, Linny	137	Seymour, Susan J.	67
Schier, Jeffrey	189	Shafer, Debra	96
Schilling, Julie	132	Shaffer, Bryan	140
Schipper, Marike	27	Shaffer, Harrison	28
Schlesinger, Laurie	80	Shahan, Andrea	109
Schmidt, Carolyn	103	Shanahan, Mary	44
Schmidt, Casey	81	Shaw, Cameron	131
Schmidt, Karen	66	Shay, Mariah	107
Schmidt, Randy	32	Shayegan, Leyli	158
Schneider, Naomi	36	Shea, Timothy	189
Schnittman, Evan	129, 130	Shear, Donna	122
Schoeffel, Ron	170	Shelly, Mary Lou	76
Schott, Susan	84	Sherer, John	33
Schrader, Rebecca	49	Sheridan, Anne	60
Schroder, Alan M.	28	Sherif, Tawhida	26
Schroeder, Amy	122	Sherwood, Gayle	75
Schroeder, Julie	104	Shestack, Alan	107
Schroeter, Alice	180	Shew, Stephen	45
Schuetz, Richard	114	Shields, Charlie	30

Sullivan, Tim	137	Toff, Nancy	129
Summerfield, Mary	43, 45	Toff, Nancy	130
Sutton, Amanda	114	Tolen, Rebecca	75
Swain, Beth	28	Tom, Henry Y.K.	81
Swope, Pamela K.	91	Tom, Linda	180
Sykes, Amy	135	Tomé, Jesús	139
Szuter, Christine R.	28	Toole, Jenny	95
Tadlock, Susanna	37	Torii, Mikako	172
Takahashi, Tomohiko	169	Torrey, Kate Douglas	117
Takayanagi, Mitsuo	169	Townsend, Larry	151
Takenaka, Hidetoshi	169	Trachtman, Dan	107
Tallon, Andrew	91	Tran, Yune	96
Tam, Yvonne	46	Tranchita, Sue	45
Tambeau, Renee	182	Tremblay, J.D.	151
Tamminen, Suzanna	183	Trenchard, Judy	154
Tan, Elisa	82	Trostle, Kevin	134
Tandysh, Melissa	114	Trueblood, Marilyn	180
Tannenbaum, Janey	147	Trummer, Erin	110
Tanner, Annette	98	Tryneski, John	43
Tarbet, Cathy	176	Tucker, Ginger	102
Tarry, Candace	76	Turner, Debra	109
Tartar, Helen	60	Turner, Emily	115
Tate, Ben	137	Twombley, Ann	120
Tate, Lori	158	Twomey, John	182
Taus, Ellen	130	Tyler, Diane	147
Taverez, Carmen	168	Tyler, Johnny	178
Taylor, Jean	181	Tyson, Julie	55
Taylor, Nicholas	115	Underwood, Will	85, 197
Taylor, Rob	109	Unkel, Jana	153
Taylor, Robyn	59	Upton, Pamela	117
Tenorio, JoAnn	69	Vacca, Carmie	90
Terry, Chris	26	Vagner, Dawn	151
Test, Gail	30	Valencia, Mary	190
Teston, Dennis	130	Valentine, Anne	154
Thatcher, Sanford G.	134, 198	Van Cleve, John Vickrey	62
Theilgard, Anne	42	Van Der Dussen, Rhonda	75
Thomas, Alan	43	Van Norman, Patty	55
Thomas, Hargis	130	van Omme, Arnout	27
Thomas, Kristin	97	van Rheinberg, Brigitta	136
Thompson, Joy	102	van Rijn, Erich	37
Thomson, Jan	58	Vance, Diana	164
Tierney, PJ	31	Vance, Eddie	108
Tietge, Rosemary	198	Vanderberg, Alison	100
Tietz, Angelika	126	Vanderbilt, Sarah	49
Tifft, Douglas	112	Vargas, Liz	28
Tingle, Leslie	162	Vaughn, Kathy	134
Tippett, Lesley	55	Vaughn, Terry	129
Tobia, Mirette	26	Vazquez, Aureliano	158